PUBLIC RELATIONS
RESEARCH ANNUAL
Volume 3

PUBLIC RELATIONS RESEARCH ANNUAL
Volume 3

A publication of the Public Relations Division, Association for Education in Journalism and Mass Communication.

EDITORS

Larissa A. Grunig
James E. Grunig
University of Maryland at College Park

EDITORIAL BOARD

PUBLIC RELATIONS RESEARCH ANNUAL
Volume 3

Edited by

Larissa A. Grunig
James E. Grunig

LAWRENCE ERLBAUM ASSOCIATES, PUBLISHERS

1991   Hillsdale, New Jersey   Hove and London

Lawrence Erlbaum Associates, Inc., Publishers
365 Broadway
Hillside, New Jersey 07642

Library of Congress Cataloging in Publication Data
ISBN 0-8058-0930-9
ISSN 1042-1408

Printed in the United States of America
10 9 8 7 6 5 4 3 2 1

Contents

Preface

In their arguments for new technology in publication, Rogers and Hurt (*Chronicle of Higher Education*, 18 October 1989) recently asserted that "scholarly journals are obsolete as the primary vehicle for scholarly communication." They have not seen the *Public Relations Research Annual*. In our view this, the third volume of the fledgling periodical, is anything but obsolete.

Instead, we consider the *Annual* to be alive, contemporary, almost trendy. And what is the trend?—toward more solidly grounded, theoretical research in a field that has only begun to mature. Even a glance at the table of contents should indicate that the studies and reviews presented here represent the most contemporary thought and investigation brought to bear on the subject we all teach or practice. As long as academics and practitioners who do research continue to share their findings with the larger community—you, the readers of the *Annual*,—a scholarly journal such as this one never will be obsolete. Its form may change, but the basic idea remains a viable one.

One cornerstone of that basic idea is peer review. We take this opportunity to thank the members of our editorial advisory board for their timely and insightful critiques. Last year, in the preface to the second volume of the *Annual*, we suggested that such conscientious reviews should become part of one's file for promotion or tenure purposes. This year, we're intrigued with the suggestion from one of our reviewers that we consider a forum for publishing the best of the reviews themselves. Indeed, there is much to be learned from the pages and pages of single-spaced copy we received in response to a good share of the manuscripts submitted.

Still, as Henri Poincaré pointed out in his *Mathematical Creation*, "To know how to criticize is good but to know how to create is better." So now, on to the contents of Volume 3. What follows is a brief overview of the creations therein—or what the novelist and essayist Arthur Koestler called "the glory of science." As he reminded us in *The Act of Creation:* "The scientist's discoveries impose his own order on chaos, as the composer or painter imposes his; an order that always refers to limited aspects of reality, and is based on the observer's frame of reference, which differs from period to period as a Rembrandt nude differs from a nude by Manet."

We hope you will find here both the excitement of such individual expression and the comfort of cohesiveness characteristic of any community of scholars. Within the paradigm we share, we value the unique contribution of each re-searcher.

Our two review pieces, for example, both speak to communication roles. Pincus, Rayfield, and Cozzens focus on the CEO's role in communicating with employees. Culbertson, on the other hand, looks at the spectrum of roles the practitioner can play—from the managerial or counseling responsibility on through the more tech-nical tasks.

The next two chapters, which are reports of original research, both deal with women's issues in the feminization of the field. Creedon, continuing the line of inquiry about public relations roles, asks us to reexamine the assumptions underly-ing some reactions to the gender switch. Grunig explores the implications of a recent victory in court for women working in communication for the Foreign Service.

The concepts of symmetry and game theory distinguish the next three chapters. Murphy recasts the familiar asymmetrical and symmetrical models of public rela-tions in terms of zero-sum and pure-cooperation games, concluding that symmetric approaches raise questions of ethics and feasibility. She suggests that a mixed-motive game describes the behavior of public relations practitioners better than does the pure game. Theus, too, studies the efficacy of different public relations practices. She finds that the news media cover an open organization more accu-rately than a closed one, leading her to suggest that we find ways of balancing cooperative and competitive strategies. Pincus, Acharya, Trotter, and St. Michel use game theory in an effort to understand the conflict that too often characterizes the agency–client relationship.

The final three chapters all deal with publics. With Van Leuven and Slater, we come full circle: back to the concept of roles. More specifically, they look at the roles played by organizational communicators, the media, and publics in the public opinion process. Ferguson, Valenti, and Melwani focus on communication with one special public: risk takers. Heath and Douglas report on two studies that add to our understanding of the ways in which audiences receive, process, and retain messages on public policy issues. Contrary to the assumptions of involvement theory, their findings do not show a significant correlation between self-interest and involvement.

Thus, we validate the contention of Guillaume Apollinaire, the poet who contended in "The Three Plastic Virtues" that "reality will never be discovered once and for all. Truth will always be new."

And scholarly journals such as the *Public Relations Research Annual* will always be propitious, not obsolete—as long as they maintain the quality of submissions and reviews that we hope characterize this volume. As its editors, we welcome your comments in response.

Larissa A. Grunig
James E. Grunig

PART I

RESEARCH REVIEWS

Chapter 1

The Chief Executive Officer's Internal Communication Role: A Benchmark Program of Research

J. David Pincus
Robert E. Rayfield
Michael D. Cozzens
California State University, Fullerton

Organizational communication and public relations researchers and practitioners have long been concerned with the effects of management communication on employee attitudes and organizational performance. This concern has sparked considerable research on the influential role of the immediate supervisor on the effectiveness of the manager–employee communication relationship. For many years, research focused exclusively on this immediate supervisor–subordinate association.

A facet of management communication that researchers have largely overlooked, however, is the special role of top-level management—namely, the chief executive officer (CEO)—in the organizational communication process. The emergence of early research efforts on top management communication appears to parallel society's growing interest in CEOs' professional and personal lives. This elevated attention on the CEO has no doubt been fueled by the increased public exposure of CEOs as authors, advertising personalities, talk show guests, and media spokespersons.

Rising concern with the importance of the CEO's internal management role was highlighted in a recent *Fortune* magazine cover story on the "trust gap" existing between CEOs and their employees, and the pressing need for CEOs to come out of their offices and get in closer touch with workers' attitudes and concerns (Farnham, 1989).

The public's and business media's increasing fixation with CEOs has consisted mostly of anecdotal information. Relatively few scholarly investigators have launched empirical research projects into the nature, scope, and impact of the

CEO's communication role. A small body of research exists on how employees perceive top management communication activities, but to date no systematic efforts have been reported on how CEOs view and practice their own internal communication role.

This article reports on a two-part program of exploratory research on CEOs' views and self-reported practices of their internal communication role. This effort, guided by a new top management communication model and designed as a precursor to more systematic theory-building research, consists of longitudinal data collected in two recent national studies of CEOs of large American companies. Through this developmental research, we hope to better describe the phenomenon of CEO communication in order to, as J. Grunig (1978) argued, use those descriptions "to model the phenomena and eventually build theory which can be used in a wide range of public relations situations" (p. 4).

The manuscript begins with an analysis of the relevance of CEO communication to public relations. This is followed by a comprehensive review of prior research on the effects of management–employee communication. Then, guided by a top management communication model developed by two of the authors, the research questions are outlined. The next section outlines the methods used to collect the data. This is followed by a presentation and comparative analysis of key findings from each study. We then discuss the implications for development of public relations theory and CEO internal communication strategies. And, finally, an agenda for future research on CEO and top management communication is forwarded.

RELEVANCE TO PUBLIC RELATIONS

Internal Communication and Public Relations.   As recently as 10 or 15 years ago, many public relations professionals and researchers might have defined public relations as being primarily an externally focused communication function (e.g., media, customers, government). Today, however, the practice of public relations appears to naturally encompass both internal—commonly referred to as *organizational* or *employee* communication—and external communication systems (Grunig & Grunig, 1989). Indeed, a cursory analysis of some of the major public relations textbooks (e.g., Cutlip, Center, & Broom, 1985; Grunig & Hunt, 1984; Newsom & Scott, 1985; Seitel, 1989; Wilcox, Ault, & Agee, 1989) reveals that portions of several chapters are normally devoted to discussing strategies for communicating with publics within organizations.

Common to the internal and external relationship-building of contemporary public relations is the concept of *managing communication systems*. Grunig and Grunig (1989), for example, maintained that "public relations is organizational communication," yet they argued that organizational communication inherent in public relations is "managed communication" as opposed to the unplanned, informal "communication behaviors that occur naturally within an organization (i.e., without the intervention of a communication professional)" (p. 28).

This notion is central to Crable and Vibbert's (1986) definition of public relations, which they argued contains two essential variables: "communication and management" (p. 9). They proposed that communication management is the process through which an organization maintains relationships with its key internal and external publics. They suggested that public relations involves two different kinds of communication—task and enabling. Task communication involves the formal process of producing and sending written, oral, or action-oriented messages (e.g., newsletter, videotape). Enabling communication, however, is less formal and is designed to help create the appropriate climate for task communication to be effective (e.g., a staff meeting of key employees to plan a new company-wide program).

The Vital Role of the CEO.   Communication management, then, seems to be the linchpin between public relations and internal or organizational communication. A long-accepted principle in public relations (and organizational communication) is the need for "management's" approval and participation. Relatively little attention in public relations textbooks or research has been given to the single manager whose approval is essential to all organizational activities: the CEO. The CEO's support of and participation in public relations programs, both internally and externally, are vital. As a management function, public relations is an extension of the CEO, the top communicator of the organization. Obviously, if the CEO doubts the value of public relations, the function will receive little funding or support from top management—and efforts are likely to be ineffective.

The CEO, because of his or her standing and unique organizational vantage point, is, as Crable and Vibbert (1986) might argue, the key "enabling" communicator; that is, the CEO creates the appropriate context in an organization so that the public relations department can effectively manage the communication systems. This enabling role appears to loosely parallel the environment-enhancing "manager" or "process facilitator" roles described in the public relations roles research (e.g., Broom & Dozier, 1986).

Fortunately, CEOs today seem to be increasingly supportive of public relations and, at the same time, appear to recognize the power of their personal involvement in the communication process. For instance, Phillip Hawley, CEO of Carter, Hawley & Hale, says that "our ability to communicate *effectively*, as opposed to just communicating, makes a big difference in the results . . . and that is true internally as well as externally" (Steiner, 1983, p. 56).

In summary, public relations involves the management of communication with publics inside and outside organizations. This paper focuses on the internal communication process and the importance of the key manager's—the CEO's—special role in that process. We begin with a review of prior research on management communication.

MANAGEMENT COMMUNICATION RESEARCH

The research program reported here grew out of our in-depth examination of the body of management communication research. Early research attention on the first-line supervisor's communication effectiveness has gradually spread upward to include upper level management's role in the organizational communication process. Our desire to understand how all managers view and play their communication roles served as the backdrop for this literature review.

This review comprises three sections: (a) immediate supervisor–subordinate communication, (b) top management communication, and (c) CEO communication. Prior research on these topics was obtained through a comprehensive computer-assisted investigation of all relevant academic and popular data bases within the fields of communication, business management, psychology, organizational behavior, and sociology.

Immediate Supervisor–Subordinate Communication

The thrust of most research on management communication effectiveness has been on the immediate supervisor–subordinate communication relationship, and its impact on subordinate work attitudes and behavior. A large and varied body of studies has shown that different types of superior–subordinate organizational communication—including a range of both information flow and relationship-building variables—are positively related to employee job satisfaction (Falcione, Daly, & McCroskey, 1977; Goldhaber, Porter, Yates, & Lesniak, 1978; Jablin, 1979; Pincus & Rayfield, 1989; Richmond, Wagner, & McCroskey, 1983). For example, in Goldhaber et al.'s (1978) state-of-the-art review of organizational communication, one of the key predictors of employee job satisfaction was found to be an employee's communication relationship with his or her immediate supervisor.

Another substantially smaller group of studies has revealed a positive relationship between immediate supervisor–subordinate communication and subordinate job performance or productivity (Daly & Korinek, 1982; Hellweg & Phillips, 1981; O'Reilly & Roberts, 1977). Findings from these studies, however, are somewhat less consistent, probably due to the inherent complexity of the productivity-performance variable.

A serious limitation in this body of literature is the absence of clear-cut definitions of various terms used to denote *management communication*. Although the meaning of *immediate supervisor* is relatively clear, other terms used in reported research, such as *superiors, managers, or management,* are too broad to interpret or lack common definitions. As a result of this definitional void, it is difficult, if not impossible, in most studies to pinpoint differences among various levels of management. This is not surprising, because most studies did not seek to compare findings between levels within the management hierarchy. Nevertheless, in Pincus and Rayfield's (1989) metaresearch analysis of the communication–job satisfaction relationship, they concluded that despite varying definitions, "a consistent and strongly positive relationship" exists between an employee's job satisfaction and an employee's perceptions of the immediate supervisor's credibility, communication activities with the supervisor, and the supervisor's receptivity to employee participation in decision making (p. 194).

Top Management Communication

Rising Concern. Research interest in the supervisor–subordinate communication relationship remains strong today. Recently, however, that interest has begun to extend to the influence and role of upper levels of management on the organizational communication process. Perhaps not coincidentally, this surge of research activity parallels mushrooming public exposure to and interest in top managers, especially the CEO. This trend is reflected, for example, in CEOs' increasing spokesperson roles in company advertisements (e.g., Chrysler, Wendy's, American Airlines), the growing spate of books on and by successful CEOs (see e.g., Horton, 1986; Iacocca, 1984; Levinson & Rosenthal, 1984; Morita, 1986), and CEOs' increasing openness to accommodate business media requests for interviews and appearances on business-oriented TV/radio talk shows.

The CEO's View. CEOs themselves appear to have recognized and, to some extent, accepted—at least conceptually—the importance of top management's communication role. Although Barnard (1938) argued some 50 years ago that a top executive's first responsibility is to develop and maintain a communication system, his message was largely ignored until the 1970s. Within the last 20 years, however, researchers and top managers alike are discussing openly the external and internal communication activities of upper management.

In 1977, for example, Hamley pointed out that internal communication had become a "major top management responsibility relating directly to the success and survival of the organization" (p. 8). Former Sperry Rand Chairman and CEO J. Paul Lyet has called communication "one of the most important facets of my job" (1978, p. 18). Added former Dupont CEO Irving Shapiro, ". . . a CEO is first and foremost in the human relations and communication businesses. No other item on the chief executive's duty list has more leverage on the organization's prospects" (1984, p. 157). And retired General Motors Chairman Roger Smith maintained that communication "should be treated with as much thoughtful planning and attention as quality, finance, engineering and manufacturing" ("Our Top People Need Help," 1985, p. 7).

Top managers also appear to be increasingly cognizant of the importance of effective communication in meeting their own objectives. Harold Burson, president of Burson–Marsteller, emphasized that point: "The communications process has become recognized by the CEO as absolutely critical to the accomplishment of his mission" (Horton, 1986, p. 189). More specifically, Pincus and Rayfield

(1985) have argued that the top manager's key responsibilities as chief communicator include: (a) serving as "the catalyst in forming an organization's communication philosophy and style" (p. 1071), (b) establishing management's credibility with employees, (c) creating forms of two-way communication that foster trust, and (d) selecting the "right" communication medium for each situation.

Top Management and Job Satisfaction. Several studies in the early 1980s revealed a link between employee perceptions of top management in general (no special focus on communication variables) and employee work attitudes. Although these researchers did not set out to explore the implications of top management's communication responsibilities, the importance of these responsibilities nevertheless surfaced in their reported findings.

Ruch and Goodman's (1983) study in 1972–1973 of 3,500 General Motors hourly employees from 14 different U.S. plants was one of the earliest efforts to identify any differences in how employees view various levels of management. In addition, their findings uncovered empirical evidence—apparently for the first time—linking employee perceptions of upper management to employee job satisfaction. The researchers found that employees responded differently to questions that used the word *supervisor* than to questions that used *foreman.* According to Ruch and Goodman (1983), employees did not "consider management to be a single entity" (p. 15). And, after analyzing dozens of demographic and work factors, they concluded that employees' perceptions of top management had the "single greatest impact on worker job attitudes . . ." (p. 16).

Ruch and Goodman (1983) cited similar findings from two other studies. Sen found among AT&T employees and Holtfreter found among professional employees of an international accounting firm that employees' attitudes toward top-level management had the single most influence on positive work attitudes.

Employee Views of Top Management Communication. Despite Ruch and Goodman's (1983) revelation some 20 years ago of top management's distinctive communication role, relatively little empirical research attempting to explore the relationship between top management communication and key employee effectiveness variables, such as job satisfaction and job performance, has been reported. The pace of research related to this topic has picked up markedly since the mid-1980s, however.

Several early studies offered signs of employees' perceptions of top management's unique communication role. For instance, in a study of perceived dimensions of job satisfaction among nurses, Everly and Falcione (1976) found that the most influential of four factors was *relationship orientation.* Interestingly, the loading for relations with general supervisory personnel was equal to that for relations with fellow workers and higher than that for relations with immediate supervisors. And in a 1979 study of communication consistency and job performance, Penley and Hawkins (1979) found that when communication from top management and immediate supervisors was consistent, positive employee performance could be predicted.

Several later studies of management communication effectiveness revealed evidence of a statistically significant association between employees' perceptions of top management communication and employee job satisfaction and performance. In Pincus's (1986) study of hospital nurses, findings demonstrated empirical support for the top management communication-employee job satisfaction link. Canonical correlation analysis showed that the strongest influences on nurses' job satisfaction and job performance were first and foremost employee perceptions of immediate supervisor communication, followed by employee perceptions of top management communication. He concluded that these results did not lessen the importance of the superior–subordinate communication relationship, but revealed "the emergence of a second, somewhat different vertical organizational communication relationship" (p. 414).

Two later studies added support to and expanded on Pincus's (1986) initial findings of a top management communication-job satisfaction relationship. Heng (1988), in a study of 545 line and management employees at a semigovernment agency in Singapore, explored the relationship between communication satisfaction and job satisfaction among employees at all levels within the organization. Correlation analysis revealed a positive, significant association between employees' perceptions of top-level managers' communication activities (trust, openness, and participation in decision making) and employees' overall job satisfaction. This relationship was strongest among junior staff members, weakest among mid-level staff, and moderate among senior staff members. These findings seem to suggest that employees at various levels in large organizations have varying communication needs.

In a 1985 study of the communication climate–job satisfaction relationship among bank supervisory employees, Pincus, Knipp, and Rayfield (1990) found via factor analysis that a new factor, which they termed "organizational trust and influence," was most responsible for explaining supervisors' job satisfaction. This new factor—formed from items related to employees' perceptions of top management communication and participation in workplace decisions—explained most (three fourths) of the variance in employee job satisfaction. Superior–subordinate communication accounted for most of the remaining variance. This finding among first-line managers was in stark contrast to prior research results, which have consistently reported immediate supervisor–employee communication as the driving influence on employee job satisfaction. The researchers suggested that as employees rise in organizations, their "desire for communication with top management may increase" and they may need more information about their organizations, which "frequently emanates from top-level management" (p. 185).

A Management Communication Model. The residue of these various studies suggests that employees' views of and need for communication with management are complex. Employees at different levels within an organization may expect a different type of communication relationship with upper management. For example, a line employee and a mid-level manager in a large organization are likely to each want and need different types of information from and relationships with successively higher levels of management.

In addressing this notion of employees' varying communication needs and preferences, Pincus and Rayfield (1986) have proposed a "Top Management Communication Outcomes" model (see Fig. 1.1). In this model, the researchers hypothesize that employees prefer to receive information about the organization (e.g., future plans, policies) from top-level management and information about their jobs (e.g., performance feedback) from their immediate supervisors. The model further suggests that these varying and complex communication relationships, if healthy, will generate somewhat different, yet positive, outcomes. For instance, the top management–employee relationship is portrayed as mainly affecting organization-wide factors such as morale and productivity. In contrast, the immediate supervisor–employee relationship is presented as most directly influencing individual job-related outcomes such as job satisfaction and turnover. The dotted lines in the model depict the transactional nature of the effects of each communication relationship on the other, which may highlight the need for thoughtful communication management.

From a public relations perspective, the implicit underlying notion of this model is that *managed two-way communication* will enhance management–employee relationships. This model helped establish the questions that guided our research (see Research Questions section).

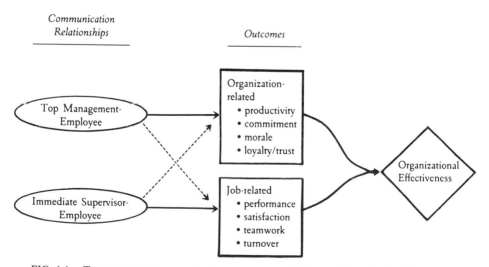

FIG. 1.1.   Top management communication outcomes model. Source: Pincus & Rayfield (1986).

What Employees Want from Top Management. A number of different general employee communication surveys have been conducted by management consulting firms since 1980. When viewed together, these survey findings tend to confirm Goldhaber et al.'s (1978) conclusion that information from top management is "of lower quality than that from other key sources" (p. 84). More precisely, employees have consistently indicated dissatisfaction with the amount, quality, and candor of top management's communication efforts. The thrust of these research activities suggests that employees want a closer, more open communication relationship with top managers, particularly with CEOs (Foehrenbach & Rosenberg, 1982; Gildea, 1981; Ruch & Goodman, 1983; Special Report, 1983; Wyatt Report, 1986).

Employees report that top management does not communicate with them as much as they would like. In a 1980 survey of some 45,000 employees in 40 United States and Canadian organizations, conducted by the International Association of Business Communicators and management consulting firm Towers Perrin, respondents ranked top executives 12th among 15 current sources of information. In contrast, top executives were ranked as the third most preferred source of information, after immediate supervisors and small group meetings (Gildea, 1981). This study was repeated 2 years later among 32,000 employees and the results were largely the same. Researchers, therefore, concluded that "employees' perceptions of top management are very closely linked to their overall perceptions of the organization as a place to work and the general state of morale" (Foehrenbach & Rosenberg, 1982, p. 7).

As a result of top management's infrequent communication with workers, employees view upper-level executives as increasingly isolated from and insensitive to their concerns. This was highlighted in a 1982 special report on human resource management compiled by Opinion Research Corporation (ORC).The research team found that employees were dissatisfied with their companies in general and with top management in particular. And in comparing 1982 worker attitudes with those of the late 1970s, ORC reported that employees believed top management had become more isolated from them and less responsive to their needs (Opinion Research Corporation, 1983).

More recently, the Wyatt Company, a management consulting firm, and ORC surveyed 1,200 executives in the United States on the state of their formal employee communication programs. When asked to rate the quality of communication between senior management and employees at other levels within their organizations, responding executives reported progressively lower quality communication moving down the hierarchy from middle management to supervisors to nonmanagement. The second most desired major change reported by employees was for increased communication with senior management ("Wyatt Report," 1986).

The essence of these survey findings highlights the existence of a "communication gap" between top management and employees. Employees consistently report dissatisfaction with both the quantity and quality of communication with upper levels of management, particularly concerning the two-way aspects of the communication process. Simply put, employees appear to desire more open, more frequent, and more give-and-take communication with their top managers.

CEO Communication

The thrust of research on the top manager's or CEO's communication role is based on how employees perceive this role. Empirical research on how CEOs view their internal communication role is practically nonexistent. Clearly, if we are to better understand this "communication gap" between employees and top managers, then we need a more complete picture of each party's attitudes and behaviors concerning the communication process.

Most prior research on how CEOs view their particular role is anecdotal, most often based on a handful of interviews, and makes little, if any, effort to investigate the communication components of the CEO's management responsibilities. For instance, a number of management researchers (Barmash, 1978; Mintzberg, 1973; Shook, 1981) have explored how CEOs view their management roles in general, usually focusing on factors such as use of time (Mintzberg, 1973), views on power (Nader & Taylor, 1986), reflections on key business decisions (Lamb, 1987), and thoughts on corporate leadership (Levinson & Rosenthal, 1984). Several broad-based surveys of CEOs have been conducted during the past 15 years, but they too have, at best, touched communication issues only superficially (Bonfield, 1980; Godiwalla, Meinhart, & Warde, 1979; Lahiff & Hatfield, 1978).

But because most traditional management texts do not identify communication as a key function of management, most management researchers have not asked CEOs about their communication activities. Our knowledge, then, of how CEOs view their communication role—internal or external—is based largely on speculation and isolated anecdotal information.

One study serves as an exception, however. In 1984, Grubbs studied 97 "Fortune 500" CEOs' external communication practices, including areas such as target publics, activities, electronic information technologies, and media. This work offered a useful early profile of how CEOs of America's largest organizations practice their communication role with audiences outside their companies. Simply put, Grubbs found that CEOs see themselves as needing to be active communicators and that their communication with external publics follows certain patterns. For example, she reported that: (a) CEOs communicate most frequently with professional colleagues, customers, and stockholders; (b) they rely most heavily on conventional oral and written media, such as letters and telephone; and (c) their most active personal participation in communication activities includes civic/community organizations, speaker at public events, and attendance at professional conferences. Although quite revealing, these data on CEOs' external communication behavior did not explore CEOs' deeper beliefs about CEO communication in general or their internal communication role in particular. But this study opened the door for more research into the CEO's communication role.

The Research Questions

Our analysis of the largely anecdotal body of literature revealed how little we know about the nature and impact of the CEO's internal and external communication roles. Most prior research on CEOs has not sought to investigate the human resource management or communication aspects of the top executive's job. Nevertheless, our assessment of contemporary communication and business publications suggests that interest in and the potential impact of CEOs as leaders, managers, and public spokespersons have grown substantially. Yet, despite the emergence of the CEO as a public figure and as an object of research, the body of reliable, empirical data on the CEO's corporate communication role is scarce. Analysis of the extant literature suggested four major areas needing additional research:

1. Top managers' increasing sensitivity to the importance of their organizational communication role.
2. Employees' perceptions of top management's communication efforts and their impact on employees' job satisfaction.
3. Employees' desire for distinctive communication relationships with different levels of management.
4. Despite employees' general dissatisfaction with top management communication, employees want more frequent and better quality communication with upper management.

Our focus is on the first area. Data on the CEO's internal communication role are meager, and are largely based on how employees see the CEO as communicator. At this point, we know very little about how the CEO sees his or her role as communicator. Are employees' and CEOs' perspectives on the CEO communication role similar or different? Understanding the nature of the "gap" between CEOs' and employees' viewpoints should eventually help pinpoint changes needed to enhance the organizational communication environment.

This line of research sought to learn how CEOs feel about and practice their internal communication role. Because there was virtually no body of prior research on the subject, these initial efforts were exploratory in nature. As such, both studies were guided by the same set of general research questions.

Reliance on a Guiding Conceptual Model. These research questions, however, grew out of some of the assumptions rooted in Pincus and Rayfield's (1986) "Top Management Communication Outcomes" model noted earlier (see Fig. 1.1).

This model posits that employees prefer to have different types of communication relationships with upper and lower level managers. In other words, employees see various types of management as fulfilling different communication roles. As yet, however, no research has uncovered data revealing how managers, particularly the top executive, see management's internal communication responsibilities and how their views may differ from employees'. The model argues, in broad terms, that one of top management's key communication objectives should be to provide informa- tion to employees on organization-wide issues and that immediate supervisors' role is to generate job-related information. The model does not distinguish between the CEO's internal communication role and that of other top- or mid-level managers. And it is based, to a large extent, on employees' information needs, and does not formally consider other noninformation aspects of a manager–employee commu- nication relationship (e.g., two-way communication, perceptions of source credi- bility).

The model was not formally tested as part of this research. Nevertheless, com- ponents of the model served as a valuable guide in conceptualizing the research focus and generating specific research questions. Most importantly, however, this model, in our view, offers a framework on which to build more solid theory— beginning with data reported here (see Discussion section).

Our interest was in probing CEOs' perceptions of their internal communication responsibilities and analyzing how those perceptions square with their reported communication practices.

The three core questions and their accompanying subquestions that directed our studies were:

1. *What are CEOs' attitudes toward the nature and impact of their internal communication role?* (a) To what extent do CEOs believe their communication activities positively influence employees and the organization? (b) To what extent do CEOs believe their internal communication role is different from other manag- ers? (c) To what extent do CEOs believe their employee communication programs are cost-effective?

2. *How do CEOs actually practice their internal communication role?* (a) How much of their time do CEOs devote to communicating with employees? (b) With which publics (internal and external) do CEOs communicate most frequently? (c) What types of communication channels do CEOs use most frequently? (d) What types of feedback channels do CEOs consider most effective? (e) In which types of organizational situations do CEOs believe they should assume the lead commu- nication role?

3. *To what extent does a CEO's background and type of organization influence his or her communication attitudes and behaviors?* (a) Do organization size and type (industrial vs. service) affect a CEO's communication role? (b) Do a CEO's age,

longevity as a CEO, and prior management experiences influence his or her communication beliefs and activities? (c) Do a CEO's experience and training in communication practices affect his or her communication role?

METHODOLOGY

This article incorporates results from two national studies, one conducted in May 1987, and the other in May 1989. The latter study was both a replication and an extension of the initial one. Therefore, the methodologies were practically identical. So rather than present duplicate descriptions of the methods employed in each study, we offer a single description and note any important differences.

Sample

The target population consisted of all the CEOs (president and/or chairman) from the "Fortune 500" industrial and "Fortune 500" service firms. Widely used, these rankings, compiled annually by *Fortune* magazine, comprise the largest U.S. organizations in each market sector, based on annual revenues.

Instrumentation

The primary data collection instrument was a four-page printed questionnaire. A driving concern in designing the questionnaire was to make it inviting to busy chief executives. Therefore, layout, time required (10 min), and simple response scales were prime considerations. The questionnaire contained three major sections: CEO attitudes toward the CEO communication role (14 items), CEO communication behaviors (about 40 items), and demographic information (about 20 items). The final question was open-ended and sought CEOs' personal thoughts on how their communication has changed and will change in the years ahead.

The 1987 and 1989 versions of the questionnaire contained, for the most part, the same questions. Several new items were added in the latter study, language was clarified, and some of the response scales were made more precise. Most items relied on 3- or 5-point Likert response scales. A definition of CEO communication was offered in order to seek consistency in CEOs' responses: "the CEO's active involvement in communicating with employees in the organization."

For each version of the questionnaire, pretesting was conducted among five top-level executives at various types of organizations. None of these managers were included in the sampling frame. Feedback prompted only incidental alterations in language, format, and response categories.

Administration

Questionnaires were mailed to CEOs along with cover letters explaining the purpose and importance of the study. Postage-paid return envelopes were also included. In the 1987 study, the "Dear CEO" cover letter was signed by the researchers. In the letter, a special appeal asked CEOs to complete the questionnaire themselves. In the 1989 study, the personalized cover letter came from the CEO of the management consulting firm sponsoring the study (Foster Higgins); therefore, an "honesty" reminder seemed neither appropriate nor necessary. In both cases, CEOs were offered preliminary summaries of results as an enticement to and a "thank you" for participation.

In an effort to garner support within the CEO's organization for his or her participation in the study, a personalized letter (with copy of questionnaire) signed by the lead author and the national leader of Foster Higgins' communication practice was mailed to the organization's top-ranked member of IABC or PRSA, the largest professional communication associations. Two weeks after the initial mailing, a follow-up letter and another copy of the questionnaire were mailed to all CEOs.

RESULTS

Our primary emphasis in this benchmark research effort was to generate a descriptive account of CEOs' beliefs and practices related to their internal communication role. We also sought to uncover differences in communication beliefs and behaviors affected by a number of organizational variables, such as size, industry type, CEO experience, and CEO age. In addition, results were tested for temporal stability across the 2 years between the 1987 and 1989 surveys.

The first (CEO attitudes & beliefs) and second (CEO communication practices) research questions are answered by examining the tabulation of frequencies and corresponding percentages (see Tables 1.1–1.7). In order to test for differences due to organizational or CEO demographic variables (research question #3), t tests (to compare means) and correlation analysis (e.g., Pearson's r, regression models) were used. The relevant significant statistical results are presented and discussed.

Finally, in order to test for stability across time, t tests were used to compare differences in means (where scale properties permitted) or chi-square tests of independence were used to compare frequency distributions of CEO responses from 1987 and 1989.

Results are presented in four sections. First, survey response rates are discussed. Second, stability of findings across the two surveys is analyzed. Third, the large volume of descriptive findings are simplified in a "typical CEO communication profile," including accompanying tables. Finally, results of tests exploring relationships among the demographic, organizational, and communication variables are presented.

Response Rates

The Actual Response. In the 1987 study of a large sampling (about 900) of Fortune 500 industrial and service CEOs, 132 usable questionnaires were returned, representing a 14.6% response rate. In the 1989 study of all 1,000 CEOs in these categories, 164 usable questionnaires were received, which was a 16.4% response rate. These responses were fairly representative among the range of organizations comprising the sampling frame. In the 1987 study, 47% of the returns were from industrial organizations and 44% were from service organizations; 47% had less than 10,000 employees and 52% had more than 10,000 employees. A similar distribution of responses occurred in the 1989 study.

The Reason Why. These response rates are quite low, which is problematical. Compared to other studies of this heavily surveyed target public, however, these response rates are realistic. For instance, Grubb's (1984) study of Fortune 500 CEOs yielded only 101 usable returns (24%). There is a reason for this, which is revealed by the companies themselves. Because of the high visibility and easy access to mailing lists of the Fortune 500, these companies have become popular sampling frame targets of researchers. As a result of this heavy demand on their executives' time, many of these organizations have adopted policies refusing to participate in any surveys. In the 1989 study, for example, we received 39 letters explaining why companies (e.g., Chrysler, Kodak) will not complete survey questionnaires. One letter indicated that the company receives, on average, 50 such requests a week.

Unfortunately, knowing the reasons for a low response rate does not resolve the problems associated with generalizations based on such a relatively small sample. It is possible that respondents reflect a self-selection bias of those CEOs who hold positive attitudes toward communication. The extent of this possible bias, however, is unknown. This abnormally low response rate represents a common dilemma for those who study "hard to reach" target populations, such as CEOs. Nevertheless, the approximately 300 chief executive officers represented in these two surveys are a substantial number from this target population. Although these findings must be considered somewhat tentative, they do reflect an important first step in the systematic study of this group of influential individuals.

Stability of Findings

CEO Attitudes and Beliefs. Findings from the 1987 and 1989 studies were generally similar. A number of statistical tests were performed (e.g., chi-square tests of independence, t tests of means) to compare the 1987 and 1989 results. CEO communication perceptions and practices appeared stable over the 2-year interim between surveys. This finding strengthens our confidence in the validity of our findings and conclusions.

CEO Communication Practices.   The average amount of time CEOs devoted to communication activities in the 1989 sample was 18%. This figure is slightly more than the average of 15% reported in the 1987 survey. The difference between these means was statistically significant ($p < .01$). Thus, the major difference in the two surveys was that CEOs reported spending more time in communication activities in 1989.

The CEO as Communicator: A Descriptive Profile

The first and second research questions sought to uncover CEOs' perceptions of the impact of their communication role and how they play that role. Data from the 1987 and 1989 studies—when analyzed together—offer a first-ever composite picture of how CEOs of large organizations see themselves as communicators. From this composite, we have created a descriptive profile of the CEO as communicator (see tables for complete findings). Selected written comments from responding CEOs are included to bring "life" to the data. Most data presented are from the 1989 study; only findings from the 1987 study that illustrate shifts over the 2-year period are included.

The General Profile.   Overall, the typical CEO as communicator appears this way:

1. He is a middle-aged business leader of considerable experience and success.
2. He believes his internal communication role to be important to employees and the organization, and that his communication role is unique.
3. He appears to be most comfortable and believes he is most effective with face-to-face communication.
4. He believes in the value of employee feedback and uses mostly informal communication channels to obtain it.
5. He has increased his communication activities over the past 2 years, but would be more involved if not for so many other demands on his time.

Demographics.   The typical CEO is a man between 56 and 65 years of age who has been a president or CEO for 8 years. He runs an industrial company of about 7,500 employees. Profits of his company have increased recently and the employee turnover rate has been stable.

Prior to becoming a CEO, he most likely has held management positions in operations and/or sales and marketing. Although he does not have a degree in communication, he reads books on the subject occasionally and receives coaching from his communication staff. He sometimes receives advice from outside communication counsel and has completed a few university courses and/or professional seminars on communication topics.

His top professional communicator probably reports directly to him. The CEO believes he should be involved in decisions concerning organization-wide communication activities (see Table 1.1 for details of demographic characteristics).

CEO Perceptions. The typical CEO strongly believes that his communication with employees directly influences their job satisfaction, job performance, and organizational commitment, and positively affects the organization's "bottom line."

TABLE 1.1
A Profile of CEO Respondents—Demographic Results

	% Response	
Size of Organization		
under 10,000 employees	48%	
10–25,000	25	
25–50,000	17	
over 50,000	10	
Type of Organization		
Industrial	52%	
Service	38	
Other	10	
Age		
35–45	12%	
46–55	31	
56–65	52	
66–75	4	
Top Communicator Reports to CEO		
Yes	51%	
No	49	
Prior Management Experience[a]	*1989*	*1987*
(1) Operations	60	41
(2) Sales/Marketing	38	47
(3) Finance/Accounting	32	23
(4) Manufacturing/Engineering	32	25
(5) Planning	28	17
(6) Research and Development (R & D)	12	11
(7) Hum Resource Management	9	11
(8) Legal	9	14
(9) Communications/Public Relations	9	9

[a]Number of respondents indicating some prior experience (multiple responses permitted).

One CEO of an industrial firm commented, "Communication has been recognized as a key activity, vital to an organization's success." The CEO of a service firm in Ohio added, "Today, more than in the past, the board holds the CEO accountable for developing the 'culture' of the organization . . . and leading the way to its attainment."

The CEO finds himself less involved in organizational communication activities than he wants to be, but has increased his time communicating with employees over the past couple of years. "The need for open, frequent, direct, creative communication," said a new, young CEO from New York, "will continue to grow and will be much more important in the future." The average CEO believes that his internal communication role is different from that of other managers and that the organization would be hurt if his communication activities were significantly reduced. "The role of the CEO is to provide the vision . . . ," noted the CEO of a large company in Pittsburgh. "Interpretation of that vision," he wrote, "is the responsibility of operating unit managers."

More and more convinced of the usefulness of communication, he is less likely to reduce his organization's employee communication budget today than he was 2 years ago. "This CEO," wrote a Minneapolis-based leader, "believes communication (internally) needs lots of work; we are moving away from an autocratic leadership culture." (See Table 1.2.)

Time Devoted to Communication. Three years ago, the typical CEO spent 10% or less of his time communicating with employees. Today, he devotes closer to 15% of his work day to employee communication, and he would like it to be about 23%. He is unable to devote more time to employee communication because there are "just too many other demands" on his time. (See Table 1.3.)

Use of Media. Almost half of the CEO's communication efforts rely on interpersonal means. There will be "more and more emphasis on frequent contact with all levels of employees," said a CEO of a service company headquartered in New Orleans, because "more day-to-day, hands-on management makes for more daily contacts." More than a third of CEO communication is written and just 15% is via mass communication media. The CEO is comfortable communicating face-to-face with employees, but tends to think CEOs who are not comfortable as communicators should not do it. Commented one experienced Boston CEO: "Pity the CEO who is not effective or who does not want to communicate. Note: You cannot force it—it won't be effective."

The CEO communicates frequently with employees through "management by walking around," one-on-one meetings, articles in internal publications, group meetings with employees, speeches, memos, and phone calls—in that order. The average respondent writes letters and/or memos to his employees approximately every 3 weeks, uses mass media techniques about once each quarter, and is satisfied with these frequencies.

He believes himself to be very effective in face-to-face communication and

TABLE 1.2
CEO Perceptions of Communication Issues

	SA	A	HD	D	HD
Positive Impact of CEO Comm on . . .					
Job satisfaction	59	38	3	—	—
Job commitment	43	52	5	—	—
Job performance	19	56	24	1	—
Bottom line	25	54	20	1	—
CEO Comm Role					
CEO primary spokesperson	12	36	11	39	2
CEO comm role *no* different than other mgrs.	4	19	3	53	21
CEO should comm only on special occasions	0	1	2	43	54
Employees believe CEO comm candid/ honest	7	58	31	4	—
Employees possess info to help CEO decisions	39	55	5	1	—
Company's Employee Communication Programs					
Bring good return on investment	13	65	21	1	—
Primary purpose is to send info to employees	2	51	9	37	1
Employees receive sufficient info to do jobs effectively	—	17	34	47	2

Note: All data are presented in percentages.
N = 164; SA = Strongly Agree; A = Agree; HD = Hard to Decide; D = Disagree;
SD = Strongly Disagree.

TABLE 1.3
CEO Time Devoted to Internal Communication

	Today	3 Years Ago	Ideally
% of CEO's Time Communicating w/ Employees			
0%–5%	23	34	12
6%–10%	23	25	14
11%–15%	15	9	16
16%–20%	14	14	20
21%–25%	7	6	9
26%–30%	5	3	10
more than 30%	14	9	19
Mean	18.7	15.2	23.2
Median	15	10	20

Note: All data are presented in percentages.
N = 164.

moderately so in written communication. But he assesses himself as only "somewhat effective" when using mass media. However, some see use of mass media as a key to the future. A 9-year veteran of a large midwestern industrial firm wrote: "A greater emphasis on technology has made timeliness possible. Through the video medium, I've been able to take a greater personal role in communicating with employees" (see Table 1.4).

Issues and Situations.   The CEO holds a distinct role in the organizational communication process. He expects to assume the lead role in communicating with employees on major organization-wide issues, such as year-end reviews, layoffs, and product recalls. "Employees want to hear from their CEO," noted an East-Coast-based CEO. "They need to know more about their company, its direction and future."

He expects other top managers to take prime responsibility for more narrowly focused organizational issues, such as benefits, sagging sales, and employee recognition. "The CEO must set a tone," said the top executive of an industrial firm in New Jersey, "but total communication is the role of every supervisor" (see Table 1.5).

The Employee Communication Function.   The typical CEO is far more positive about the effectiveness of his personal internal communication role than he is about his organization's employee communication program. He sees the primary

TABLE 1.4
CEO Communication Channels

	Usage			Effectiveness		
	D/W	M/Q	Less	VE	SE	IN
Type of Communication						
Face-to-face (e.g., speeches, meetings, MBWA)	74	24	2	88	12	—
Written (e.g., letters, memos)	45	49	6	38	59	2
Mass media (e.g., video, articles)	4	67	28	22	62	16

Note: All data are presented in percentages.
N = 164; D/W = Daily/Weekly; M/Q = Monthly/Quarterly; Less = Less Than Quarterly; VE = Very Effective; SE = Somewhat Effective; IN = Ineffective.

TABLE 1.5
Lead Management Communication Role

	CEO	Top Mgt	Mid Mgt	Super
Issue or Situation				
Sagging sales	30	49	17	3
New overtime policy	5	28	41	26
New benefits program	27	52	19	2
Product recall	57	35	7	1
Recognize money-saving suggestion	19	42	28	10
Announce layoffs	69	27	2	2
Year-end reviews	75	15	1	9

Note: All data presented in percentages.
N = 164.

purpose of employee communication as one-way communication: management sending vital company information to employees. But 4 out of 10 of his colleagues disagree, perhaps implying they see the purpose as broader. Wrote one CEO of a very large corporation: "It's my responsibility to encourage environments in which employees feel free to take risks, participate, grow with the corporation. I'm trying to remove barriers which prevent employees from doing their best job."

The CEO believes the employee communication program brings a good return on investment, but does not think management provides employees all the information they need to perform their jobs effectively. He thinks many, but not all, of his employees believe he communicates candidly and honestly with them. He soundly rejects the notion that a CEO should communicate with employees only on special occasions or during crises. "There is less and less tolerance of hiding behind the 'corporate veil,'" said a CEO of a Houston-based service company (see Table 1.2).

Target Publics.   Inside the organization, the CEO communicates most frequently with his top managers, professional and technical staff, middle managers, and board of directors. Line employees and shareholders receive infrequent communication from the top manager.

Externally, the CEO tends to believe he should be the organization's primary spokesperson. "The increased demand for public accountability by corporations makes it imperative that the CEO be the public point-man," wrote a CEO with 10 years of experience. The CEO is in contact with customers, other CEOs, and community leaders at least monthly. Interestingly, only about 1 in 10 CEOs communicates with media on more than a weekly basis. He rarely communicates with suppliers or union leaders (see Table 1.6).

Feedback Channels.   The CEO believes strongly that information from employees can help him make better decisions. "Communication—to be effective,"

TABLE 1.6
Frequency of CEO Communication with Target Publics

	D/W	M	Q	Less
Publics				
Top management (I)	98	2	—	—
Professional/technical				
staff (I)	59	21	15	5
Middle management (I)	45	36	15	4
Customers (E)	43	20	18	19
Other CEOs (E)	34	42	11	13
Community leaders (E)	27	34	18	21
Board of directors (I)	22	55	18	—
Hourly employees (I)	22	23	28	27
Financial community (E)	20	35	36	9
Government officials (E)	15	24	15	46
Shareholders (I)	12	11	66	11
Media (E)	11	31	37	21
Union leaders (E)	2	10	16	72

Note: All data presented in percentages.
N = 164; D/W = Daily/Weekly; M = Monthly; Q = Quarterly; Less
= Less Than Quarterly; (I) = Internal Public; (E) = External Public.

says the top manager of a consumer products giant in New York, "must be two-way. I just can't talk to them—I must also listen." The average CEO says that casual conversations and meetings with employees provide him with the most effective feedback. Somewhat less effective are employee attitude surveys. He does not believe that the suggestion box or the telephone hotline are particularly effective feedback vehicles (see Table 1.7).

TABLE 1.7
Effectiveness of CEO Feedback Channels

	Very Effective	Somewhat Effective	Ineffective
Casual conversations	57	42	1
Employee meetings	39	57	4
Employee attitude surveys	29	55	16
Memos/letters from employees	29	60	11
Written progress reports	17	70	13
Grapevine	11	61	28
Formal complaints/grievances	7	70	23
Suggestion box	5	52	43

Note: All data presented in percentages.
N = 164.

The CEO as Communicator: Demographic Influences

Predicting CEO Communication Behavior. Respondents were very consistent in their beliefs about specific effects of CEO communication. As a result, four questionnaire items indicating CEO beliefs about the positive effects of their communication (i.e., job satisfaction, commitment, job performance, and organizational profits) were used to construct a general scale. The scale was found to be reliable (Cronbach's α = .81). This "CEO communication effects" scale was subsequently used in several analyses.

Initially, we sought to predict actual time devoted to communication activities in a regression model using the effects scale as the primary predictor with several other organizational variables as controls, such as years as a CEO, age, type of organization, size of organization, and CEO background in communication. None of these control variables significantly contributed to the model after the effects scale was entered into the formula. Thus, the model reduced to a simple regression model in which CEO beliefs in the value of CEO communication predicted CEO time devoted to communication activities (b = 2.27, p < .01, R^2 = .07). This finding suggests that CEOs who believe more strongly that their communication positively influences employee attitudes and organizational performance devote more time to communication activities. The regression model showed that organizational factors, such as organization size or type, and individual factors, such as age, tenure as CEO, and prior management experience, were unimportant compared to CEO beliefs about their communication effectiveness.

Predicting CEO Communication Beliefs. In addition to predicting communication behavior from beliefs, several factors were considered that might predict CEO beliefs in communication effectiveness. A regression model was estimated with the CEO communication effects scale as the dependent variable and several organizational and individual variables as predictors, including type and size of organization, CEO communication background, age, and tenure as CEO. Most of these variables proved nonsignificant to the model.

However, one organizational variable and one individual CEO variable were significant. The final reduced model predicted CEO beliefs about positive effects of communication from type of organization (b = $-$.49, p < .05, one-tailed test) and previous management experience in sales and marketing (b = .59, p < .01). These coefficients imply that CEOs from industrial organizations have less positive beliefs about the impact of CEO communication and CEOs with previous experience in sales and marketing have more positive beliefs about the value of CEO communication. These two predictors combined to explain 5% of the variance in the CEO communication effects scale.

Although CEO tenure was unrelated to the CEO communication effects scale described in the aforementioned regression model, the zero-order correlation revealed a significant, small negative association between CEO tenure and the belief that there would be adverse organizational effects with less CEO communication (r

$= -.21, p < .01$). CEOs of longer tenure seem to believe that their communication efforts have a smaller impact on organizational success (see Table 1.8).

Predicting the CEO Communication Role.   Zero-order Pearson correlations revealed a significant association ($r = -.21, p < .05$) between CEOs' time on communication and their perceptions of the CEO communication role. This correlation indicated that as CEOs spend more time on communication, they are less likely to view their communication role as "different from other managers." Thus, those CEOs who devote more of their time to communication activities are more likely to view their communication role as similar to that of other managers (see Table 1.8).

Predicting Effectiveness of Feedback Channels.   An association was found between CEO longevity and beliefs in the effectiveness of feedback channels. The more years as CEO predicted less agreement with the statement that "employees possess information that can help CEOs make better decisions" ($r = -.18, p < .05$). Age was associated with beliefs in the effectiveness of formal complaint feedback channels. Specifically, older CEOs were more inclined to rate formal complaints as an effective form of feedback ($r = .16, p < .05$). Size of organization was also found to correlate with beliefs about the effectiveness of feedback channels. CEOs of larger organizations tended to believe that employee attitude surveys

TABLE 1.8
Pearson Product-Moment Correlation Results—CEO Communication
and Demographic Variables

	Size of Organization	Tenure as CEO	Age
Communication Variable			
Perception			
Employees possess info help CEO decisions	ns	$-.21^b$	$-.17^a$
Media			
Frequency of use of mass media	$.30^b$	$-.21^b$	ns
Effectiveness of written comm	$.25^b$	ns	ns
Effectiveness of mass media	$.25^b$	ns	ns
Feedback			
Effectiveness of employee attitude surveys	$.20^b$	$-.16^a$	ns
Effectiveness of formal complaints	ns	ns	$.16^a$
Effectiveness of grapevine	$-.15^a$	ns	ns

Note: This table includes only statistically significant results.
$N = 164$.
$^a p < .05; {}^b p < .01$.

are an effective form of feedback ($r = .20$, $p < .01$) and, conversely, the grapevine is a less effective form ($r = -.15$, $p < .05$) (see Table 1.8).

Predicting Use of Communication Channels. Size of organization was related to CEO beliefs in effectiveness of both written and mass media. CEOs of larger organizations judged their effectiveness with written or mass media as greater compared to CEOs of smaller organizations. In both cases (written and mass media), the correlation between organization size and medium effectiveness was .25 ($p < .01$).

Several organizational factors were related to CEO use of and preference for certain communication channels. First, an examination of the relationship between use and perceived effectiveness of communication channels revealed that those who perceive written and mass communication to be more effective use those channels more regularly ($r = .30$, $p < .01$ for written; $r = .28$, $p < .01$ for mass media). However, this relationship did not hold for face-to-face communication; perceived effectiveness was unrelated to frequency of face-to-face communication. These findings suggest that CEOs who use written or mass media more frequently do so because they believe that these channels are more effective. Conversely, CEOs who avoid written or mass media do so because they view these channels as relatively less effective. When CEOs communicate through face-to-face channels, they do so even though they may not wholeheartedly believe in their effectiveness.

Finally and not surprisingly, reported use of mass media was correlated with organization size and CEO tenure. CEOs of larger organizations reported using mass media more frequently ($r = .30$, $p < .01$). CEOs of fewer years were more likely to use (and prefer to use) mass media ($r = -.21$, $p < .05$). Practical necessity may prompt leaders of large, multisite organizations to rely on media that can reach large numbers of employees quickly and simultaneously. Less experienced CEOs may view mass communication as a means to help them to communicate instantly and uniformly with the entire organization, thereby beginning to establish relationships.

DISCUSSION

In this section, we discuss the theoretical, strategic, and applied implications of the findings from this developmental research program of how CEOs of America's largest companies define and practice their internal communication role.

Building Public Relations Theory

Results of this exploratory series of studies suggest several intriguing connections to extant organizational communication and public relations paradigms that should be explored further in subsequent studies.

Developing a Management–Employee Communication Model.   Most significantly, the line of research reported here highlights the importance of understanding the complex management–employee communication relationship. Findings reinforce the underlying theoretical notion of Pincus and Rayfield's (1986) top management communication model that employees relate to managers at different organizational levels in different ways. That is, management should be segmented by levels and roles when devising internal communication strategies. In these studies, CEOs indicated that they see their communication role as different from other managers. And when asked who should assume the lead communication role in different types of organizational situations, the CEOs clearly distinguished among top, middle, and first-line managers. This research, then, seems to argue for extending—and further segmenting—the traditional focus of management communication research (e.g., immediate supervisor–employee association) to include relatively uninvestigated levels of management (e.g., middle) and organizational relationships (e.g., CEO–employee, top manager-middle manager).

Central to the efficacy of the model is the unstated need to manage two-way communication between managers and employees so as to enhance their communication relationships. This concept of mutual communication is emphasized in Grunig and Hunt's (1984) two-way symmetric model of public relations: ". . . the public should be just as likely to persuade the organization's management to change attitudes or behavior as the organization is likely to change the publics' . . ." (p. 23). Although Grunig and Hunt's research looked primarily at organizations' system-wide public relations efforts with external publics, we believe their model can be applied to internal communication as well. Interestingly, CEOs in the studies reported here said they strongly believe in the value of employee feedback to help them make better decisions. Yet, as our literature review revealed, employees tend to perceive top management as somewhat isolated, and want more and better quality communication with them. In other words, CEOs may view their internal communication role as two-way symmetric, but may actually practice more of a two-way asymmetric or public information (one-way) style. Grunig and Hunt's set of public relations models appears to offer helpful conceptual guidelines for developing internal communication theory.

In light of these new data and theoretical implications, perhaps the Pincus and Rayfield (1986) model should be reconfigured to reflect differences among levels of management (e.g., CEO, top management, middle management, first-line supervisor) and to incorporate employees' and managers' varying information needs and perceptions of their communication relationships. Such a reconfigured model may be the beginning of a contingency theory of two-way management communication that separates management's and employees' communication responsibilities and roles according to organizational level, size of organization, and information/communication needs. Obviously, more testing of these relationships is needed.

J. Grunig's Situational Theory of Publics. Another theoretical framework that may help explain internal communication relationships is James Grunig's situational theory of publics (see Grunig & Hunt, 1984, pp. 147–160). In this theory, Grunig maintained that a public's communication behavior can be predicted based on the extent of its problem recognition (information seeking or processing), constraint recognition, and level of involvement (active/passive) with a particular issue. From his research, he identified eight categories of publics and computed the probabilities of those publics' likely communication behaviors in varying situations. Essentially, Grunig's continuum spans from the very active, information-seeking public to the very inactive, information-passive public.

This theory may help in identifying variables affecting the management–employee communication relationship. However, a more precise focus is needed to uncover such information. The data from the studies behind Grunig's (Grunig & Hunt, 1984) theory were drawn from citizens' views and information preferences on a range of external (e.g., public affairs) issues. The criteria housing this situational theory of publics should, conceptually speaking, apply to any public inside or outside an organization. Indeed, internal publics, due to their special self-interests, may hold unique information needs and desires, and may perceive potential organizational constraints differently. If so, certain communication strategies and tactics may be most appropriate, as Grunig and Hunt suggested.

Focusing the Grunig (Grunig & Hunt, 1984) theory exclusively on publics within an organization, employees today—increasingly educated, professional, and hungry for information about their organizations—would probably be classified as an active public (e.g., high involvement, information seeking). If so, Grunig and Hunt maintained, organizations should respond with high profile, proactive communication strategies in order to fuel employees' activism. Yet, as internal publics are further segmented by level, longevity, job type, and so forth, these subpublics are likely to exhibit varying communication needs and tendencies, and thus require customized communication strategies.

The Grunig (Grunig & Hunt, 1984) situational theory of publics appears to be a useful conceptual framework for further studying and classifying groups of employees and managers up and down the organization. Such findings might not only broaden the applicability of Grunig's model, but also foster development of new theoretical notions related to management–employee communication.

The Impact of CEO Communication

CEOs strongly believe in the value and impact of their internal communication activities on their employees and organizations. In two studies conducted 2 years apart among the same population of CEOs, these business leaders reported a strong belief that their communication activities positively influence employees' feelings toward work and the organization's bottom line. Such strong attitudes, which were echoed throughout CEOs' written comments, may be pivotal to predicting CEOs' future decisions on communication-related matters.

Perhaps CEOs are saying what they think they are expected to say: that their communication efforts do make a difference. However, their reported actions—ranging from CEOs devoting more of their limited time to communication activities to CEOs approving larger communication budgets—suggest that CEOs genuinely endorse the importance of their own *communication leadership role.*

Although they believe in the importance of their communication role, CEOs are less certain about the extent to which they should play their role and how effectively they play it. They had mixed views on whether they should be their organizations' primary communicator, and a number of them question whether employees perceive their communication efforts as honest and credible. These doubts— possibly fueled by their limited preparation or prior negative experiences as communicators—should make CEOs receptive to suggestions for how they can more effectively fulfill their communication responsibilities.

CEO Perceptions of Employee Communication Programs

CEOs have mixed feelings about the effectiveness of their organizations' employee communication programs. CEOs are less certain of the positive influence of their organizations' employee communication programs than they are of their own communication activities. Although most believe that their internal communication programs bring a good return on investment, they expressed mixed reactions to the value of the information employees are receiving from management.

This perceived gap between how CEOs view the effectiveness of their personal communication and their company's employee communication program may be explained by CEOs' limited involvement in their employee communication programs. Also, CEO communication strategies should be tied more directly to organizational objectives so that CEOs can see the linkages between their communication activities and the attainment of organizational goals.

CEO Approaches to Communication

CEOs define their internal communication role as largely one-way communication, mostly with other managers. CEOs reported that employees possess information about the organization that can help CEOs make better decisions. This belief suggests that CEOs ought to be aggressively seeking such feedback. Yet they rely mostly on informal, irregular, limited types of feedback—casual conversations and meetings with employees—to obtain this important information. They see employee attitude surveys, which can provide a scientific view of the organization as a whole, as less effective than informal talks with small numbers of employees.

CEOs' communication behavior does not appear to be completely consistent with their perceptions of their communication role. For example, despite CEOs' expressed desire for information from employees, only about one of five CEOs said he communicates with employees daily or weekly, which is substantially less frequently than they reported communicating with most other publics. In fact, almost a third reported communicating with employees less than quarterly. Their most frequent contact is with other levels of management, customers, and other CEOs. CEOs who do not aggressively and continuously seek input from employees may never get it—or if they do, it may be what employees think the "bosses" want to hear. Although it is true that other managers should provide CEOs with input from employees, the natural bureaucratic filtering process may dilute or change employees' actual messages before they reach the CEO.

CEO communication activities, as well as the priorities attached to them, may be based too much on tradition or circumstances rather than on clear-cut, thoughtful strategies tied to organizational objectives. CEOs may be unconsciously overemphasizing the wrong audiences, inadvertently ignoring their organization's goals. This argues for the need to develop distinct CEO communication strategies that are incorporated into the organization's overall communication plan, not apart from it.

Excessive emphasis on one-way CEO communication strategies is inconsistent with today's business environment. As organizations continue to merge, restructure, and downsize, employees are forced to go through confusing, traumatic cultural transformations. Such cultural change must be supported by and involve the lowest level employees to be effective and lasting. But employees need leadership—from the top. And the top needs to know its people and their beliefs if it hopes to effectively lead. CEOs "must guide" cultural change, argued Dumaine (1990), "to make sure it happens coherently" (p. 127). This means CEOs must know their employees' true feelings about their CEO, their work, their management, and their organization before crafting appropriate communication approaches. Casual, random conversations with a handful of individuals are a weak substitute for more scientific, ongoing, organization-wide attitude research.

CEO Communication Behavior

CEOs prefer and rely mostly on face-to-face communication, and shy away from and under-utilize mass media. CEOs are primarily interpersonal communicators. Their channel of choice is face-to-face communication, marked by meetings, speeches, and management by walking around (MBWA). Written communication, mostly memos and letters, is used moderately. Mass media, such as videotapes or articles in publications, are used by CEOs sporadically and are not seen as highly effective in communicating with employees. These findings were evident in both the 1987 and 1989 studies.

Among the written comments forwarded in this study, many touted CEOs' increasing reliance on new communication technologies (e.g., videoconferencing), and predicted the need for CEOs to become more comfortable and competent with mass media. Findings suggested that this may already be happening. For instance,

CEOs of larger organizations said they actually use mass media more than their counterparts at smaller organizations. The CEO of a large, multilocation organization cannot hope to establish meaningful relationships with employees relying mostly on face-to-face forms of communication. In contrast, CEOs of smaller, single-site organizations, such as hospitals, are able to use interpersonal communication more regularly and effectively. CEOs adept at using mass communication channels, such as video, can simulate face-to-face communication with large numbers of employees.

Better training may be needed. Many CEOs today are unprepared—and, therefore, uncomfortable—to do a TV interview or appear on a talk show or speak to a large audience. Although they recognize their responsibilities, they often avoid or delegate such obligations because they are uncomfortable or untrained to handle them. Typical business education has stressed topics such as finance, operations, and marketing. Communication training has been largely overlooked. For instance, it is only since about 1970 that MBA programs have included any communication training in their curricula. And the thrust of that training focuses on basic communication skills, such as writing and speaking, and includes little, if any, emphasis on strategic communication issues, such as the role of the media or employee communication strategies (Pincus, 1988).

Typical MBA programs should incorporate a wide range of communication issues into their curricula. In addition, CEOs may need on-the-job training on special communication topics (e.g., media interviews) from their professional communication staff and/or outside consultants.

The Uniqueness of the CEO's Communication Role

CEOs see their internal communication role as situation-specific and continuous. CEOs hold strong feelings on what their communication role should be and when they should play that role. They see their internal communication responsibilities as related to, but different from, other managers' roles. And they believe they should communicate with employees regularly, yet, depending on the type of issue or situation, communication leadership should shift among management levels. When the issue has potential organization-wide impact (e.g., layoffs), they believe the CEO should be the primary communicator. Perhaps, companies should develop CEO strategic communication plans, prepared in consultation with the company's public relations staff, and integrate them into the company's objectives.

Demographic and Organizational Effects on CEO Communication

Younger and less experienced CEOs are more likely to believe in the value of CEO and employee communication than older and more experienced CEOs. What might cause such a finding? Maybe it is the natural difference between old and new guard CEOs—those who learned to manage "by the numbers" versus those who learned to consider human relations implications in their decisions. For exam-ple, findings indicated that older CEOs are less likely to believe that employee feedback is useful to executive decision-making.

If true, this difference is disturbing. It may suggest that over time CEOs are less aware of the positive effects of their own and their company's communication efforts. This might be due to weak communication strategies and tactics. Or it may be because professional communicators are failing to adequately gather evidence demonstrating the effects of communication.

On the other hand, younger and less experienced CEOs may simply see the work world in different terms than more senior CEOs. That is, maybe because of their business school training and general management orientation, they place greater emphasis on the human side of managing—and on organizational commu-nication—than did their predecessors. Or this may reflect a fundamental cultural change in a society increasingly dependent on instant communication tech-nologies.

Indeed, CEOs of the future, faced with intensifying demands to communicate with internal and external publics, may, to an increasing extent, be selected by shareholders and boards because of their ability to effectively build relationships through communication.

A FUTURE RESEARCH AGENDA

CEO/top management communication is a relatively unexplored area of commu-nication research. The studies reported here offer some useful benchmark data in understanding how CEOs view their internal communication role. Future re-search, if properly focused and methodologically sound, can pave the way for developing new, more far-reaching management communication concepts and theories. The opportunities to pursue new avenues of research are limitless. Based on our investigations, we offer suggestions for building on this emerging area of study.

Enhancing Existing Research and Theory. Most top management/CEO research to date has been largely anecdotal and void of strong theoretical foun-dations. New research in this area should, where possible, build conceptual groundwork by testing extant theoretical foundations. New research in this area should, where possible, build conceptual groundwork by testing theoretical para-digms noted earlier, such as Pincus and Rayfield's (1986) top management com-munication model and Grunig's (Grunig & Hunt, 1984) situational theory of publics.

Additionally, the longitudinal research reported here should be replicated and further developed in order to track changes and probe new issues. Special empha-sis should be given to bolstering response rates in order to increase the representativeness of the data. As a first step in this direction, one of the authors has conducted a series of 25 face-to-face structured interviews with CEOs from a cross-section of major organizations across the United States. Systematic analysis of these transcripts is currently underway.

Other Target Publics.   How other key publics perceive the CEO's communication role can add perspective to our understanding of CEO effectiveness. Two such influential publics are stockholders and boards of directors. In addition, research into the middle management–employee and CEO–middle management communication relationships needs to be pursued to further test Pincus and Rayfield's (1986) conceptual model of top management communication. The primary focus to date has been on CEOs of large organizations; new, comparative research needs to be done on CEOs and top managers of organizations of differing sizes, types (e.g., profit vs. nonprofit), and within particular markets (e.g., hospitals).

The CEO's External Communication Role.   Only a small amount of research has focused on the CEO's external communication role (e.g., Grubbs, 1984). By the very nature of their position, CEOs must maintain relationships with a number of key external publics, such as customers, community leaders, and the media. Do CEOs consciously select contrasting communication strategies and tactics for internal and external publics? If so, what factors most influence those decisions and practices? Research probing CEOs' perceptions and behavior related to their external communication—perhaps patterned on the studies reported here (e.g., perceptions, target publics, channels)—would provide a more complete profile of the CEO as public communicator.

Impact of CEO Communication.   CEOs believe that their communication efforts directly influence employees' satisfaction, commitment, and performance, as well as the bottom line. A few empirical studies have demonstrated relationships between employees' perceptions of top management communication and employees' job satisfaction and performance. Relying on self-reported perceptual data needs to be supplemented by other types of data. For example, one approach might be participant–observers of CEOs on the job to report their actual communication behavior and then compare that to their self-declared activities. A strategy for measuring the actual impact of different types of CEO communication would be a semicontrolled field experiment. It might involve simultaneous evaluation of different CEO communication styles (delivering split messages) and their effects on various employee and organizational outcomes among various units within the same organization or industry.

Communication and Leadership.   How does a CEO's communication competence influence his ability to be an effective organizational leader? Is communication a critical factor in leadership? What types of communication approaches have the greatest impact on leadership effectiveness? Testing the influence of communication factors on leadership theories and models might shed new light on the role of interpersonal and mass communication strategies in leadership behavior.

Conclusion.   Despite the almost limitless potential for research in the area of CEO communication, focus is needed in order to build a meaningful body of literature. Use of comparable definitions, variables, and methodologies should be sought whenever possible. As Pincus and Rayfield (1989) noted in their review of the communication-job satisfaction literature, conclusions were difficult because of the many differences in study approaches and designs. Cooperation among researchers on terms and measures, as well as rapid promulgation of findings, would enhance the development of useful data bases on CEO and top management communication. The authors are fully prepared to cooperate in such an effort.

REFERENCES

Barmash, I. (1978). *The Chief Executives*. Philadelphia: Lippincott.

Barnard, C. I. (1938). *The functions of the executive*. London: Cambridge University Press.

Bonfield, P. (1980). *U.S. business leaders: A study of opinions and characteristics*. Conference Board Report No. 786. New York: Conference Board.

Broom, G., & Dozier D. (1986). Advancement for public relations role models. *Public Relations Review, 12*(1), 37–56.

Crable, R. E., & Vibbert, S. L. (1986). *Public relations as communication management*. Edina, MN: Bellwether.

Cutlip, S. M., Center, A. H., & Broom, G. M. (1985). *Effective public relations* (6th ed.). Englewood Cliffs, NJ: Prentice Hall.

Daly, J. A., & Korinek, J. T. (1982). Organizational communication: A review via operationalizations. In H. W. Greenbaum & R. L. Falcione (Eds.), *Organizational communication: Abstracts, analysis and overview*. (Vol. 7, pp. 11–46). Beverly Hills, CA: Sage.

Dumaine, B. (1990, January 15). Creating a new company culture. *Fortune*, pp. 127–131.

Everly, G. S., & Falcione, R. L. (1976). Perceived dimensions of job satisfaction for staff registered nurses. *Nursing Research, 35*(5), 346–348.

Falcione, R. L., Daly, J. A., & McCroskey, J. C. (1977). Job satisfaction as a function of employees' communication apprehension, self-esteem, and perceptions of their immediate supervisors. In B. D. Rubin (Ed.), *Communication Yearbook I* (pp. 363–376). New Brunswick, NJ: Transaction.

Farnham, A. (1989, December 4). The trust gap. *Fortune*, pp. 56–78.

Foehrenbach, J., & Rosenberg, K. (1982). How are we doing? *Journal of Organizational Communication, 12* (1), 3–9.

Gildea, J. (1981). 45,000 employees judge effectiveness of internal communication. *Journal of Communication Management, 2*, 3–11.

Godiwalla, Y. M., Meinhart, W. A., & Warde, W. D. (1979). Environment and technology: Strategic contingency mixes for overall corporate strategy. *University of Michigan Review, 31,* 26–32.

Goldhaber, G. M., Porter, D. T., Yates, M. P., & Lesniak, R. (1978). Organizational communication: 1978 (state-of-the-art). *Human Communication Research, 5,* 76–96.

Grubbs, L. (1984). *Chief executive officer communication in the American corporate environment.* Unpublished doctoral dissertation, University of Texas at Austin.

Grunig, J. E. (1978, August). Theory and research in public relations. Paper presented at the Association for Education in Journalism & Mass Communication Convention, Public Relations Division, Seattle, WA.

Grunig, J. E., & Grunig, L. A. (1989). Toward a theory of the public relations behavior of organizations: Review of a program of research. In J. E. Grunig & L. A. Grunig (Eds.), *Public relations research annual* (Vol. 1, pp. 27–63). Hillsdale, NJ: Lawrence Erlbaum Associates.

Grunig, J. E., & Hunt, T. (1984). *Managing public relations.* New York: Holt, Rinehart, & Winston.

Hamley, W. A. (1977). Communicators: Next in the spotlight. *Journal of Organizational Communication, 4,* 8–9.

Hellweg, S. A., & Phillips, S. L. (1981). Communication and productivity in organizations: A state of the art review. In K. H. Chung (Ed.), *Academy of management 1981: Proceedings* (pp. 188–192). Wichita, KS: Academy of Management.

Heng, T. H. (1988). *Management communication and employee job satisfaction: A study of a semi-government agency in Singapore.* Unpublished master's thesis, California State University, Fullerton.

Horton, T. R. (1986). *"What works for me": 16 CEOs talk about their careers and commitments.* New York: Random House.

Iacocca, L. (1984). *Iacocca: An autobiography.* New York: Bantam.

Jablin, F. M. (1979). Superior–subordinate communication: The state of the art. *Psychological Bulletin, 86,* 1201–1222.

Lahiff, J. M., & Hatfield, J. D. (1978). The winds of change and managerial communication practices. *The Journal of Business Communication, 15,* 19–28.

Lamb, R. B. (1987). *Running American business: Top CEOs rethink their major decisions.* New York: Basic.

Levinson, H., & Rosenthal, S. (1984). *CEO: Corporate leadership in action.* New York: Basic.

Lyet, P. J. (1978, April). Excerpt of remarks to employee publications conference, cited in Stand Tall Without Apology. *Journal of Communication,* p. 18.

Mintzberg, H. (1973). *The nature of managerial work.* New York: Harper & Row.

Morita, A. (1986). *Made in Japan: Akio Morita and the Sony Corporation.* New York: Dutton.

Nader, R., & Taylor, W. (1986). *The big boys: Power and position in American business.* New York: Pantheon.

Newsom, D., & Scott, A. (1985). *This is PR: The realities of public relations* (3rd ed.). Belmont, CA: Wadsworth.

Opinion Research Corporation. (1983, January 10). Special report: Managing human resources/1982—A strategy briefing for executives. *Behavioral Sciences Newsletter.*

O'Reilly, III, C. A., & Roberts, K. H. (1977). Communication and performance in organizations. In K. H. Chung (Ed), *Academy of Management Proceedings 1977* (pp. 375–379). Wichita, KS: Academy of Management.

Our top people need help. (1985, June/July). *Communication World,* p. 63.

Penley, L. E., & Hawkins, B. L. (1979). *Communication consistency as a factor in the prediction of motivation and performance.* Paper presented at the Southwestern Academy of Management Convention, Houston.

Pincus, J. D. (1986, August). Communication satisfaction, job satisfaction, and job performance. *Human Communication Research, 12,* 395–419.

Pincus, J. D. (1988). *The study of the role of business communication education in the University of Southern California's MBA program.* Unpublished manuscript.

Pincus, J. D., & Rayfield, R. E. (1985). The emerging role of top management communication: "Turning on" employee commitment. *Personnel Communications Management, 28,* 1291–1296.

Pincus, J. D., & Rayfield, R. E. (1986). *The relationship between top management communication and organizational effectiveness.* Paper presented at Association for Education in Journalism & Mass Communication Convention, Public Relations Division, Norman, OK.

Pincus, J. D., & Rayfield, R. E. (1989). Organizational communication and job satisfaction: A meta-research perspective. In B. Dervin & M. Voigt (Eds.), *Progress in communication sciences,* (Vol. IX, pp. 183–207). Norwood, NJ: Ablex.

Pincus, J. D., Knipp, J. E., & Rayfield, R. E. (1990). Internal communication and job satisfaction revisited: The impact of organizational trust and influence on commercial bank supervisors. In J. Grunig & L. Grunig (Eds.), *Public relations research annual* (Vol. 2, pp. 173–191). Hillsdale, NJ: Lawrence Erlbaum Associates.

Richmond, V. P., Wagner, J. P., & McCroskey, J. C. (1983). The impact of perceptions of leadership style, use of power, and conflict management style on organizational outcomes. *Communication Quarterly, 31,* 27–36.

Ruch, R. S., & Goodman, R. (1983). *Image at the top: Crisis and renaissance in corporate leadership.* New York: Free Press.

Seitel, F. P. (1989). *The practice of public relations* (4th ed.). Columbus, OH: Merrill.

Shapiro, I. (1984). Managerial communication: The view from inside. *California Management Review, 27*(1), 157–172.

Shook, R. L. (1981). *The chief executive officers: Men who run run big business in America.* New York: Harper & Row.

Steiner, G. A. (1983). *The new CEO.* New York: MacMillan.

Wilcox, D. L., Ault, P. H., & Agee, W. K. (1989). *Public relations: Strategies and tactics* (2nd ed.). New York: Harper & Row.

Wyatt communications survey report. (1986). Chicago: The Wyatt Company.

Chapter 2

Role Taking and Sensitivity: Keys to Playing and Making Public Relations Roles

Hugh M. Culbertson
Ohio University

Sensitivity to others—clients, bosses, publics, and colleagues—has long been seen as an ingredient of effective public relations (Wilcox, Ault, & Agee, 1986). Such sensitivity, which involves role taking, is especially important when a practitioner acts as a communication manager—assessing, reacting to, and devising ways of relating to publics and clients in a dynamic, ongoing way (Broom & Dozier, 1986).

In a changing world with increasing interdependence among and within larger and larger organizations, communication and understanding within and across organizational boundaries have become both more important and more difficult. In simpler times, public relations (PR) practitioners, their clients, and their bosses could doubtless often get by with role taking at a basic level—putting themselves "into others' shoes" to predict specific behaviors, decisions, and beliefs. In the modern world, however, issues management, environmental scanning, proactive public relations, and other buzz words imply a need for a deeper level of sensitivity. That, in turn, involves predicting and understanding often subtle meanings—as well as long-term and short-term effects—of anticipated behaviors, beliefs, and decisions as these affect varied publics and stakeholders.

This chapter reviews literature on role taking to help define such sensitivity. First, we look at fundamental concepts helpful in understanding role taking. Then we draw on symbolic-interactionist and other literature in spelling out 12 dimensions or attributes of role taking and role creation.

Having laid this foundation, the paper next discusses several hypotheses linking the dimensions to six oft-noted trends in modern society and communication. And finally, we use the role-taking process and proposed dimensions to elucidate five rather popular topics in communication literature. These are public relations role theory, the two-way symmetric model, maturational theory of ethics, clashing perspectives or schemata, and bureaucratic propaganda or organizational impression management.

SOME KEY CONCEPTS

Mead (1955), often called the father of symbolic interactionism, saw role taking as the process by which infants become truly human. No person is an island, as the poet, John Donne, said. We all deal with and learn from others most of the time. An infant or young role taker (hereafter labelled P) becomes human largely by: (a) behaving, often in seemingly random, unsystematic ways; (b) observing how others react to that behavior; and (c) imitating these reactions, incorporating them (and accompanying evaluations and assessments of P) into P's cognitive and behavioral repertoire.

Thus, P gains the tools to define his or her self. Further, because two or more others normally come into play, the maturing P learns that he or she can be defined and assessed in various ways. This realization suggests that any one definition of P is arbitrary—not absolute and beyond question. That, in turn, paves the way for P to see him or herself *as an object*—as something to be evaluated and altered where needed in light of apparent probable reactions by others.

Mead (1955) referred to other people (hereafter called Os) whose reactions to P figure in this process as *significant others*. The fact that different significant others react to P differently has at least two implications for socialization.

First, it drives home the point that different people have different expectations and define P differently. To gain a positive response, P must behave differently—and become a somewhat different person—depending on the situation and the significant other being considered. This process makes it clear that any role (father, professor, wife, or whatever) that one plays changes with contexts and the others who help define it. Roles are in flux; they are not simply slots or niches handed down by a monolithic society that force people to behave in completely predetermined ways (Turner, 1962).

Second, it taxes one's ability to think and solve problems. Learning a completely unique way of behaving for each of hundreds of significant others would be unbearably complex and demanding. The human copes partly by developing a concept of self as a reasonably stable, consistent behaver. That unification, in turn, stems from a stable, consistent view of significant others—a kind of weighted average of their responses—which Mead called the *generalized other*.

The weighting process is not very precisely defined. But clearly some significant others count more than others in any given case. Also, some creative synthesis occurs—the whole is not simply the sum of its parts or even very clearly related to them (Mead, 1955, p. 155).

P's self—more or less an internalized *generalized other*—has two aspects, according to Mead (1955, pp. 175–178, 200). First is the *me*, those elements that are incorporated with little change from society's view of P. Alongside that is the *I* —the aspect that is creative, spontaneous, and unique to the individual role taker. The I helps ensure that people adapt to changing situations and contexts. No two people have identical lives, so no one is simply a clone of another.

Clearly Mead (1955) and his followers emphasized two assumptions about humans as is apparent from the aforementioned analysis:

1. They are purposeful and goal oriented in their behavior. When they enact roles, they do so in particular situations and with reference to particular role definers (significant others) as well as to additional *relevant others* who are taken into account. In fact, when an infant incorporates significant others' behavior into his or her own repertoire, the infant engages in a conversation of gestures. A gesture is a behavioral symbol that represents, in one's mind, a purposeful act. For instance, a chair is something to sit in. The word chair symbolizes to its user the act of sitting, which is implicit in the word's definition (Mead, 1955, p. 15).

2. They construct their own unique worlds. Human percepts and concepts do not simply mirror a God-given reality that is uniform for all. Meanings are in people, as Berlo (1960, p. 175) has said. And researchers or PR persons had best not assume, without confirmation, that their definitions of stimuli, situations, goals, and other entities are shared by diverse others (Blumer, 1962).

Before discussing role taking in its various aspects, we examine briefly the concept of role as generally used in sociology. A role implies at least these elements:

1. A position in a social group (i.e., the referent for a word such as judge, father, doctor, or public relations practitioner).

2. A person who occupies (or, at least, a view that someone might exist who could occupy) the position.

3. A set of persons (here called relevant others) who consensually assign individuals to the position.

4. A set of behaviors (including covert attitudes and opinions) that relevant others agree relate to the position. How they relate varies. Some are prescribed for anyone occupying the position (i.e., he must bring a paycheck to continue enacting the husband role). Some are proscribed (i.e., performance of them, such as wife or child beating, might invalidate the enactor's right to continue as a husband). And some are optional—the occupant can conform or not without risk of invalidation.

5. One or more *reciprocal positions*. At least some of the position occupant's validating behaviors are directed at a specific reciprocal position. For example, certain behaviors by a father (i.e., teaching one to box) are seen as appropriate

when directed toward a son but not a daughter. Also, certain behaviors by the reciprocal-position occupant (e.g., working to learn to box), and by varied significant others (a wife who grants legitimacy to such behavior) are needed to validate the position occupant's occupancy.

6. A set of sanctions—rewards and punishments consensually defined by people within society as appropriately used by relevant others to encourage role-occupant conformity to expectations (Turner, 1962).

Relevant others need to be defined at this point. They are people whom P must take into account in playing a role, even though they may have no part in P's definition of self. For instance, a merchant must meet the needs of customers, taking their probable reactions into account, without necessarily adopting those views as his or her own (C. J. Couch, personal communication, July 28, 1965).

Now some roles are very tightly defined (Blau, 1963, pp. 28–31). That is, they entail very clear, complete specifications of "must and must-not" behaviors. Little room is left for the I—for idiosyncratic, creative, unique behavior by an individual role occupant. For example, the author once marched in close-order drill as a United States Marine. As third man in a four-man squad, he behaved in a prescribed way at the command "column left." He stepped off at a 30° angle on the first count following the command, and he did the same on counts of two and three. The behaviors needed to continue enacting the role were:

1. Codified or written in a manual so new recruits could learn precisely how to execute the commands. Also, old-timers could agree quickly on who performed adequately, who did not, and what needed to be corrected.

2. Routinized or carried out in the same way time after time—with little regard for unique attributes of a given marching situation, marcher, or drill sergeant.

3. Consensually defined, with little or no disagreement among people within society (and in particular, among people empowered to impose sanctions) as to what behavior was appropriate—or as to the acceptability of rewards for conformity and punishments for noncompliance (Berger, 1963, p. 66–92).

Obviously some roles are much looser (Turner, 1962). The author, for example, experienced real culture shock when he became a college professor shortly after leaving the Marine Corps. He had been accustomed to playing rather tightly defined roles as a Marine. And he was a bit startled when his dean said he could probably gain tenure by excelling in any two of four areas of endeavor—research, teaching, advising, and service. There was but one clear constraint—research or teaching had to be one of the chosen two. Such freedom of choice seemed liberating, but a bit scary to one not accustomed to it and not knowledgeable about professoring.

Symbolic interactionists (SI) are inclined to emphasize that even the most tightly defined roles are not perfectly tight. The Marine in close-order drill can step with a snap and flare not completely spelled out in the Marine Corps manual. Further, some drill sergeants are much more apt than others to lower the boom on a recruit who marches slightly out of step. Recruits learn these variations and adjust their behavior accordingly.

SI adherents seemingly tend to emphasize loosely defined roles—and idiosyncratic behavior carried out even by those enacting tightly defined roles. In fact, interactionists often study "deviants" such as gays, drug addicts, ex-cons, and prostitutes (Becker, 1973, pp. 1–18). These roles are somewhat loosely defined by society, partly because many people seldom deal with such folks and have not developed clear expectations of them.

Clearly, PR practitioners need to assess the looseness or tightness of roles played by bosses, clients, and others (Blumer, 1969). Persuading a person to buy beer will prove difficult at best—even given a secretly held favorable attitude toward beer—if the individual happens to be a devoted member of the Women's Christian Temperance Union. Also, PR-practitioner roles may vary as to tightness. For example, a communication technician probably often follows a clearly defined, repetitive sequence of steps—a routine—more closely than does a communication manager (Broom & Dozier, 1986).

Failure to study tight roles can lead to public relations snafus. As a Marine, the author spent time in a U.S. Naval Hospital. On Christmas day, a charitable organization gave bottles of cologne to him and some fellow recruits. No doubt the givers meant well. But they should have realized that anyone bringing cologne back to marine boot camp would face endless push-ups and worse. The recruits did not think nice thoughts about these benefactors when tossing their cologne into the wastebasket on the way back to active duty!

We now turn to 12 dimensions of role taking suggested by interactionists and allied scholars. These dimensions should help practitioners plan and assess role-taking efforts.

DIMENSIONS OF ROLE TAKING

Dimension 1—Level of Accuracy. Each person lives within a unique social context and has had a unique learning history. Consequently, no two people have precisely the same meanings for and expectations about any role or other object. And of course, language and other symbol systems are imperfect tools for describing one's experience to another. Thus a person can never get "completely inside another's skin" as might be required for perfect role taking (Berlo, 1960).

A good deal of social-science theory and research suggests that changing long, intensely held attitudes, beliefs, and behavioral intentions is difficult (Klapper, 1964, pp. 15–52). When practitioner or client and a public hold differing views, agreement is often unattainable. Practitioners would have to change the public's opinions/attitudes—and/or their own—so the two would agree.

However, as Bowes and Stamm (1975) have noted, accuracy of interpersonal perception is often within reach. One can learn about another's point of view without accepting that position as his or her own. And this can pave the way for tolerant, active information seeking and dialogue (Stewart & Hoult, 1956).

We now provide a partial definition[1] of a popular theoretical tool—the Chafee–McLeod coorientation model—as a means of further understanding of role taking.

Chaffee and McLeod (1968) noted that, when one predicts the priorities, preferences, or behaviors of another, three sets of reactions are involved: (a) the predictor's (P's) own set of reactions; (b) P's perception or prediction of how the other person, O, would react; and (c) O's actual reactions.

As shown in Fig. 2.1, the coorientation model hinges on three measures of similarity or difference among these sets of reactions:

1. *Agreement* between P's and O's own responses.

2. *Congruency* or similarity between P's own reaction and that which she or he attributes to O. Further, extremely low congruency seems synonymous with polarization—the complete absence of apparent shared meaning between self and other. There is reason to believe polarization, like projection, can discourage understanding and dialogue among people (Dalton, 1962).

3. *Accuracy*—the level of similarity or difference between P's prediction of O's response and O's actual behavior.

Similarity or difference in these concepts can be defined in at least two ways—in terms of distance between ratings given or pattern of responses. For example, baseball fan A may rate all modern baseball teams as more capable than B defines them. Yet A and B may agree that the Tigers are now much better than the Orioles, who are superior to the Indians. In such a case, distance similarity would be low, pattern similarity high. Methodological and conceptual problems relating to this distinction are complex—and beyond the scope of this chapter.

We have now laid a foundation for a second dimension of role taking.

Dimension 2—Method of Role Taking.   Because role taking is important and difficult, the method used seems important. Few rigorous studies have compared different methods, or even defined them clearly. However, approaches seem to fall in three basic categories:

---

[1]Chaffee and McLeod (1968) posited symmetry and mutuality of role taking, with P taking O's role and the converse, as necessary for true coorientation. We ignore the question of symmetry for simplicity's sake here, simply examining the case in which some P takes some O's role.

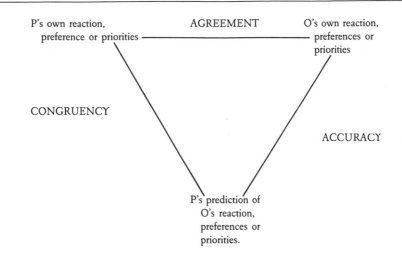

FIG. 2.1. Modified coorientation model of Chaffee and McLeod (1968). Each line represents a measure of similarity or dissimilarity between the arrays of responses that it connects. The index of similarity in each case is denoted by a word in capital letters.

1. *Projection*—attributing P's own beliefs or intentions to the person (hereafter called O) whose role is being taken. Because people differ, this approach seldom yields perfect accuracy. Psychoanalytic thinkers often regard projection as dysfunctional (Hall & Lindzey, 1957, pp. 50, 195–199). And social critics see it as ethnocentric (when carried out by many within a racial, ethnic, or national group with respect to those in another group) or egocentric (when practiced by one individual toward another) (Hartley & Hartley, 1952, pp. 302–303).

In short, projection, which amounts to high congruency, fails to take into account differences between individuals. However, the technique seems easy to use if one buys the assumption that we know (or, at least, think we know) ourselves better than we know others. Gans (1980) found that journalists with national media sometimes project their own views to news consumers because the latter seem too numerous and diverse to analyze. Further, as noted later, projection yields high accuracy under certain conditions.

2. *Reading about and studying role expectations, rules, and contexts.* This can help one predict another's behavior and views if that other's role is tightly defined (i.e., codified, consensually defined, and routinized). The author could pretty well predict the behavior of marching marines by reading his drill manual. He could not predict the behavior of professors, however, from reading their faculty handbook (Steiner, 1963).

3. *Personal interaction with the person, O, whose role is being taken.* One can "get to know" another by constant association and careful observation over time. Formal survey research can be useful in predicting reactions by a group. Predictive games can also help. Here one interacts with a person, predicts his or her priorities or reactions, calculates the level of similarity between P's predictions and O's actual or stated reactions, and then discusses with O bases for prediction errors. The author has used this approach successfully in teaching news judgment to journalism students (Culbertson & Scott, 1978).

Two propositions about the viability of the three role-taking approaches follow logically from the aforementioned definitions.

First, given high agreement, high congruency (i.e., projection) yields high accuracy. This translates into the truism that P can accurately predict O's thinking and behavior by assuming P resembles O only if, in fact, the resemblance (i.e., high agreement) is present.

Second, given low agreement, fairly low congruency is a necessary but not sufficient condition for high accuracy. In short, where P differs from O, P cannot safely use his or her beliefs or preferences as a basis for predicting where O stands. P must look elsewhere for guidance in figuring O out. And Strategies 2 (studying O in context, and with regard to rules, systematically) and 3 (getting to know O through purposeful observation and interaction) can help fill the bill (Culbertson, 1975–1976).

As noted earlier, Strategy 2 should work well only with tightly defined, codified roles. Thus, Strategy 3—laborious, time consuming, and uncertain though it may be—seems to be the only workable approach where agreement with O is low and roles are in a state of flux and uncertainty.

When P takes O's role, he or she attempts to predict or estimate O's reaction or definition with regard to some entity, X. We now turn to two dimensions of role taking that address the nature of X.

Dimension 3—Is the Object the Role Taker's (P's) Self or Someting Else?.
Turner (1956) refers to prediction by P of O's perception of P as *reflexive* role taking. Other types are *irreflexive*.

Clearly reflexive role taking lies at the heart of impression management, an important concern of social psychology and communication. Where people depend on each other, O's impression of P usually bears on P's success in reaching goals. Thus, P has reason to try harder, like Avis, when role taking reflexively. Snodgrass (1985) noted this in attempting to explain why, in an experiment focusing on perceptions of relationships, reflexive role taking proved more accurate than irreflexive.

Dimension 4—Is the Object P's or O's Self, Given It Is One of the Two?.
Goffman (1956) referred to communication by P about P's self as demeanor

behavior and communication by P about O's self as deference. In line with Bateson (1972, pp. 201–211), he argued that most communicative acts have deference and demeanor implications, intended or not.

Say, for example, that you give a smooth, polished, well-researched speech to a chamber of commerce. Your actions tell chamber members that you are a careful, competent, respectful person (a demeanor implication), and that you think they merit your best effort (a message of positive deference). As another example, successful PR people promptly send thank-you letters to speakers whom they have hosted. Such letters, mailed quickly, have positive implications as to both deference (respect for the recipient) and demeanor (showing the sender is thoughtful).

The next two dimensions focus on how one uses a role-taking prediction once it has been made.

Dimension 5—What Is the Role Taker's Standpoint?.   As advanced by Turner (1956), this variable has three values:

1. The *first-person* standpoint. Here, role taker P more or less automatically accepts O's definition of the role-taking object, X, as P's own personal reaction. Such imitative behavior, which amounts to high congruency, does not take account of differences between P and O. First-person role taking is used widely by infants—and perhaps by adults who, for reasons such a mental illness, have lost the ability to interact in a thoughtful, creative, adaptive way.

2. The *third-person* standpoint. In this mode, P attends to O's reaction, but sees it as separate and distinct from P's own. P may use O's presumed reaction as a frame of reference in interpreting P's own view. For example, when the author gives a B grade to a student, he may define that as a relatively low grade if most other instructors have given that person As. Also, when he gives a grade way below that student's academic average, he may hunt for explanations (ill health, a parent's death, etc.) to explain and make sense of the discrepancy without invalidating his own judgment. In either case, the author predicts and considers or infers O's (the colleague's) reaction to the student, but does not imitate it, in forming his own judgment.

3. The standpoint of *interactive effect*. Here P considers the joint implications of his or her own definitions and O's. Subtle and intricate relational behavior—the stuff of good literature and drama—can result. For example, salesperson P can try to make a potential customer (O) feel P is "plain folk." The hoped-for result may be a sale—if the potential customer likes ordinary people—even though P may continue with some distress (dissonance) to see him or herself as a sophisticate and not plain folk.

Table 2.1 provides examples of role taking at each possible value of both reflexivity and standpoint. Clearly, as one moves from the upper left to the lower

TABLE 2.1
Examples of Role Taking at Each Level of Reflexivity and Standpoint

	Standpoint		
	First-person	Third-person	Interactive Effect
Irreflexive	Practitioner blindly ac-cepts boss's assessment that press release is best means of gaining press coverage.	Practitioner views client's ideas about adequacy of press coverage as one factor in making his/her own assess-ment.	Practitioner goes along with client suggestion which he or she dis-agrees with, thinking that the project being completed will succeed anyway, so challenging this suggestion is not worth the hassle it might involve.
Reflexive	Practitioner blindly ac-cepts client's view that he/she has capability of playing only commu-nication technician role.	Practitioner views client's ideas about his/her per-formance skeptically, noting that client is a hyper-critical person who thinks only of the bottom line and the short term.	Practitioner makes special effort to sell him/herself as a researcher, believ-ing this message, if bought by client, will open the way to future valuable research op-portunities.

right in this table, role taking becomes more intricate and subtle. Changing, complex environments require flexibility and adaptability. Of course, subtle role taking requires time and effort sometimes not available when crises demand imme-diate action—and when P lacks the training, wisdom, and information needed. We explore this issue further in the section entitled Implications.

Reedy (1987) attributed very subtle irreflexive role taking from the standpoint of interactive effect to Clark Clifford, secretary of defense under President Lyndon B. Johnson.

Clifford felt that continued American participation in the Vietnam War was untenable by the late 1960s. However, he quickly concluded that overtly arguing to the president for a pull-out would be futile. According to Reedy, Clifford responded by intentionally giving weak arguments in favor of staying in the war. He hoped that Johnson and other top officials would come to see the fallacy of continued U.S. involvement—and would feel that they themselves had reached that conclusion. In this way, defenses against persuasion allegedly were overcome.

The concept of interactive-effect role taking relates closely to the PR practi-tioner's oft-proclaimed desire to function at a management level (Broom & Dozier, 1986). The pure communication technician seemingly focuses mainly on how others look at messages and events that he or she develops almost as ends in themselves. As a strategist, however, the manager must predict and discern people's reactions to the results (i.e., interactive effects) of those efforts. A high level of subtle role taking seems required in the latter instance.

Where role taking occurs from the third-person or interactive-effect standpoint, to what extent does the role taker, P, follow or comply with O's preferences behaviorally? This question leads to another dimension.

Dimension 6—Followership Versus Autonomy. In his news-orientation model developed when studying journalists, Culbertson (1983, pp. 7–9) defined three related concepts as shown in Fig. 2.2. Once again, we view P as the role taker, a PR practitioner, and O as some audience or audience member with whom P communicates.

Given that Ps believe they differ from audience members in prioritizing possible message content, Ps can follow audience preferences when choosing such content. They can act autonomously, behaving on the basis of their own priorities. Or they can do some of both.

The underlying question here—does one follow or lead—has widespread implications for responsible, effective communicator behavior. Extremely high autonomy but low followership can lead one to lose touch with a client or audience. At the other extreme, very high followership but low autonomy can amount to conformity and subordination.

From an ethical standpoint, P's following of O can pose interesting problems where O also follows P. Here each party looks to the other for leadership—a classic case of the blind leading the blind! David Broder (1981, pp. 474–475), among others, has suggested that modern politicians who rely heavily on polls tend

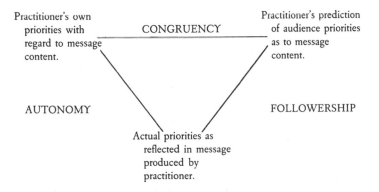

FIG. 2.2. News-orientation model adapted for use with practitioners. Each line represents a measure of similarity or dissimilarity between the arrays of responses that it connects. The index of similarity in each case is denoted by a word in capital letters. Adapted with permission from Hugh M. Culbertson (1983). Three perspectives on American Journalism. *Journalism Monographs, 83,* p. 8.

to follow their constituents slavishly. Yet constituents probably also follow the politicians. Practitioners and clients in public relations must define carefully what they regard as appropriate levels of autonomy and followership.

The followership–autonomy distinction relates closely to key interactionist concepts discussed earlier. For one thing, high autonomy seems required for an active I in Mead's (1955, pp. 175–178) terms. That, in turn, involves behaving and thinking in creative, idiosyncratic ways, not simply reflecting generally accepted consensual definitions and suggestions.

On the other hand, high followership suggests a predominant role for the me— a tendency to accept and behave on the basis of consensual definitions and prescriptions without altering or changing these.

In Ralph Turner's (1956) formulation, role taking from the first-person standpoint implies high followership. Central here is a tendency to accept beliefs and behavioral dictates of others unquestioningly and automatically. On the other hand, role taking from the standpoints of the third person, and often of interactive effect, involves attending to distinctions between self and other as a basis for defining one's self and organizing one's behavior. Low or medium followership seems to be required.

In a final area, Turner's (1962) notion of role making implies autonomy— playing an existing role creatively so as to provide a basis for change. Such change, in turn, may be noted consensually within a social system and accepted as appropriate or inappropriate for future enacters of the role in question.

Some autonomy, it would seem, is needed for creative, adaptive role taking. This suggests another dimension.

Dimension 7—To What Extent Are Roles Being Created or Changed?. Turner (1962) refers to these processes as *role making.* He and Klapp (1958) suggested that they often happen roughly as follows:

1. A role enacter uses a new and different approach. For example, a public relations instructor arranges a series of panel discussions by members of a class.

2. Word about this new wrinkle in playing the instructor role gets around to incoming students, academic administrators, and faculty colleagues.

3. These people discuss and evaluate the instructor's approach, articulating features of it that seem useful and worthy of emulation. They provide the instructor with feedback and suggestions as to how the panels might be refined.

4. Talk of the instructor's innovation reaches colleagues around the state and even nation via the grapevine—and perhaps through seminars at regional and national meetings. While taking part in such discussions, the instructor describes what she or he has done so others can follow suit.

5. Eventually, if response is positive, panel discussions become an accepted part—almost a must—in public relations teaching. Books, articles, and conference papers codify the approach so it becomes accepted practice. Young professors may

ultimately be evaluated for tenure partly on the basis of whether and how well they implement panel discussions!

Lack of change in roles sometimes leads an organization to rigidify and fail. Several processes can contribute to this. For example, elites tend to perpetuate themselves if left unchecked. They strive to win permanent support from certain factions, closing out others who might bring conflicting or new viewpoints. Stone (1987) called this process *elite distemper*.

As noted earlier, interactionists contend that role taking almost always is re-ciprocal (at least, if it is accurate, viable, and adaptive) (Stryker, 1981). This, in turn, suggests a need for people to relate in ways that are symmetrical—P operat-ing at the same level as O—with respect to resources, dependency, and power. We now consider each of these aspects in turn.

Dimension 8—Symmetry of Resources. Exchange theory, a popular area of socio-psychological work, focuses largely on the assumption that two people will seldom keep interacting unless each feels he or she is deriving benefit at least roughly in line with resources he or she contributes. Resources can be financial, physical (owning equipment), or service oriented (having information, wisdom, or help to offer). If P has a monopoly on resources, O may come to feel dependent on P, straining their relationship (Emerson, 1981). (For example, an elderly lady usually feels comfortable about accepting service from someone only if she believes she has repaid or somehow will repay that person in some way.)

This brings us to three dimensions also involving symmetry.

Dimension 9—Symmetry of Dependency. When O depends on P but P does not depend on O for happiness or success, P's monopoly on the "chips" in the relationship may give her or him power over O.

Dimension 10—Symmetry of Power. Interactionists suggest that free, open, accurate, and complete communication becomes difficult when some hold power over others. The Watergate scandal and other governmental disasters presumably occurred partly because subordinates refused to be the "messengers who might get killed" when they passed bad news up the line to the chief executive (Dean, 1977, p. 200). Smugness and arrogance—antithetical to effective mutual role taking—resulted in the oval office itself.

Dimension 11—Symmetry of Communication. The aforementioned suggests that big shots often get an incomplete or inaccurate story from their underlings. Hersey and Blanchard (1969, p. 95) and other management scholars have noted this.

At the same time, underlings apparently need accurate information about their superiors' perceptions of them to survive. In an experiment, subordinates within problem-solving groups showed greater sensitivity to superiors than superiors did to them (Snodgrass, 1985). Apparently asymmetry applies to the accuracy and completeness of messages, as well as their formality and subtlety, with upward communication being quite formal but ranking lower on the other three of these attributes.

A rather vast literature links the first three types of symmetry to complete, accurate communication at the international and societal levels. Asymmetry as to resources and education allegedly contribute to growing differences in knowledge (hence power based on knowledge) between society's haves and have-nots (Gaziano, 1983). And asymmetric information flow between rich and poor nations has been a main concern of the New World Information Order debate (Wells, 1974). Extension by analogy to the interpersonal or role-taking level seems reasonable, but it requires further testing.

The notion of symmetry, along with that of subtle, nonimitative thinking, suggests that effective role takers recognize differences in perspective. This, in turn, leads to a final dimension.

Dimension 12—How Many Roles Does P Take, and How Varied Are These Roles, in Organizing P's Behavior?. Culbertson (1989) has referred to this dimension as breadth of perspective. He has reviewed varied arguments suggesting that breadth of perspective is an important public relations concept. It apparently contributes to adaptability, innovativeness, success, and satisfaction in varied human endeavors. PR implications of this are discussed later.

This completes a look at 12 dimensions of role taking. We now turn to ways in which role-taking dimensions can help articulate and define practitioner behavior amid six current trends affecting public relations.

UNDERSTANDING SOME MODERN TRENDS AND ISSUES

An explosion of knowledge (Toffler, 1971), rapid social change (Klapp, 1978), new communication technology such as videotex and direct broadcast satellite (Wicklein, 1981; Williams, 1982), and other modern phenomena have created new and fast-changing environments for public relations. It has become almost a cliche that practitioners must change to survive in such a context.

We now turn to a trend within public relations and allied fields. Professional communicators have come to segment audiences more than ever. For example, one can find magazines designed for such small, narrowly defined groups as managers of downtown athletic clubs and owners of bed-and-breakfast establishments. This, in turn, has led to careful study of audiences so as to define their needs and interests and market a saleable product (Frank & Greenberg, 1980; Haley, 1985).

Culbertson (1983, 1989) has reported evidence that, where people believe in studying the audience carefully, they tend to favor following it. Bordewich (1977) and Hoyt (1990) have suggested this can lead to shallow, low-quality messages. However, Meyer (1978) has contended that such shallowness need not result from careful audience study if researchers look carefully at common tastes of and relations among audience segments.

These considerations suggest the following hypothesis.

Hypothesis 1. The greater a practitioner's tendency to define his or her audience narrowly and study it carefully, the greater his or her inclination to exercise high followership and low autonomy vis-à-vis that audience.

As noted earlier, role taking through personal interaction seems most workable where a communicator deals with a specific, narrowly defined audience (Tunstall, 1971, p. 230). Even with specialized audiences, gathering and interpreting data about idiosyncracies of individuals is difficult. However, in marketing, this has involved profiling individuals on lifestyle or psychographic dimensions (Frank, Massy, & Wind, 1972; Haley, 1985, p. 13) as a tool in audience segmentation. This suggests another hypothesis.

Hypothesis 2. The more narrowly practitioners define their audiences, the more likely they are to relate to audience members through personal interaction as opposed to projection or rule-context study.

We now turn to five trends said to prevail in modern society.

First, people and institutions all over the world have become increasingly interdependent (Cutlip, Center, & Broom, 1985, pp. 110–111). Industrialization, dependency on other nations for resources and markets, the realization that natural resources are finite, new communication technology, and the growing role of the federal government in people's lives are among many factors supposedly contributing to this trend.

Second, society has become more and more fragmented, with narrowly defined interest groups and political parties focusing on one or a few issues and/or one or a few small subgroups of people (Cutlip et al., 1985, pp. 517–557). Often such groups emphasize emotional, inflammatory issues such as abortion or nuclear safety to the exclusion of other concerns that coherent, well-planned public policy must address.

Third, decentralization within very large organizations has contributed to intense competition for status and resources among units within those organizations (Bower, 1983, pp. 187–220; Peters & Waterman, 1982).

Fourth, organizations and society as a whole are changing with unprecedented frequency and speed as reflected in mergers, bankruptcies, the demise of formerly booming religious institutions, political revolutions, and other developments (Klapp, 1978; Naisbitt, 1982; Toffler, 1981).

Fifth, client organizations often operate in threatening environments with considerable uncertainty about the future and how to prepare for it (Grunig, 1984).

Viewing these changes in light of the role-taking dimensions yields five additional hypotheses for further testing.

Hypothesis 3. In those sectors of society with greatest dependency on other organizations, greatest competitiveness, and most rapid change, successful practitioners are most apt to be the ones who practice role taking from the standpoint of interactive effect extensively.

In line with this hypothesis, Grunig and Grunig (1989) have called attention to the need for sophisticated boundary spanning and two-way communication in uncertain, complex political, regulatory, and product environments. These authors note some evidence that modern organizations have begun to meet such a need, though the data are not conclusive. Role taking at the interpersonal level is not addressed explicitly in related research. However, anecdotal literature clearly suggests that, as competitiveness grows in large organizations with many competing power centers, subtle demeanor implications and interactive-effect, reflexive role taking assume added importance.

For example, McCabe (1987, p. 42) reported an act by Diane Sawyer, then with CBS News, allegedly calculated to tell staffers around her that she was an insider and thus a power to be reckoned with at the network. One day, CBS President Bill Paley called Sawyer who, in the presence of startled executives, replied, "Tell him I'll call him back." At that time, according to McCabe, very few CBS people felt free to refuse to answer a Paley call. In doing so, Sawyer walked a delicate line. Had she misjudged, staffers in a position to block her career progress might have defined her as a hated, ruthless opportunist and a bluffer. Apparently reports at that time that she had recently dined several times with Paley offset these concerns in her calculations by suggesting that her insider status was genuine.

In a different vein, Kruckeberg and Starck (1988) have called for public relations practitioners to emphasize a search for a sense of *community* while also focusing on partisan goals such as votes, favorable legislation, increased purchases, and so forth. The authors believed that such a sense has been lost in the face of trends such as fragmentation, audience segmentation, and decentralization within large organizations. And they contend that, in the absence of a sense of shared purpose and a universe of discourse, practitioners and their clients may often win battles but lose wars.

It would seem that role-taking diversity or breadth of perspective is needed to appreciate the parts that make up society's mosaic—and to find common elements and interesting differences needed to grasp the whole as implied in a sense of community. Perhaps in a world of specialists, PR practitioners may be among the very few able to look at an organization's "total picture," making breadth of perspective especially important for them.

The aforementioned suggests the next hypothesis.

Hypothesis 4—As society becomes more fragmented, organizations more decentralized, and audiences more segmented, public relations practitioners who are successful will have high role-taking diversity (that is, a tendency to take the roles of varied and numerous individuals and groups).

Hypothesis 4 seems especially worthy of testing in a cross-cultural context. It implies that practitioners have a less urgent need for breadth of perspective in a homogeneous, traditional society than in a pluralistic, complex Western nation. (At least, this may hold in intranational public relations.)

In a competitive, fragmented society or organization, someone is almost bound to lose often, creating a high probability of resource, dependency, and power asymmetry. As noted earlier, this apparently can reduce accuracy of communication and role taking, creating a special need for effort to ensure communication symmetry in such contexts. This implies the following.

Hypothesis 5—In highly competitive communities, societies, and organizations, resource, dependency, and power asymmetries will be common. And, in the absence of fully developed public relations and boundary-spanning systems, role-taking accuracy by PR practitioners will be low.

Studies of collective behavior and social movements have shown that cultural, economic, and political change comes about through a process of discarding old rules, definitions, and modes of operation, searching for new rules in a rather loosely defined pattern of behavior for a time, and then institutionalizing and establishing legitimacy of new patterns (Blumer, 1969). This suggests hypothesis 6.

Hypothesis 6. In periods of rapid change within an organization or society and its environments, successful public relations practitioners will often be the ones who role-take a great deal through individual interaction (not via rules, which are then in a state of flux, or by simple projection).

This coin has another side, however. Rokeach (1960, pp. 54–70) suggested that operation in an uncertain environment perceived as threatening has two counter-productive tendencies. First, it requires flexible, adaptive behavior. But second, it tends to lead to slavish, unquestioning adherence to rules and leaders—first-person role taking, projection, and high followership in role-taking terms. Clearly, the second of these tendencies seems apt to mitigate against successful adherence to the first. All of this suggests Hypothesis 7.

Hypothesis 7. In threatening, uncertain environments, public relations roles tend to be tightly defined and many practitioners role-take extensively through the study of rules and contexts. Role taking will often be more inaccurate in such contexts than in others.

If people feel well prepared and seem successful, it would seem threat levels specified in Hypothesis 7 would tend to decline. Thus the more optimistic Hypothesis 6, involving subtle role taking in conditions of change, might "kick in." Peters and Waterman (1982, pp. 292–305) seemed to recognize this when urging large firms to "stick to their knitting" and avoid moving into fields where they have little competency.

Of course, the validity of these hypotheses doubtless hinges on a multiplicity of contingent factors. Nonetheless, they constitute a starting point for future research.

Now we turn to possible implications of role-taking theory in six areas of public relations scholarship and practice.

Public Relations Roles: Some Additional Questions

Broom and Dozier (1986), among others, have sought to clarify the roles that practitioners play. Some appear to act largely as communication technicians, producing and distributing messages. Others serve as PR managers, often playing at least three different roles in the process. These are:

1. Expert prescriber—viewed by top managers as an authority on public relations. Such a person defines PR problems and tries rather autonomously to solve them.

2. Communication facilitator—acting as a liaison, interpreter, and mediator between an organization and its publics. The focus here is on two-way communication, removing barriers to information exchange, and keeping channels open.

3. Problem-solving process facilitator—guiding managers and their organizations through rational processes in defining problems as well as in planning and programming.

Culbertson (1985) found that some educators conceive of two communication-technician roles. One was called the pure production technician, attending almost exclusively to the art and mechanics of message production. A second subrole involved communication planning, dealing with campaign planning and the study of media uses and techniques.

Role research has focused largely on the tasks that various practitioners carry out, their purposes, and environmental as well as organizational-structural factors affecting role choice (Acharya, 1981; Grunig, 1984). Interactionists might call for a focus on one's choice and variety of significant others as well as on role-playing dynamics. Specific hypotheses might include the following: First, communication-technician roles are highly codified and repetitive—hence tightly defined. In particular, tightness might be high with pure production technicians who deal constantly with production schedules, printers' bids, mailing-list updates, and other mechanical matters.

Second, communication and problem-solving process facilitators have many and varied significant others (i.e., high role-taking diversity) relevant to their understanding of process—and of strategic consequences in a changing world. Furthermore, such practitioners emphasize role making and adaptation to change. And in doing so, they become (or are expected to become) proficient at subtle role taking—especially of the reflexive type and from the standpoint of interactive effect.

Of course, measurement problems would be many and varied in studying these matters. However, the payoff in articulating public relations roles might be worth the effort.

Support for Two-Way Symmetric Thinking

Careful study of SI can articulate and add substance to the two-way symmetric model of public relations. Grunig and Hunt (1984) argued persuasively that this model represents a step forward in many contexts for the evolving public relations function.

Mead (1955) and his followers (Stryker, 1981) provided a firm philosophical foundation here. In their view, two-way interaction—behaving and attending to others' reactions in defining one's future behavior—both depends on and adds to a pool of significant symbols about which people share meaning. Such symbols, in turn, are basic to human development and function. People simply cannot *not* do two-way communication without, in some sense, compromising their humanity.

Reedy (1987, pp. 107–111, 135–137) extended the same argument to the American presidency. He noted that the White House is a communication technician's dream. Reporters keep a constant vigil, noting the president's eating habits as well as his stands on issues. Television networks set up expensive equipment on the grounds at their own expense. And rules governing TV press conferences almost guarantee that the chief executive can use reporters as "straight persons" in getting a message across his way.

Despite all that, presidential performance and credibility have suffered, in Reedy's (1987) view, from factors limiting real two-way communication with constituents. Given such isolation, even astute politicians like Lyndon Johnson and Richard Nixon became paranoid and out of step. They grossly misjudged probable reaction to the Vietnam War, prospects for the 1972 election, and other things. Resulting snafus drove both presidents from office in disgrace.

What broke the bond between the president and public? The answers are many and complex, according to Reedy (1987). Most have a strong interactionist flavor. Also, they seem apt to bother both problem-solving process facilitators and communication-liaison people. Included are these points:

1. Presidents are driven, ambitious people with large egos. Those lacking such attributes probably would not run for the office. Thus presidents feel able to change society and see the change as urgent. Their political backgrounds lead them to sort people into three groups: staunch supporters of desired change, implacable foes, and uncertain folk who might be converted. Such a stereotypic view does not set the stage for careful listening to many diverse groups (Reedy, 1987, pp. 127–139).

2. Presidents live in regal surroundings. Almost anyone would come to feel god-like under such circumstances. And those who see themselves as semidivine seldom listen carefully to ordinary mortals (Reedy, 1987, pp. 15–27).

3. In recent years, the threat of assassination has led to security measures that prevent a president from "pressing the flesh" with ordinary people very often. Television campaigning had much the same effect, largely replacing schoolhouse gatherings (except those that are carefully scripted), whistle-stop campaign speeches from the backs of trains, and so forth (Reedy, 1987, pp. 127–138).

4. Bureaucratization, the knowledge explosion, and computers have helped create a need for many specialists to absorb and interpret knowledge so the president can use it in making decisions (or delegating them to others). Further, within the past 20 to 30 years, presidents have found it increasingly necessary to hire aides whom they can control rather than rely on cabinet-level departments. Because such aides have vaguely defined roles, power and prestige get allocated among them based largely on personal closeness to the president and his immediate subordinates. Results are excessive deference to those people and reluctance to report bad news to them (Dean, 1977, pp. 83–121).

These and other factors have limited the effectiveness of incumbent presidents—and of the presidency as an institution—in Reedy's (1987) view. And surely, many if not most such problems fall within the realm of public relations.

One practical implication of such two-way thinking centers on the role and evaluation of exchange programs, roundtable discussions, faculty internships, symposia, and other programs designed to promote interaction. Such programs are sometimes carried out ostensibly to gain acceptance and knowledge of a firm, agency, or industry by the persons invited. Interactionists would argue that such intrapersonal goals are only part of the story. Evaluation should also focus on role-taking accuracy, reflexivity, and standpoint as well as shared meaning—interpersonal objectives.

Maturational Ethics—A Current Rage?

In the area of ethics, SI role taking shows up in a popular contemporary notion—John Rawls's (1971, pp. 118–192) veil of ignorance. Rawls urged ethical decision makers to back away from a situation psychologically, stand behind an imaginary veil of ignorance, and assume they do not know whether they will be self, or affected others, when coming out from the veil. Such a procedure encourages one to take others into account fully, and to avoid taking unfair advantage, especially of those with little power and few resources.

The fruitfulness of taking roles of varied others—and of striving for breadth of perspectives—seems in line with several other strands in contemporary ethics. These are as follows:

1. Kohlberg (1981, pp. 408–412) built on the underlying notion that, as people mature ethically, they develop and subscribe to principles that apply more or less universally. This, in turn, implies applicability to varied persons and groups in varied contexts. Surely such thinking places a premium on role-taking diversity.

2. The very concept of the generalized other focuses on a rather abstract, global construction of one's social world. This, in turn, suggests a tendency to take into account the community or society as a whole. Culbertson (1973) has argued that the truly professional public relations person must work for the benefit of society as well as one's boss or client.

3. Taking of varied roles requires openness to divergent viewpoints (Hampden-Turner, 1971, p. 389). This openness is often sacrificed when people focus on a narrow range of significant others and turn inward, becoming unduly concerned with serving themselves as a professional or vocational group rather than working for society as a whole. Habenstein (1962) has found such a tendency within the emerging funeral directors' profession, and Carey (1978) has warned against it in a critique of journalism education. Also, Stone (1987) has noted a similar phenomenon among self-perpetuating elites, calling it "elite distemper."

Katz (1984) has argued that medical doctors have moved onto ethical thin ice by promoting authoritarian one-way relationships with their patients. In most cases, he believes, doctors do have genuine concern for people. However, a tendency to talk rather than listen when dealing with patients has had several results detracting from complete, mutual role taking needed for mature ethical performance.

First, doctors and patients have failed to appreciate that they have somewhat different goals. For one thing, doctors tend to view longevity as the main objective of treatment. Patients, on the other hand, sometimes stress quality of life, appearance, and the opportunity to function somewhat normally even if only briefly (Katz, 1984, p. 96). The author's ailing mother once commented, "I'd rather be 90 years old and free to move about and do things than 91 and miserable."

Second, physicians sometimes imply falsely that they have great confidence in the success of a treatment. Such implications stem partly from the notion that patients can best recover if they relax and feel sure they are in good hands. These arguments doubtless have merit. But unrealistic public expectations may result—after all, health care is about as much art as science. Letdowns in the wake of all this can lead to widespread public disaffection as well as poor recovery (Katz, 1984, pp. 165–206).

Clashing Perspectives: Cause for Serious Role Taking

Symbolic-interactionist studies suggest basic problems in organizational functioning when groups, or persons within a group, who are presumed to share a common perspective really do not. A perspective here is a set of organizing beliefs—sometimes called schemata (plural for schema)—that help shape people's information seeking, overall understanding, and behavior (Graber, 1984, pp. 178–200). Failure to accurately perceive disagreements as to perspective can have devastating results.

Anthropologists such as Sahlins (1976, pp. 170–179) emphasize the importance of such schemata. For example, Sahlins noted that Americans eat beef (cattle) and pork (pigs) while according near-sacred status to horses and dogs. In fact, selling of horse meat at American stores has led to vehement protests and cries of sacrilege. This has occurred despite the fact that horses and dogs are quite nutritious and are widely eaten in certain parts of the world.

Such beliefs hinge on complex sets of values and assumptions, according to Sahlins (1976, p. 171). Some examples follow:

1. The central role of meat, particularly beef, in American diets may stem in part from the fact that meat evokes the masculine pole of a sexual code of food, which must go back to the Indo-European identification of cattle or increasable wealth with virility.

2. Horses symbolize the frontier on which they played a prominent role. That role suggests notions such as bravery, individualism, and stamina which are thought to be part of the American character.

3. Dogs have been given familiar names and have assumed a role in the American nuclear family. In the process, they have come to symbolize and be intertwined psychologically with the family as a principal socializing agent and have connotations of warmth, obedience, and friendliness.

Now, when Americans meet people who routinely slaughter and eat dogs and horses, they are apt to disparage those people unless they understand their supporting schemata. Such understanding requires careful thought and, possibly, extensive interaction. It also entails some risk because the American involved may have disquieting thoughts that acknowledging the edibility of horses and dogs might challenge important beliefs that rest on the assumption of inedibility (Rokeach, 1960).

Resolution of such semicrises may be painful, and may require unusually skilled, thoughtful role taking. However, it may lead to new understandings and syntheses contributing to a more satisfactory sense of human community (Kruckeberg & Starck, 1988).

At a more mundane level, Matthews (1979, pp. 153–158) noted that 1974 federal legislation led to construction of many day-care facilities for elderly women. This, in turn, required a new breed of professionals (or, at least, expansion of an existing breed) to run the centers.

Conventional wisdom held that the professionals were supporters and servants of the elderly, with both sharing a common definition of how the two groups would interrelate. However, Matthews's (1979) observations convinced her that the professionals and the elderly had conflicting perspectives, which lay at the heart of potential PR problems.

In one center, for example, elderly "customers" sought to be active in politics in the tradition of the Grey Panthers. (After all, 70-year-olds are not all senile and decrepit just because a law so defines them.) (Matthews, 1979, p. 20). Far from being supportive, the professionals covertly opposed the political bid by withholding information from the elderly (Matthews, 1979, 155–158).

Why? Matthews contended that the professionals' jobs, and the legitimacy of their work, hinged largely on the dependent, inferior status of the elderly (Matthews, 1979, pp. 155–158). Neither the professionals nor the elderly perceived this motivation clearly. Nonetheless, the overall picture was not a promising one for smooth interaction within the care centers—or for reporters trying to enhance public understanding. Nor was it a healthy setting for the birth of a profession (based, by definition, on a concept of broad, genuine public service) (Rivers & Schramm, 1969, p. 24). In-depth analysis in line with management-oriented public relations roles would be needed to address these matters.

In a literature review, Culbertson and Shin (1989) traced police public relations problems back to differing viewpoints between cop and citizen regarding police work.

On one hand, citizens have been led by popular lore, movies, and TV shows to equate police work largely with apprehending bad guys and bringing them to justice. Also, police training and recognition tend to emphasize and reward such activity more than community service broadly defined (Trojanowicz, 1973).

However, in the wake of social unrest in the 1960s and 1970s, American police came to realize that they cannot prevent or solve crimes alone. They must rely on help and support from varied citizens. In light of this, police began working with citizens in neighborhood watch and other community-service oriented efforts. In fact, things have progressed to the point where the police now spend only about 20% of their time enforcing the law in a narrow sense (Bard, 1973).

In point of fact, police cannot do community service very well unless citizens—and cops themselves—expect and want them to. Culbertson and Shin (1989) found widespread support for such activity in one small town, but only insofar as people linked the activity with prevention of specific, salient crimes. Career counseling in public schools, escorting parades, unlocking car doors, and other non-crime-related police activities received little public support. Such factors as a siege mentality among inner-city cops (Whittington, 1971) and widespread use of patrol cars (Cain, 1973, pp. 238–246) reduce informal, supportive, friendly interaction needed to achieve real police–citizen understanding on such matters.

Organizational Impression Management: Sensitive Business

In a different area, the truly accomplished expert prescriber might profit from studying different strategies involved in presenting one's organization.

A seminal writer in this area is Canadian sociologist Erving Goffman. In a book called *The Presentation of Self in Everyday Life*, Goffman (1959) argued that we all act on the stage of life most of the time. That is, we take into account how others might react to our behavior and thoughts. And we behave accordingly.

Organizational impression management involves "bureaucratic propaganda," defined in a book with that title by sociologists David L. Altheide and John Johnson (1980). These authors defined propaganda very broadly, focusing largely on records kept and objective-looking measures of success or failure backed up by sophisticated, reflexive role taking from the standpoint of interactive effect.

A bureaucratic organization needs to present itself as successful, as having achieved a great deal (Altheide & Johnson, 1980, pp. 187–203). Thus, it frequently develops tangible measures of success or failure—usually spelling out the methodology behind these measures so skeptics can assess their adequacy and even replicate research that uses them.

Often scholars are called upon to develop such measures. Scholarly labels and sophisticated procedures give an appearance of validity, careful thought, and independence from special interests (Altheide & Johnson, 1980, pp. 77–107). To help on the latter front, related research is often conducted by ostensibly independent university professors.

In fact, however, indices of success are usually developed and chosen with the sponsoring profession's or occupation's interests in mind. Both private and public programs must demonstrate efficiency and achievement to bring in additional funds and/or customers. And public agencies must toe an especially fine line to show they have accomplished a lot—yet they could do much more if only additional funds were allocated for the coming year!

Complex methodologies and terminology mask the fact that performance evaluation in service and information fields is almost always arbitrary and subjective. Take welfare work. Number of visits per day is a tangible index of activity, but it hardly reflects success to a reasonable observer. Yet welfare departments seek to impress people by stressing visits when they appeal for grants and legislative appropriations. Altheide and Johnson (1980, pp. 145–149) found a tendency to overclaim or "normalize" visits so each worker in a welfare unit had about 140–150 visits per month. Such a figure was viewed as impressive, yet credible. Workers would count or discount phone visits—and count or discount visits with people not yet officially on the rolls—to approach this range.

Bureaucratic propaganda would seem to be a necessary element in modern public relations. Scholars would contend that there simply are no god-given indices of success that avoid subjective choice. And they would add that organizations are bound to think of their own interests in a world where most behavior is, in some sense, purposeful and goal oriented.

However, such indices of success can backfire in the long run if investigative reporters and others learn that sponsoring agencies have paid off scholars or chosen only "friendly" ones. Such under-the-table efforts clearly contravene the Public Relations Society of America (PRSA) Code of Professional Standards. In particular, Article 6 of the Code precludes corrupting the integrity of communication channels and government processes. Also, Article 9 rules out making use of an individual or organization purporting to be independent and unbiased but actually serving undisclosed interests (PRSA Register, 1986).

Olasky (1987a) noted that special interests have sometimes hired academic researchers to provide supportive results with just the appearance of independent, scholarly validation. And Bok (1979, p. 182) asserted that perpetrators of such deceit often realize short-term gains but fail to assess realistically the possibility of getting caught—of losing the war despite having won the battle.

CONCLUSIONS

In sum, a symbolic-interactionist view of roles and role taking suggests several lessons for public relations scholars and practitioners.

First, two-way symmetric practice has its roots in basic human functioning. The so-called fourth model of public relations has foundations far beyond those usually provided by professors and practitioners within public relations (Grunig & Hunt, 1984, pp. 41–48). And it obviously suggests a growing role for the activities of expert prescriber, communication facilitator, and problem-solving process facilitator.

Second, practitioners frequently seek to foster interaction. But in evaluation, they tend to stress intrapersonal objectives such as acceptance, support, and knowledge. Interpersonal goals—accuracy of perception included—merit more attention.

Third, the roles that people play—what they do and what they are expected to do—deserve careful study. In such analyses, role tightness or looseness can be critical. Persuading one to do things proscribed by salient others is sometimes akin to forcing a camel through the eye of a needle! Also, successful performance in loosely defined roles requires subtle role taking, knowledge, and self-confidence.

Fourth, in applied planning and research, conflicting perspectives between two organizations or individuals contribute to many public relations problems. In-depth study of these is needed for accurate role taking.

Fifth, personal impression management and its organizational equivalent, bureaucratic propaganda, merit careful study. Such analysis should be searching and critical, but not with universal condemnation. Organizations can hardly be expected not to present themselves as attractive in a world where they depend on various publics.

Sixth, public relations ethics, often accused of shallow, self-serving development in practice (Olasky, 1987b, pp. 143–145), may profit from study of breadth of perspective in role taking—and from varying abstractness (mixing individual-level role taking with efforts to consider one's community or society as a whole). Nonpartisan or societal goals would then come to the fore.

Seventh, role research should broaden its base. To date it has dealt largely with the behaviors that different types of practitioners carry out, and for what reasons.

Future research could focus on role tightness or looseness, role making, inter- and intrarole differences as to ethical maturity and breadth of perspective, possible clashing viewpoints (for example, communication managers may resemble Bower's [1983] people-oriented politicians whereas communication technicians act as hard-headed, measurement-oriented technocrats), and bureaucratic propaganda or impression management as practiced by public relations people in their own behalf.

In sum, the study of role as process—as purposeful construction of meaning—can inform role research within public relations in many ways.

ACKNOWLEDGMENTS

Dr. Culbertson acknowledges the useful contributions to this paper by Carl J. Couch and Chorpaka Kaewyai.

REFERENCES

Acharya, L. (August 1981). *Effect of perceived environmental uncertainty on public relations roles.* Paper presented to Public Relations Division, Association for Education in Journalism and Mass Communication, East Lansing, MI.

Altheide, D. L., & Johnson, J. M. (1980). *Bureaucratic propaganda.* Boston: Allyn & Bacon.

Bard, M. (1973). The role of law enforcement in the helping system. In J. R. Snibbe & H. M. Snibbe (Eds.), *The urban policeman in transition: A psychological and sociological review* (pp. 407–420). Springfield, IL: Thomas.

Bateson, G. (1972). *Steps to an ecology of mind.* New York: Ballantine.

Becker, H. B. (1973). *Outsiders: Studies in the sociology of deviance.* New York: Free Press.

Berger, P. L. (1963). *Invitation to sociology: A humanistic perspective.* New York: Doubleday.

Berlo, D. K. (1960). *The process of communication.* New York: Holt, Rinehart & Winston.

Blau, P. M. (1963). *Bureaucracy in modern society.* New York: Random House.

Blumer, H. (1962). Society as symbolic interaction. In A. M. Rose (Ed.), *Human behavior and social processes* (pp. 179–192). Boston: Houghton Mifflin.

Blumer, H. (1969). *Symbolic interactionism: Perspective and method.* Englewood Cliffs, NJ: Prentice-Hall.

Bok, S. (1979). *Lying: Moral choice in public and private life.* New York: Random House.

Bordewich, F. M. (1977). Supermarketing the newspaper. *Columbia Journalism Review, 11*(3), 24–30.

Bower, J. L. (1983). *The two faces of management.* New York: Mentor.

Bowes, J. E., & Stamm, K. R. (1975). Evaluating communication with public agencies. *Public Relations Review, 1,* 23–37.

Broder, D. S. (1981). *Changing of the guard: Power and leadership in America.* New York: Penguin.

Broom, G. M., & Dozier, D. M. (1986). Advancement for public relations role models. *Public Relations Review, 12,* 37–56.

Cain, M. E. (1973). *Society and the policeman's role.* London: Routledge & Kegan Paul.

Carey, J. W. (1978). A plea for the university tradition. *Journalism Quarterly, 55,* 846–855.

Chaffee, S. H., & McLeod, J. M. (1968). Sensitization in panel design: A coorientational experiment. *Journalism Quarterly, 45,* 661–669.

Culbertson, H. M. (1973). Public relations ethics: A new look. *Public Relations Quarterly, 17,* 15–17, 23–25.

Culbertson, H. M. (1975–1976). Gatekeeper coorientation: A viewpoint for analysis of popular culture and specialized journalism. *Mass Comm Review, 3,* 3–7.

Culbertson, H. M. (1983). Three perspectives on American journalism. *Journalism Monographs, 83,* 7–9.

Culbertson, H. M. (1985). Practitioner roles: Their meaning for educators. *Public Relations Review, 11,* 5–21.

Culbertson, H. M. (1989). Breadth of perspective: An important concept for public relations. *Public Relations Research Annual, 1,* 3–25.

Culbertson, H. M. (1989). Should journalists follow or lead their audiences?: A study of student beliefs. *Journal of Mass Media Ethics, 4,* 193–213.

Culbertson, H. M., & Scott, B. T. (August 1978). *Some editorial games for the magazine editing and writing class.* Paper presented to Magazine Division, Association for Education in Journalism, Seattle, WA.

Culbertson, H. M., & Shin, H. (1989). Police in America: A Study of changing institutional roles as viewed by constituents. *Public Relations Research Annual, 1,* 155–174.

Cutlip, S. M., Center, A. H., & Broom, G. M. (1985). *Effective Public Relations.* Englewood Cliffs, NJ: Prentice-Hall.

Dalton, M. (1962). Cooperative evasions to support labor-management contracts. In A. M. Rose (Ed.), *Human behavior and social process: An interactionist approach* (pp. 267–284). Boston: Houghton-Mifflin.

Dean, John (1977). *Blind ambition.* New York: Pocket.

Emerson, R. M. (1981). Social exchange theory. In M. Rosenberg & R. H. Turner (Eds.), *Social psychology: Sociological perspectives* (pp. 30–65). New York: Basic.

Frank, R. E., & Greenberg, M. G. (1980). *The public's use of television.* Beverly Hills, CA: Sage.

Frank, R. E., Massy, W. F., & Wind, Y. (1972). *Market segmentation.* Englewood Cliffs, NJ: Prentice-Hall.

Gans, H. J. (1980). *Deciding what's news: A study of CBS Evening News, NBC Nightly News, Newsweek and Time.* New York: Vintage.

Gaziano, C. (1983). The knowledge gap: An analytical review of media effects. *Communication Research, 10,* 447–486.

Goffman, E. (1956). The nature of deference and demeanor. *American Anthropologist, 58,* 473–502.

Goffman, E. (1959). *The presentation of self in everyday life.* New York: Doubleday/Anchor.

Graber, D. (1984). *Processing the news.* New York: Longman.

Grunig, J. E. (1984). Organizations, environments and models of public relations. *Public Relations Research & Education, 1,* 6–29.

Grunig, J. E., & Grunig, L. A. (1989). Toward a theory of the public relations behavior of organizations: Review of a program of research. In J. E. Grunig & L. A. Grunig (Eds.), *Public Relations Research Annual, 1,* 27–63.

Grunig, J. E., & Hunt, T. (1984). *Managing public relations.* New York: Holt, Rinehart & Winston.

Habenstein, R. W. (1962). Sociology of occupations: The case of the American funeral director. In A. M. Rose (Ed.), *Human behavior and social processes* (pp. 225–246). Boston: Houghton Mifflin.

Haley, R. I. (1985). *Developing effective communication strategy: A benefit segmentation approach.* New York: Wiley.

Hall, C. S., & Lindzey, G. (1957). *Theories of personality.* New York: Wiley.

Hampden-Turner, G. (1971). *Radical man.* Garden City, NY: Anchor.

Hartley, E. L., & Hartley, R. E. (1952). *Fundamentals of social psychology.* New York: Knopf.

Hersey, P., & Blanchard, K. H. (1969). *Management of organizational behavior.* Englewood Cliffs, NJ: Prentice-Hall.

Hoyt, M. (1990). When the walls come tumbling down. *Columbia Journalism Review, 28* (6), 35–40.

Katz, J. (1984). *The silent world of doctor and patient.* New York: Free Press.

Klapp, O. (1958). Social types: Process and structure. *American Sociological Review, 23,* 674–678.

Klapp, O. (1978). *Opening and closing: Strategies of information adaptation in society.* New York: Cambridge University Press.

Klapper, J. T. (1964). *The effects of mass communication.* New York: Free Press.

Kohlberg, L. E. (1981). *The philosophy of moral development: Moral stages and the idea of justice.* New York: Harper & Row.

Kruckeberg, D., & Starck, K. (1988). *Public relations & community: A reconstructed theory.* New York: Praeger.

Matthews, S. H. (1979). *The social world of old women.* Beverly Hills, CA: Sage.

McCabe, P. (1987). *Bad news at black rock: The sell-out of CBS news.* New York: Arbor House.

Mead, G. H. (1955). *Mind, self and society.* Chicago: University of Chicago Press.

Meyer, P. (1978). In defense of the marketing approach. *Columbia Journalism Review, 11* (5), 60–62.

Naisbitt, J. (1982). *Megatrends.* New York: Warner.

Olasky, M. N. (1987a). The development of corporate public relations, 1850–1930. *Journalism Monographs, 102,* 22–23.

Olasky, M. N. (1987b). *Corporate public relations: A new historical perspective.* Hillsdale, NJ: Lawrence Erlbaum Associates.

Peters, T. J., & Waterman, R. H., Jr. (1982). *In search of excellence.* New York: Warner.

Public Relations Society of America Register (1986–1987). New York: Public Relations Society of America.

Rawls, J. (1971). *A theory of justice.* New York: Basic.

Reedy, G. E. (1987). *The twilight of the presidency: From Johnson to Reagan.* New York: New American Library.

Rivers, W. L., & Schramm, W. (1969). *Responsibility in mass communication.* New York: Harper & Row.

Rokeach, M. (1960). *The open and closed mind.* New York: Basic.

Rokeach, M. (1969). *Beliefs, attitudes and values.* San Francisco: Jossey-Bass.

Sahlins, M. (1976). *Culture and practical reason.* Chicago: University of Chicago Press.

Snodgrass, S. E. (1985). Women's intuition: The effect of subordinate role on interpersonal sensitivity. *Journal of Personality and Social Psychology, 49,* 146–155.

Steiner, I. D. (1963). Interpersonal behavior as influenced by accuracy of social perception. In E. P. Hollander & R. G. Hunt (Eds.), *Current perspectives in social psychology* (pp. 263–268). New York: Oxford University Press.

Stewart, D., & Hoult, T. (1956). A social-psychological theory of the authoritarian personality. *American Journal of Sociology, 65,* 274–279.

Stone, C. N. (1987). Elite distemper versus the promise of democracy. In G. W. Domhoff & T. R. Dye (Eds.), *Power elites and organizations* (pp. 239–265). Newbury Park, CA: Sage.

Stryker, S. (1981). Symbolic interactionism: Themes and variations. In M. Rosenberg & R. H. Turner (Eds.), *Social psychology: Sociological perspectives* (pp. 3–29). New York: Basic.

Toffler, A. (1971). *Future shock.* New York: Random House.

Toffler, A. (1981). *The third wave.* New York: Bantam.

Trojanowicz, R. C. (1973). Police-community relations: Problems and process. In J. R. Snibbe & H. M. Snibbe (Eds.), *The urban policeman in transition: A psychological and sociological review* (pp. 119–138). Springfield, IL: Thomas.

Tunstall, J. (1971) *Journalists at work: Specialist correspondents.* London: Constable.

Turner, R. H. (1956). Role-taking, role standpoint and reference group behavior. *American Journal of Sociology, 61,* 316–328.

Turner, R. H. (1962). Role-taking: Process versus conformity. In A. M. Rose (Ed.), *Human behavior and social processes* (pp. 20–40). Boston: Houghton Mifflin.

Wells, A. (1974). *Mass communications: A world view.* Palo Alto, CA: National Press Books.

Whittington, H. G. (1971). The police: Ally or enemy of the comprehensive community mental health center? *Mental Hygiene, 55,* 55–59.

Wicklein, J. (1981). *Electronic nightmare.* New York: Viking.

Wilcox, D. L., Ault, P. H., & Agee, W. K. (1986). *Public relations strategies and tactics.* New York: Harper & Row.

Williams, F. (1982). *The communication revolution.* Beverly Hills, CA: Sage.

PART II

REPORTS OF ORIGINAL RESEARCH

Chapter 3

Public Relations and "Women's Work": Toward a Feminist Analysis of Public Relations Roles

Pamela J. Creedon
The Ohio State University

Practitioners and researchers alike have expressed concerns about the potential for a decline in status and salaries in public relations due to the increasing number of women entering the practice (e.g., Bates, 1983; Cline et al., Hunt & Thompson, 1988). Underlying this position is the belief that the new female majority in the practice of public relations will soften the image of the field and cause it not to be seen as a "heavy-hitting top management function" (Lesly, 1988, p. 5). David Dozier (1988) suggested that the "fate of women in public relations—particularly their participation in management decision-making—is inexorably linked to the survival and growth of public relations as a profession" (p. 6).

An examination of news stories about the increasing number of women in other fields—including medicine and law—uncovers similar concerns. For example, the increasing number of women entering the professional fund-raising and development field resulted in a story in the *Chronicle of Philanthropy* in March 1989, which has a hauntingly familiar sound to that being heard in public relations:

> As female development officers have come to outnumber their male colleagues for the first time, some veteran fund raisers and consultants say they are worried about what they see as a troubling paradox.
>
> Those observers, male and female alike, say that the "feminization of fund-raising" may be simultaneously helping and harming the profession. They note that women are enjoying tremendous success in a vocation for which they appear to be especially well suited. But at the same time, those observers say that if women come to dominate the field, their presence could depress the salary levels and prestige of this traditionally male career. (Goss, 1989, p. 2)

Why is the repetitive theme about the troubling paradox of "feminization" repeated as "news" each time the number of female workers exceeds the number of male workers in a previously male-dominated occupation?[1] A possible explanation comes from sociologist Barbara Reskin (1988). She suggested that "the primary method through which all dominant groups maintain their hegemony is by differentiating the subordinate group and defining it as inferior and hence meriting inferior treatment" (Reskin, 1988, p. 58).

She also asserted that the conventional explanation for the wage gap—job segregation—is wrong because it ignores the dominant group's "incentive to preserve their advantages and their ability to do so by establishing rules that distribute rewards" (Reskin, 1988, p. 58). Elizabeth Toth (1989) hinted that just such a rationale also might explain some of the reactions to "feminization" in public relations when she asked: "Are men attempting to maintain their perceptions of power in public relations instead of seeking to learn as the contexts change, that their roles can change as well? Are male public relations practitioners seeking to maintain their own positions of power?" (p. 9).

Sociologists have articulated several patterns that typically occur when occupations switch from a predominantly male to a predominantly female work force. The first pattern is that males concentrate in the highest status, highest paying jobs (as we have observed in public relations); and the second is that, as women gain access to formerly male-dominated occupations, changes occur in work content, autonomy, and rewards (Reskin, 1988).

For example, in the field of pharmacy, at about the same time that women began to predominate in pharmacy schools, the content, autonomy, and rewards of the occupation began to decline. Large manufacturers took over the preparation of many drug compounds and chain and discount store pharmacies undercut independently owned pharmacies, forcing the retail pharmacists to become increasingly like retail sales clerks, simply dispensing prepared drugs and keeping records (Reskin, 1988, p. 70). Similar patterns of decline in content, autonomy, and rewards have been described in more than a dozen "feminized" occupations including book editing, real estate, and baking.

This chapter explores the concept that not only might the content, autonomy, and rewards in public relations practice be changing, but that we may also be ignoring the promise of "feminization" by overreacting to a perception that "feminization" poses a "threat" to the growth of the public relations function (e.g. Creedon, 1989a; Rakow, 1989). The fundamental premise is that the "threat" scenario is a socially constructed interpretation for "feminization" tied to a much deeper struggle to establish value and equity for gendered work in this culture. Rakow (1989) suggested that the struggle for equity in the workplace is rooted in

---

[1] I put "feminization" and "women's work" in quotes throughout the chapter because of the perjorative manner in which they are usually used. Webster's definition of "feminize" as "to make or to become effeminate" only adds fuel to the "fear of feminization" by males in our culture.

our "gendered core that makes us *feel* male or female" (p. 3). Similarly, Benderly (1987) asserted that "gender comes down to what life revolves around anyway: earning a living" (p. 65).

The goal of this chapter is to stimulate discourse about the societal values and assumptions that support attempts to construct the meaning of "feminization" in public relations. It also examines the notion that one possible side effect from these attempts has been the trivialization and devaluation of what has come to be called the technician's role where the majority of women in public relations are employed. The chapter also explores how devaluing the technician's role affects students' perceptions of the communication-producing or information-processing role of public relations and their employment expectations.

The analysis that shapes this chapter is based on 15 years of professional experience, 5 years of classroom interactions, a review of the literature, in-depth interviews with several female public relations executives, a group interview with several mid-level practitioners, an exploratory survey of 20 seniors in the public relations sequence at The Ohio State University, and conversations with other educators.

A Review of Role Research

A role is "a culturally prescribed mode of behavior" (DiCaprio, 1974, p. 14). Individuals in a given culture have both life roles and occupational roles, which generally fit into societal norms for patterns of behavior (Betz, in press). Often early childhood socialization, reinforced by parents, teachers, religion, the media, and so forth, presents these life roles and occupational roles in terms of sex role stereotypes. Betz (in press), for example, reported on research that suggests that children as young as $2\frac{1}{2}$ years are able to distinguish masculine and feminine occupations and that these stereotypes are highly resistant to change. She also suggested that "although attempts have been made to justify the existence of occupational stereotypes on the grounds that certain kinds of job content are more congruent with the skills of males, while others are more congruent with female abilities, there is strong and consistent evidence that the proportion of men and women in an occupation is the best predictor of its job sex-type."

Formal occupational role research in public relations began in the late 1970s.[2] First, Glen Broom and George Smith (1979) conceptualized and reported on five different role concepts (expert prescriber, technical service provider, communication process facilitator, problem-solving/task facilitator, and acceptant-legitimizer)

---

[2]The description of the chronology and genealogy of the development of public relations role research in this section of the chapter is a secondary analysis of reports from Ferguson (1987) and Wetherell (1989). Ferguson was a student of Broom's at Wisconsin, and Wetherell was a student of J. Grunig's at Maryland. Further primary research into the historical development of public relations role concepts that describes various aspects of the work would be useful.

at the Association for Education in Journalism (AEJ) convention in Seattle in 1978. According to Wetherell (1989), these "roles were theoretical and derived from the practitioner and consulting literature" (p. 45).

In 1980 Broom (1982) consolidated the five roles into four categories (expert prescriber, communication facilitator, problem-solving process facilitator, and communication technician), and compared the roles played by men and women in a paper presented to the Public Relations Division of AEJ in Boston. He also suggested that some roles in his schema overlap because individuals do activities found in several roles, but he maintained that over time a dominant role emerges. Since then others have suggested that the scale used by Broom and Smith (1979) to differentiate between role functions may be ambiguous (Reagan, Anderson, Sumner, & Hill, 1989).

In the early 1980s David Dozier began to collaborate with Broom by correlating Broom's four role concepts with such variables as sex, salary, education, and experience (Broom & Dozier, 1986). Dozier's factor analysis of Broom's data base identified two primary role typologies (the manager and the technician) and two lesser categories (media relations and communication liaison).

By the mid-1980s, research into public relations roles was rapidly gaining in popularity. *Public Relations Review* published a theme issue on role research in 1985 (Brody, 1985; Cottone, Wakefield, Cottone, & North, 1985; Culbertson, 1985; Selnow & Wilson, 1985) and a number of other researchers—several of whom who had studied with Broom—continued to examine public relations roles on their own.

Among this group were several female researchers who suggested further refinements on Broom's role concepts. For example, Mary Ann Ferguson (1987), who studied with Broom at Wisconsin, started her own program of empirical research on public relations roles beginning in 1979. She has continued this work and two of her female students at the University of Florida (Linda Childers and M. Dayrit) completed their master's theses in the area (Ferguson, 1987).

It is interesting to note that although this group of female researchers also found clear evidence of distinct manager and technician typologies in their work, they each identified a role category (called researcher-problem solver by Childers, researcher by Ferguson, and monitor by Dayrit) that had not been identified as a separate role category in either Broom's[3] or Dozier's work. However, of greater interest to this paper are their findings related to the role category described by Dozier as communication liaison. In Dozier's schema, the communication liaison functions as an advisor to decision makers, but is not held accountable for program outcomes.

Childers's research suggested that the variables associated with the liaison role appear to change over time, and Dayrit described the role as an information-processing and linking function in her research (Ferguson, 1987). In Dayrit's schema, which relied heavily on boundary spanning theory by Miles (1980), the linker establishes and maintains relationships between the organization and its publics, whereas the information processor interprets the meanings of information and translates its implication to decision makers or to the organization's publics.

The thread that appears to tie the categories of liaison, linker, and information processor together is some evidence of decision making in a nonmanagerial role. Additional evidence of decision making in a nonmanagerial role was found in a study by Johnson and Acharya (1982) who suggested that women participate in decision making but a lower level. Moreover, in one of the few cross-cultural studies of public relations roles and decision making, two female Canadian researchers (Piekos & Einsiedel, 1989) found that Canadian women participate in higher-order decision making as frequently as men, especially at the managerial role level.

The support found in these studies for a role category in which decisions are made by nonmanagers is significant. One need only to examine commonly cited textbook descriptions of the manager and technician typologies to understand the significance. For example, James Grunig and Todd Hunt (1984), who proposed that three of Broom's (Broom & Smith, 1979) roles (expert prescriber, communication facilitator, and problem-solving process facilitator) are actually subroles of the manager role, described communication managers as: " . . . practitioners (who) systematically plan and manage an organization's public relations program, counsel management, and *make communication policy decisions. They are involved in all segments of public relations decision making.* They frequently use research to evaluate their work" (p. 91, emphasis added).

They describe communication technicians as: " . . . practitioners (who) provide the communication and journalistic skills—writing, editing, audiovisual production, graphics, and production of messages—needed to carry out public relations programs. *Communication technicians do not make organizational decisions.* They implement the decisions of others, and do not do research to plan or evaluate their work" (Grunig & Hunt, 1984, p. 91, emphasis added).

These descriptions clearly suggest that the fundamental difference between a public relations manager and technician is the ability or power to make organizational decisions. However, as the previously cited studies suggest (e.g. Childers, 1986; Dayrit, 1986; Ferguson, 1987; Johnson & Acharya, 1982), evidence of decision making has been found in an apparently nonmanagerial category variously described as a linking, liaison, or information-processor role.

Who Are the Technicians?

Research has shown that American public relations practitioners are segregated by sex within the two dominant role typologies (Cline et al., 1986; Dozier, 1988). Women are clustered in the technician role, whereas men predominate in the manager role.

In fact, in a panel survey of 206 members of the Public Relations Society of

America conducted by Broom and Dozier (1985), the number of female respondents who were classified as technicians increased from 38% to 52% from 1979 to 1985, whereas the number of female respondents who were classified as managers moved only one percentage point from 18% to 19% over the same time period. This finding was considered especially disturbing because the same 206 practitioners responded to the survey, suggesting that female job status actually declined as experience increased.

In striking contrast, the cross-cultural study of public relations roles by Piekos and Einseidel (1989) found that, although Canadian public relations practice paralleled the United States with significantly more women than men in the role of communication technician, when *"age and years of experience are controlled for, the relationships between gender and communication technician, and gender and expert prescriber become insignificant"* (p. 16). They found that in the roles of communication facilitator and problem-solving process facilitator, women were just as likely as men to assume these roles. However, they did find that overall women earn significantly less than men in all role categories except for that of problem-solving process facilitator.

In the United States, Dozier (1988) suggested that the "segregation of women in the technician roles does more to predict income differences than do years of professional experience, span of employment with present employer, education and age" (p. 7). Over the course of a career, this role segregation can result in a $300,000 to $1.5 million penalty for being a woman in public relations (Cline, 1989).

Why is a Technician of Less Value?

There is no simple causal explanation of why predominantly female job and occupational categories like that of the public relations technician are perceived as less valuable than predominantly male categories.

Feminist analyses suggest that such systematic devaluation probably began with the first re-presentation—also known as historical account—of life in primitive hunting and gathering societies. Accounts of primitive man-the-hunter portray a culture in which violent, venturesome men killed wild animals to feed the helpless, homebound women and children of the tribe (Benderly, 1987; Eisler, 1987).

However, many scholars and anthropologists, including Richard Leakey, endorse the position that "the notion of the club-swinging caveman killer is a wishful fantasy" and that more than likely the truth is that the men came back empty-handed or not at all from their hunting excursions, whereas the women cultivated the crops and gathered the food that provided most of the village or tribe's diet (Benderly, 1987, p. 137).

Thus, feminist theory traces the systematic devaluation of women's contributions to its roots in assumptions underlying anthropological, archaeological, and historical traditions that trivialized work not associated with male values like phys-ical power and dominance.

In the American workplace, feminist scholars suggest that "women's work" has been systematically devalued since the industrial revolution, when we moved from a communal-like, agrarian-based economy to an economic system that split life and labor into public and private spheres. In the industrial economy, value—which was linked to wages—was linked with the public or masculine sphere. Conversely, the private or feminine sphere—which was not associated with wage value—was assigned little or no public value (Rakow, 1989; Scott, 1988).

Why Do Women Cluster in the Technician's Role?

Some have argued that women are clustered in the technician role because the skills required by this role attract them to it. This research reports that women are attracted to public relations careers primarily to write and to be creative, and that often these preferences are the result of socialization patterns (e.g., Bates, 1984; Cline, et al., 1986; Selnow & Wilson, 1985).

Suggesting that the socialization process explains different outcomes is both useful and dangerous. From a feminist perspective, it is useful because it allows us to see the influence of various values (e.g., gender, race, class) on the outcome in a white, male, American culture. However, it is also troubling from a feminist perspective because the explanation is often turned into a justification for different outcomes. In this sense, socialization becomes a vehicle through which the victim is blamed for the rape or the victim is encouraged to blame herself.

For example, Hunt (1988) found that male and female students may approach the study of public relations with differing self-perceptions of competence and differing conceptualizations of basic skills before and after training, presumably due in some part to socialization patterns. However, in contrast to what a socializa-tion paradigm might lead one to expect, a review of occupational self-efficacy studies by Betz (Betz & Hackett, 1986) did not support a general hypothesis of gender differences in overall occupational self-efficacy.

Instead, she found evidence of socialization patterns in studies that examined occupational self-efficacy in traditional and nontraditional occupations. That is, whereas "men's occupational self-efficacy was equivalent for traditional male and traditional female occupations; women's self-efficacy expectations were lower than men's for nontraditional occupations and significantly higher than men's for tradi-tional occupations" (Betz & Hackett, 1986, p. 281).

Thus, Hunt's (1988) finding of difference in gender-related self-perceptions of competence before training may relate more to the students' perceptions of the occupation than to their perceptions of their own abilities. There is also some evidence that the gender differences in occupational self-efficacy may be crum-bling. Some studies are now suggesting that women are becoming as interested in status-related careers as men are, and that there are more similarities in the reasons why men and women choose careers than there are dissimilarities. One recent national study found increasing similarity in the values and life plans of male and female college students (Fiorentine, 1988). It reported a "dramatic increase in the value women place on status-attainment goals" and a resulting overall congruence in the high-status career goals of first-year college students.[3]

Fiorentine's (1988) finding of a high-status career orientation among college students was supported in an exploratory study of 20 seniors in the public relations sequence at Ohio State.[4]

The students, 14 women and 6 men, responded to a questionnaire that measured their interest in performing various public relations roles. The items used were statements developed by Dozier (Broom & Dozier, 1986) to measure his four public relations role categories—technician, manager, communication liaison, and media relations. A five-point Likert-type scale was used in which students indicated their interest in performing each of the functions listed.

A preliminary analysis of the responses found strong interest scores for both men and women in items describing the manager role. Moreover, women were only slightly more likely than men to agree that they were interested in being the person responsible for writing communication materials. (The media relations role and the communication liaison role produced moderate and comparable interest scores for both men and women.)

Further support for the hypothesis that women may not be attracted to public relations careers because of a desire to perform the technician's role was found in a group interview with six female mid-level practitioners in Columbus, Ohio. Only two of the six practitioners, who ranged in age from 28 to 35 years, had originally selected public relations because of an interest in writing.[5] Both women stated that this interest had been encouraged by secondary school teachers, who were not in journalism or public relations, but who thought that the best way to make a living as a creative writer was in some form of journalism.

The other four members of the group suggested that their interests were based on perceptions of the opportunities in public relations to use problem-solving and organizational skills, promotional and sales skills, and people skills. Two women actually expressed a dislike for writing and suggested that they "write only when they have to."

---

[3]The study was a time series analysis of data from the American Freshman study conducted by the American Council on Education. The survey employs a representative sampling of college freshmen from about 350 schools, surveying nearly 250,000 students each year since the late 1960s. The data set used in this study are reported from 1969–1984.

[4]My original plans were to repeat the survey for the next several quarters and to eventually have a large enough group of men and women to complete some statistical analysis. But since then we have changed the course entirely.

[5]The practitioners in this group were all part of an IABC accreditation study group. Because they belong to a professional organization and are studying for accreditation, they are likely to be more highly motivated than the typical practitioner.

Public Relations as a Management Function

A great deal of recent research has focused on the need to elevate public relations to a management function (J. Grunig, 1989; J. Grunig & L. Grunig, 1989; J. Grunig & Hunt, 1984). The theme is advanced for several reasons.[6]

First, as management function, public relations could more easily become part of an organization's dominant, policy-making coalition. Membership in the dominant coalition is important because it has been hypothesized that the coalition members select the manner in which public relations will be practiced in an organization.

The dominant coalition's power to control the way organizations practice public relations is explained by power-control theory (Childers, 1989; J. Grunig, 1989; J. Grunig & L. Grunig, 1989). Simply put, power-control theory states that organizations behave the way that they do because those with power choose that behavior.

In an article forecasting the future of public relations, Judy VanSlyke Turk (1986) cautioned that: "Public relations professionals have a choice: Become skilled strategists, even strategic innovators, and establish themselves as a central part of management as planners and decision-makers, or hold on to a preoccupation with techniques, which will limit the practitioners' role to being the "chairman's boys or girls'" (p. 13).

James Grunig (1989) amplified the need for a management orientation in public relations with his description of excellent public relations departments:

> Communication managers conceptualize and direct public relations programs. Communication technicians provide technical services such as writing, editing, photography, media contacts or production of publications. Technicians are found in all public relations departments, but managers are a necessary component of excellent departments. Less excellent departments consist mostly of technicians whose work is supervised by managers outside of the public relations department. . . . (pp. 28–29)

The preceding assessments of the technician and manager roles vigorously promote the concept that public relations should be a management function. But, it can be argued that they also contain the subtle message that although technicians may be present in excellent public relations departments and will be in the future, their contributions to an organization have less value than those of managers.

Overall, two general message themes emerge from these comments and other recent literature. First, public relations must become a management function or

---

[6]Led by Dr. James Grunig of the University of Maryland, a team of researchers—funded by the International Association of Business Communicators (IABC) Foundation in what may be the most comprehensive research project undertaken in public relations to date—has set out to examine this hypothesis and to define what constitutes excellence in public relations management. It is their view that in excellent organizations the communications function and the organization operate in a two-way symmetrical model of communication that contributes to overall organizational effectiveness. This model is "based on research that uses communication to manage conflict and improve understanding with strategic publics" (Grunig, 1989, p. 28).

else the occupation will decline in status and salaries will decrease. Second, if we agree that a dualistic role schema (manager and technician) exists, a managerial role is preferable.

What Skills Are Needed to Practice Public Relations?

As we move toward defining public relations as a management function, are we conscious that we may be reframing its occupational content? Are we ignoring research that suggests that writing skills remain critical for entry-level jobs?

In a study of the values of communication students from four geographically disparate universities, Parsons (1989) found that the public relations students in the study (80% of whom were women) expressed "extreme discomfort" with creative work, including writing. He reported that one "of the most dramatic and surprising findings of the study was the degree to which public relations students disliked all proffered forms of creative work" (p. 165). He concluded that: "While public relations students, for example, appear protectionistic of business—their future employment area—they also seem averse to writing. This may imply a desire to go right into management, even though the road to management often leads through employee communications" (p. 167).

However, these future practitioners may be surprised by what skills they find are required of them in the workplace. Wakefield and Cottone (1987) asked owners and presidents of agencies and firms and public relations directors of corporations and governmental and nonprofit organizations their opinions of the knowledge and skills necessary to practice public relations. The respondents, the majority of whom were employed at agencies and firms, reported that the top two skills required of practitioners were decision making/problem solving and customer/client relations. Various writing, editing, and design skills ranked next in this survey as very to moderately important.

In other surveys conducted to determine what skills are necessary for entry-level jobs, professionals continued to suggest that writing skills are fundamental for beginning practitioners (Baxter, 1986).

Enhancing the Value of the "Technician's" Role in Public Relations

Elizabeth Toth (1989) suggested that from "a feminist ideological perspective, women may fulfill an influential communication function for an organization—the creation of messages" (p. 8). But, because the masculine value is to ascribe status to a managerial role, "we may be searching for proof of influence on the managerial function of an organization when the technical role may be the operative one" (p. 8).

In her review of feminist theory, Larissa Grunig (1988) has suggested that the decision as to what phenomena are found to be problematic is distorted by gender needs and desires. Because there is evidence that when any male occupation becomes "feminized," a formula-like, prepackaged interpretation of the potential negative impact of the switch is advanced, it may be instructive to examine strategies used in other occupations to address gender-related job segregation.

Comparable worth theory is one strategy that some feminists have suggested can help establish value for work that is seen as gender-related or "women's work." They suggest that although affirmative action has challenged discrimination in hiring, "comparable worth challenges the allocation of rewards" on the basis of stereotypical gender traits (Blum, 1987, p. 382). Moreover, it "extends the notion of discrimination to include the systematic underevaluation and underpayment of work women do" (Blum, 1987, p. 382–383).

In the majority of cases where comparable worth strategies have been used successfully to raise wages, jobs were evaluated in terms of their contribution to the organization in accomplishing its goals and objectives. For comparable worth to meet with success in the public relations field, it would require the strong support of strong professional organizations, because the record shows that most successful outcomes have been the result of a labor union action (Blum, 1987).

Moreover, it is especially important that any efforts to add value to the technician's role in public relations on the basis of a comparable worth strategy be initiated from within the profession. The major issue in most comparable worth studies is deciding who does the job evaluation and who decides what counts (Brenner, 1987).

It is also important to recognize that comparable worth theory has been challenged by some feminists on the grounds that it reinforces skill-based hierarchies (Brenner, 1987). Others see it as "a limited remedy for occupational segregation and the wage gap" and, because it is based on meritocracy, it becomes a potentially divisive force between groups of workers (Steinberg, 1987, p. 466). However, because it is grounded in liberal theories of equal opportunity and a free marketplace, its theoretical base may have potential for more immediate acceptance in fields like public relations.

Another value-enhancing strategy might be to change the designation of the technician's role. In advertising, often the technical role is designated as a creative role; in journalism, it is essentially that of the reporter. Perhaps a title like creative specialist, communication producer, or information producer would better describe the role in public relations.

What Does the Emphasis on Managers and Management Really Mean?

Perhaps, if we are willing to freely and critically examine what we know from other occupations and to consider what assumptions support the values associated with the technician's role and the manager's role, then we can expose our various philosophical approaches to public relations.

Ferguson (1987) challenged role researchers "to be explicit about their assumptions particularly with regard to whether any one of the roles is more desirable or to be more highly valued. Findings from other areas of organizational theory and research dictate that assertions about the manager's role as being more desirable than other roles should be documented" (p. 2).

Rakow (1989) asserted that the philosophy behind management is a hierarchy structured around masculine values (efficiency, rationality, individualism, and competition), which in turn presumes a "natural" hierarchy of workers—with white women and women and men of color generally at the bottom behind blue collar men. She also suggested that calls "for making public relations a 'hard science' led by corporate managers and calls for making public relations 'macho' to attract more men are calls for increasing the power of public relations departments and practitioners by aligning the field with the masculine tendencies of organizations" (p. 12).

Thus, by emphasizing the value of the manager's role, presumably at the expense of the technician's role, we may be moving our students and our emerging profession closer and closer to adopting the male model of values. As Rakow (1989) explained, the "'feminization' of public relations could simply be a cooptation of women's unvalued work while putting women's values to work . . . " (p. 13).

If we agree with Rakow's (1989) assessment, we may be in danger of encouraging our students to become managers only to have their potential diminished to a handmaid's tale (Atwood, 1985). In this Orwellian future scenario, public relations managers would serve a management system whose sole purpose is to procreate and preserve a white male value system. (The preceding scenario was suggested primarily to promote further discussion and research. It is not presented as an inevitable outcome.)

A Feminist Look at Role Research

Role research in public relations follows the model for such work in many disciplines. Thus, the work of dedicated male researchers like Glen Broom and Dave Dozier who have toiled to identify roles in public relations is not in question; rather, the assumptions of the science that lead us to believe that we can describe meaning and experience in compact categories is called into question.

Alpha and Beta Bias. We have some evidence that the prevailing interpretation that there are two dominant roles for public relations practitioners has both homogenized and dichotomized the meaning of work in the field. The interpretation appears to have homogenized the meaning of work by making all technicians appear to be similar, when in fact there is ample evidence that this is not the case. For example, some technicians process information, some produce creative products, and some manage the process as well as produce the product. As Rakow (1986) suggested, role categories flatten and homogenize "the meaning and evaluation of experience" (p. 13).

The two-role mindset also appears to have dichotomized the meaning of work in public relations by reducing the functions of the public relations practitioner into a hierarchy of two seemingly dissimilar roles—the manager who decides policy and the technician who implements "his" decisions.

Feminist scholarship identifies the exaggeration of differences as alpha bias and the inclination to ignore or minimize differences by assuming a male norm for human behaviors as beta bias (Hare-Mustin & Marecek, 1988). We can find evidence of both biases in role research because the tendency is to massage the data to search for statistically significant difference. This means that researchers often do not look beyond the mean to the exceptions.

Alpha bias has the additional consequence of "ignoring or minimizing within group variability. Furthermore, outgroups such as women are viewed as more homogeneous than dominant groups" (Hare-Mustin & Marecek, 1988, p. 459). Another consequence of this bias is the tendency of research to ignore differences among women—or men—that are due to race, class, age, marital status, and social circumstances.

Gender Bias. From a feminist standpoint, gender bias (substitute race, class, ethnicity, etc.) in research reflects the perspective of the researcher, which frames "his" assumptions and "his" model of the world. In essence, this bias suggests that the researcher's construction of the world influences "his" perception of the results. This model argues that the "observer's identity is a critical variable in the potential objectivity of the research results" (L. Grunig, 1988, p. 52).

Although arguments that gender bias is equally possible for men and for women are acknowledged in feminist theory, they are countered by feminists from two positions. First, because the normative assumptions of most research are based on a male worldview, a woman (or person of color) in this culture is privileged to "know" at least two realities—her own and that of the white male culture in which she lives and works. Second, a movement within feminism, deconstructionism, suggests that different perspectives among women (or men) are equally likely outcomes and, therefore, there is no singular woman's perspective, rather women's perspectives (L. Grunig, 1988.) The goal is to have various perspectives recognized and revealed openly.

In public relations role research, we can find at least a suggestion of gender bias. Although Broom and Dozier's (Broom, 1982, Broom & Dozier, 1985; Broom & Dozier, 1986; Broom & Smith, 1979; Dozier, 1988) work and interpretations have predominated in the literature, we have found additional interpretations from female researchers. For example, Piekos and Einsiedel's (1989) cross-cultural study of public relations roles found clear evidence of cultural variation in decision making when correlated with gender, lending credence to the position that a cultural gender bias might have been reflected in the models. And, Ferguson, Dayrit, and Childers (Ferguson, 1987) identified a linking role in public relations that includes a level of decision making in a nonmanagerial position that was not found in the dominant role paradigm.

Riane Eisler (1987) suggested that:

> social structures of the future will be based more on linking, than on ranking. Instead of requiring individuals to fit into pyramidal hierarchies, these institutions will be heterarchic, allowing for both diversity and flexibility in decision-making and action. Consequently, the roles of both men and women will be far less rigid, allowing the entire human species a maximum of developmental flexibility. (p. 200)

Public relations research has not addressed the possibility of a linking, rather than a ranking, role structure. Our current hierarchical pyramid suggests that the primary career path for public relations practitioners moves one from technician to manager. Not only may this approach support a rigid system of ranking, but it may also ignore the realities of the workplace.

Can We Move the Boundaries of Knowledge and Create Something That Works?

There are boundary lines around any field, drawn between the knowledge that is included and that which is excluded. Thus far, public relations has primarily dealt with knowledge strategies grounded in liberal assumptions, which suggest that if we work to reform the system by gently nudging and expanding its latitude of acceptance, eventually progress will be made.

However, these strategies reflect what Huber (1983) called the "drip, drip theory of social change" and do not address a transformative approach in which we change the form of the system by exploring fundamental issues like how the field is defined and where its knowledge boundaries really are. Transformation is an approach that suggests that we need to improve the condition of women (and cultural minorities) not only by changing their position within the existing system, but also by changing the terms of the system itself.

To do this, we must re-vision—that is, re-examine our assumptions about values in a new, critical way—in our textbooks, our lectures, our courses, and our research (Creedon, 1989a, 1989b). This is an enormous task but one that is underway. Elizabeth Toth, Larissa Grunig, Lana Rakow, and others have already suggested that it is high time for public relations "to contemplate its navel."

Overall, we need to re-vision the value of work in public relations. This means that we need to discuss the gender (race, class, ethnicity) value system in our classes and textbooks so that our students understand the assumptions that form its core. For example, in role research this means we must deconstruct the philosophical assumptions that suggest that public relations should be a management function and, then, we need to deconstruct the "trash compactor" model we have used to condense a multiplicity of experiences into two hierarchical roles.

For a field that owes much of its growth to the rise of public opinion as an arbiter of value, and for a field that has been described as the "oil that makes democracy run," this transformative approach is not only a further opportunity to grow, but a chance to lead the way in communicating diversity in values to various audiences outside of academe.

And, if values are the building blocks of culture, and if a role is a culturally determined pattern of behavior, and if, as Brenda Dervin (Dervin & Clark, 1987) has suggested, communication preserves—perhaps even produces—culture, then what is to stop us from building a culture in public relations that values creative message production, linking behaviors or liaison skills, and information-processing skills in a comparable manner with policy decision-making skills and people management skills?

Within academe, the need for critical research in public relations that seeks to understand the values and assumptions of our philosophical approach to knowledge has never been more clear. Admittedly, transforming the value system is a tall order, but it starts by moving the boundary line that forms an individual's perspective on knowledge. When this individual's research program, course, textbook, or lecture reflects the multiple realities that exist in a diverse culture, it gives energy to the process that moves the boundary line of knowledge in the entire field closer to something that works.

ACKNOWLEDGMENTS

I wish to thank several individuals for their suggestions and comments that contributed to the development of this chapter. They include: Rebecca Rooney, Mary Margaret Fonow, Lauri Grunig, Leslie Steeves, and Elizabeth Toth.

REFERENCES

Atwood, M. (1985). *The handmaid's tale.* New York: Fawcett Crest.

Bates. (1983.) A concern: Will women inherit the profession? *PR Journal, (39*(7). 6–7.

Bates. (1984). Further reflections on women in the profession. *PR Journal, 40*(1), 4.

Baxter, B. L. (1986). Public relations professionals offer course recommendations. *Journalism Educator, 40*(4), 9–10.

Benderly, B. L. (1987). *The myth of two minds: What gender means and doesn't mean.* New York: Doubleday.

Betz, N. E. (in press). Women's career development. In M. Paludi & F. Denmark (Eds.), *Handbook of the psychology of women.* Westport, CT: Greenwood Press.

Betz, N. E., & Hackett, G. (1986). Applications of self-efficacy theory to understanding career choice behavior. *Journal of Social and Clinical Psychology, 4*(3), 279–289.

Blum, L. M. (1987). Possibilities and limits of the comparable worth movement. *Gender & Society, 1*(4), 380–399.

Brenner, J. (1987). Feminist political discourses: Radical versus liberal approaches to the feminization of poverty and comparable worth. *Gender & Society, 1* (4), 447–465.

Brody, E. W. (1985). Changing roles and requirements of public relations. *Public Relations Review, 11*(4), 22–28.

Broom, G. M. (1982). A comparison of sex roles in public relations. *Public Relations Review, 8* (3), 17–21.

Broom, G. M., & Dozier, D. M. (1986). Advancement for public relations role models. *Public Relations Review, 12*(1), 37–56.

Broom, G. M., & Dozier, D. M. (1985, August). *Determinants and consequences of public relations roles.* Paper presented at the meeting of the Association for Education in Journalism and Mass Communication, Memphis, TN

Broom, G. M., & Smith, G. D. (1979). Testing the practitioner's impact on clients. *Public Relations Review, 5*(3), 47–59.

Childers, L. (1986). *Salary and gender: A panel study of male and female public relations practitioners.* Unpublished master's thesis, University of Florida, Gainesville, FL.

Childers, L. (1989). Credibility of public relations at the NRC. In J. E. Grunig & L. A. Grunig (Eds)., *Public relations research annual* (pp. 97–114). Hillsdale, NJ: Lawrence Erlbaum Associates.

Cline, C. G. (1989). Public relations: The $1 million penalty for being a woman. In P. J. Creedon, (Ed.), *Women in mass communication: Challenging gender values* (pp. 263–275), Newbury Park, CA: Sage.

Cline, C. G., Toth, E. L., Turk, J. V., Walters, L. M., Johnson, N. & Smith, H. (1986). *The velvet ghetto: The impact of the increasing percentage of women in public relations and business communications.* San Francisco: International Association of Business Communicators Foundation.

Cottone, L., Wakefield, G., Cottone, R. R., & North, W. (1985). Public relations roles and functions by organization. *Public Relations Review, 11*(4), 29–37.

Creedon, P. J. (1989a) The challenge of re-visioning gender values. In P. J. Creedon (Ed), *Women in mass communication: Challenging gender values.* Newbury Park, CA: Sage.

Creedon, P. J. (1989b). Public relations history misses 'her story.' *Journalism Educator, 15* (4), 26–30.

Culbertson, H. M. (1985). Practitioner roles: Their meaning for educators. *Public Relations Review, 11*(4), 5–21.

Dayrit, M. (1986). *Boundary spanning roles: Public relations and media practitioners.* Unpublished master's thesis, University of Florida, Gainesville, FL.

Dervin, B. & Clark, K. (1987). Communication as cultural identity: The intervention mandate. Published in the *Proceedings of the 16th Congress of the International Association of Mass Communication Research* (pp. 805–812).

DiCaprio, N. S. (1974). *Personality theories: Guides to living.* Philadelphia: Saunders.

Dozier, D. M. (1988). Breaking public relations' glass ceiling. *Public Relations Review, 14* (3), 6–14.

Eisler, R. (1987). *The chalice and the blade: Our history, our future.* San Francisco: Harper & Row.

Ferguson, M. A. (1987, May). *Utility of roles research to corporate communications: Power, leadership and decision making.* Paper presented at the meeting of the International Communication Association, Montreal.

Fiorentine, R. (1988). Increasing similarity in the values and life plans of male and female college students? Evidence and implications. *Sex Roles, 18*(3/4), 143–158.

Goss, K. A. (1989, March 21). Influx of women into fund raising poses paradox: They're effective, but pay and prestige could suffer. *Chronicle of Philanthropy*, pp. 2, 10.

Grunig, J. E. (1989). *Communication, public relations and effective organizations: An overview of the book.* Manuscript submitted for review.

Grunig, J. E., & Grunig, L. A. (1989). Toward a theory of public relations behavior of organizations: Review of a program of research. In James E. Grunig & Larissa A. Grunig (Eds.), *Public relations research annual* (pp. 27–61), Hillsdale, NJ: Lawrence Erlbaum Associates.

Grunig, J. E., & Hunt, T. (1984). *Managing public relations.* New York: Holt, Rinehart & Winston.

Grunig, L. A. (1988). A research agenda for women in public relations. *Public Relations Review, 14*(3), 48–57.

Hare-Mustin, R. T., & Marecek, J. (1988). The meaning of difference: Gender theory, postmodernism, and psychology. *American Psychologist, 43*(6), 455–464.

Huber, J. (1983). Ambiguities in identity transformation: From sugar and spice to professor. In Laurel Richardson & Verta Taylor (Eds.), *Feminist Frontiers* (pp. 330–336), Reading, MA: Addison-Wesley.

Hunt, T., & Thompson, D. W. (1988). Bridging the gender gap in pr courses. *Journalism Educator, 43*(1), 49–51.

Hunt, T. (1988, July). *Do female students approach the study of public relations with different perceptions of skills from those of male students?* Paper presented at the meeting of the Association for Education in Journalism and Mass Communication, Portland, OR.

Johnson, D. J., & Acharya, L. (1982, July). *Organizational decision-making and public relations roles.* Paper presented at the meeting of the Association for Education in Journalism and Mass Communication, Athens, OH.

Lesly, P. (1988). Public relations numbers are up but stature down. *Public Relations Review, 14*(4), 3–7.

Miles, R. H. (1980). *Macro organizational behavior.* Glenview, IL: Scott, Foresman.

Parsons, P. R. (1989). Values of communication students and professional self selection. *Journalism Quarterly, 66*(1), 161–168.

Piekos, J. M., & Einsiedel, E. F. (1989, August). *Gender and decision-making among Canadian public relations practitioners.* Paper presented at the meeting of the Association for Education in Journalism and Mass Communication, Washington, DC.

Rakow, L. F. (1989, May). *From the feminization of public relations to the promise of feminization.* Paper presented at the meeting of the International Communication Association, San Francisco.

Rakow, L. F. (1986). Rethinking gender research in communication. *Journal of Communication. 36*(4), 11–26.

Reagan, J., Anderson, R., Sumner, J. & Hill, S. (1989, May). *A factor analysis of Broom & Smith's public relations roles scale.* Paper presented at the meeting of the International Communication Association. San Francisco.

Reskin, B. F. (1988). Bringing the men back in: Sex differentiation and the devaluation of women's work. *Gender & Society, 2*(1), 58–81.

Scott, J. W. (1988). *Gender and the politics of history.* New York: Columbia University Press.

Selnow, G. W., & Wilson, S. (1985). Sex roles and job satisfaction in public relations. *Public Relations Review, 11*(4), 38–47.

Steinberg, R. (1987). Radical challenges in a liberal world: The mixed success of compara- ble worth. *Gender & Society, 1*(4), 466–475.

Toth, E. L. (1988). Making peace with gender issues in public relations. *Public Relations Review 14*(3), 36–47.

Toth, E. L. (1989, August). *Whose freedom and equity in public relations?—The gender balance argument.* Paper presented at the meeting of the Association for Education in Journalism and Mass Communication conference, Washington, DC.

Turk, J. V. (1986). Forecasting tomorrow's public relations. *Public Relations Review, 12* (3), 12–21.

Wakefield, G. & Cottone, L. P. (1987). Knowledge and skills required by public relations employers. *Public Relations Review, 13*(3), 24–32.

Wetherell, B. L. (1989). *The effect of gender, masculinity, and femininity on the practice of and preference for the models of public relations.* Unpublished master's thesis, University of Maryland, College Park.

_____ **Chapter 4**

Court-Ordered Relief from Sex Discrimination in the Foreign Service: Implications for Women Working in Development Communication

Larissa A. Grunig
University of Maryland at College Park

In April 1989, the District of Columbia Court of Appeals ruled that the United States State Department had discriminated against its female Foreign Service officers in hiring, assignments, and honors between 1976 and 1985. As a result, about 600 women may be entitled to court-ordered relief—including reassignment to more responsible positions. Presumably, many of these "stretch" assignments, or jobs above an individual's personal rank, will encompass communication responsibilities in missions overseas. This chapter analyzes the lawsuit and explores its implications: more women doing public relations in developing countries.

To understand fully the implications inherent in the recent court case, we must look first at several key dimensions: the role of communication in developing countries, public relations per se, the history of women in the Foreign Service, their current status, and their role in information activities. One way to focus on these issues is through the lens of the sex discrimination suit.

Both the personnel structure of the Foreign Service and the sex discrimination case that grew out of it are complicated and have lengthy histories. In essence, then, this chapter is made up of several "minichapters" that include models of public relations, personnel practices affecting women in the Foreign Service and the sex discrimination lawsuit.

Along with the feminization of the field of public relations in the United States has come increasing interest in whatever differences might exist in the way men and women do their job. A growing body of feminist literature in public relations, management, journalism, and mass communication suggests that women would practice a more cooperative, negotiational style of public relations than would men if women saw themselves in a managerial—rather than technical—role.

The negotiational, cooperative approach to public relations characterizes what J. Grunig (1984) has called the "two-way symmetrical" model. An equally two-way but persuasive, dominating model is the "asymmetrical." One-way concepts of public relations include the press agentry/publicity and public information models.

These four normative models, as J. Grunig (1984) conceived them, developed in a linear, historical progression that began with practitioners such as P. T. Barnum, press agent par excellence. J. Grunig considered the two-way symmetrical approach the most contemporary and the most desirable. It has been developed by scholars of public relations and is most often practiced by professionals with academic training in public relations.

Research has shown that the four models reliably and accurately describe at least four typical ways in which public relations is practiced, although they have not explained well why organizations practice the models they do (Grunig & Grunig, 1989). Further, J. Grunig's assertion that the models developed sequentially is open to serious question.

Rather than being linear, the nature might be curvilinear. If—as historical evidence is beginning to suggest—19th-century practitioners of public relations included women who practiced a model that more closely paralleled the two-way symmetrical than press agentry, then P. T. Barnum and his cohorts may represent the nadir of the field. With the reemergence of female practitioners during the late 20th century, public relations may be rising once again to the heights of responsibility that might have characterized its pioneer days. Implications for developing countries include a heightened sensitivity for the people of those countries and a mutually adaptive, participatory approach to communication.

However, only by understanding each aspect of the Foreign Service's personnel practices and the legal challenge it faced in *Palmer v. Baker* (1990) can one, in turn, predict their consequences for women doing public relations work in developing countries. Ironically, these implications—which are the focus of the chapter—are relegated to its concluding section by virtue of the necessary but lengthy antecedent information.

HISTORY OF WOMEN IN THE FOREIGN SERVICE

The first women employed by the State Department (the Department) worked on a part-time basis in 1800 to prepare "taste," a silk ribbon used for affixing the Great Seal to official documents ("Women Make Their Mark," 1989). Three quarters of a century later, the Department began employing women full-time—and that was in a communicative capacity, doing copy work. By 1918, women managed to progress from this technical role to the managerial. Margaret Hanna became the first female supervisor as chief of the Department's new Correspondence Bureau.

Once again, the task involved communication; Hanna was responsible for review-ing outgoing messages.

Not until 3 years later were women permitted to take the Diplomatic Service examination. In 1922, Lucille Atcherson became the first American woman to serve in the Diplomatic Service. From that point forward, women have continued to make progress within the Department. For example, 1967 saw the inception of the Affirmative Action Junior Officer Program, which allowed members of pro-tected minority and ethnic groups to bypass the FS written examination.[1]

Beginning early in the 1970s, the Department began to change its personnel policies based on the principle that women and minorities in the Foreign Service (FS) would be treated identically to their white, male colleagues. In 1971, the Department initiated an Action Plan for Improving the Status of Women (the Plan) in response to a memo from the President to heads of executive departments and agencies. The Plan suggested ways to increase the number of women serving in presidential appointments and in senior and mid-level positions. The Plan also sought to increase the number of women on advisory boards and committees.

Perhaps more far-reaching, however, was the 1970 Policy on the Assignment of Women and Minority Personnel, which specified that "assignments to all posi-tions . . . , domestic and overseas, are made without consideration of the race, color, religion, sex, or national origin of the employee concerned" (70 CA-5901, U.S. Department of State, 1985, p.72).

In 1971, the Department issued a policy statement about the effect of marriage on the rights, opportunities, and employment conditions of female employees (71 CA-3745, U.S. Department of State, 1985, pp. 72–73). This directive made it possible for married women and those with dependents to seek or continue em-ployment in the Service *"so long as they accepted without reservation all conditions of employment, including worldwide availability"* (U.S. Department of State, 1985, p. 73, emphasis added). Until 1971, women (who made up 1.6% of the Foreign Service) were required to retire from the Service when they married.

By 1972, the Department had implemented a Reappointment Program, where-in women who had resigned from the Service because of marriage (and thus were no longer "worldwide available") could seek reappointment there.[2] At the same time, the Department reminded overseas posts that assignments were to be based on qualification, experience, and career objectives—and regardless of "local custom or prejudice" (72 A-1346, U.S. Department of State, 1985, p. 73). Posts abroad were urged to take positive action to accept and integrate women and

---

[1]By 1984, however, that program was modified so that all junior FSO candidates were once again required to take both written and oral exams because of what the Department considered "convincing evidence" that candidates who did not take the written test scored poorly as a group on the oral assessment (U.S. Department of State, 1985, p. 36).

[2]In 1974, a worldwide cable (74 State 54807) announced the Department's intention to review all pending applications from such women on a priority basis and invited all eligible women who had not applied for reappointment already to do so immediately.

minorities into official activities, in an effort to "set the tone" for host-country treatment of these employees.

Still in 1972, a group of Foreign Service Officers (FSOs) participating in various Affirmative Action programs began to acquire their job assignments through a lateral-entry process, rather than through the bottom-up procedure that had characterized job assignment previously. These candidates may have held temporary Service appointments while on detail from other agencies or may have been employed by the State Department in other career categories (U.S. Department of State, 1985).

In 1975, an interim program for hiring at middle levels was instituted for women and minorities. Its aim was to accelerate their representation in the FS (U.S. Department of State, 1985). It also was geared to increasing the number of women available to serve in the senior advisory and presidential-appointment roles alluded to in connection with the 1971 Action Plan described earlier.

These efforts resulted in significant gains for female and minority FSOs: More than 100 female officers (out of a total of between 450 and 500 mid-level officers) were added to the mid-ranks of the FS by 1986 (U.S. Department of State, 1985). Later, however, the program was phased out for two main reasons. First, the Service determined that mid-level appointments were restricting opportunities for promotion of women and minorities already employed there. Second, its previous (and preferred) system of entering from the bottom had resulted in significant numbers of women and minorities in the middle classes. (Only in the mid-1970s did the Service start hiring an appreciable number of women [Gamarekian, 1989].)

Also in 1975, the Department reaffirmed its policy of treating male and female employees abroad equitably by including both in official and social functions—despite any adverse reactions from local officials (75 A-4756, U.S. Department of State, 1985). It officially rejected the explanation that different standards of protocol for men and women, whites and minorities, were adopted to shield women and minorities from such adverse reaction. The following year, the Department reminded overseas posts that they were responsible for implementing Equal Employment Opportunity (EEO) regulations and that those principles applied to local as well as U.S. citizens employed by the Foreign Service. In 1977, an Executive Level Task Force on Affirmative Action began to explore the status of women and minorities in the Foreign Service and to recommend its own EEO solutions (U.S. Department of State, 1985, p. 75).

According to the *Personnel Narrative* (U.S. Department of State, 1985), the Task Force's 90 recommendations were implemented within 2 years. Suggestions resulted in raising the hiring goals of the mid-level entry program, appointing more women and minorities to executive positions at home and abroad, establishing EEO as a factor in appraisals of performance, and naming more women and minorities to FS selection boards.

A related committee was established in 1979. Ambassador Habib chaired a group charged with reviewing FS procedures for recruitment and examination. Of the committee's 63 recommendations, 55 were implemented; the rest were adopted with modifications. Recommendations with the greatest impact on women called for more emphasis on recruiting women, continuing the mid-level entry program for the short term, and reviewing the FS written examination to improve job-relatedness and to eliminate adverse effects on women and minorities (by having a consultant test the exam for bias and by changing the weighting of the exam's sections).

Throughout the period between 1977 and 1981, Secretaries Vance, Muskie, and Haig continued the Department's efforts to ensure that women were considered for senior positions, such as ambassadorial appointments and policy positions at the deputy assistant secretary level and above. Assistant secretaries were urged to consider women and minorities for the critical role of deputy chief of mission (DCM). When he took office in 1982, Secretary Schultz emphasized his commitment to the Department's ongoing EEO efforts. In a statement issued in 1985, he reaffirmed his personal commitment to affirmative action.

However, as a recent article in the Department's bimonthly publication ("Women Make Their Mark," 1989) pointed out: "More can and is being done. In 1988, women comprised 28% of Foreign Service officers, a figure the Department is working hard to increase" (p. 3). In fact, the Department's *Personnel Narrative* (U.S. Department of State, 1985) devoted an entire section to "Efforts to Improve the Status of Women." These efforts are aimed both at increasing the representation of women and minorities at all levels of the Foreign Service and at enhancing their status there.

CURRENT STATUS OF WOMEN IN THE FOREIGN SERVICE

Understanding the role women currently play in the Foreign Service is critically important, according to the State Department's expert on personnel (T. Whitman, personal communication, August 7, 1989). Whitman, the Department's representative most involved with the lawsuit, explained that the "nuts and bolts" of the legal case turned on personnel practices that are, in his words, "almost unique to the Foreign Service." In fact, his office submitted a brief of 50+ pages based on the FS personnel narrative document to the judge in the recent lawsuit in an effort to explain the Service's terminology and unusual personnel practices.

For much the same reason, the following section of this chapter describes those idiosyncratic procedures in some detail. Only by understanding the personnel practices of the FS can one understand both the decision in the sex discrimination suit and its implications for communication in developing countries. Thus this author has waded through the Department's 129-page *Personnel Narrative* (U.S. Department of State, 1985) in an effort to convey an understanding of sections that have a direct bearing both on women in the Foreign Service and on the lawsuit they brought.[3] Blessedly, the language of that document is more narrational than legalistic, although the system of personnel it describes is complex and hard to grasp because it is distinct from other, related (and perhaps more familiar) governmental structures.

The Foreign Service differs from the Civil Service in several major ways. An understanding of these particulars is crucial for understanding the resolution of the sex discrimination suit. First, the system is based on "rank in person" rather than "rank in position." That is, employees are appointed to a class (grade) rather than to a position as in the Civil Service. Jobs are assigned in a separate process whereby FSOs can be assigned to positions below or above (stretch) their personal rank. Promotions are made to a higher class rather than to a higher position. Second, the FS system is "up or out," wherein members who fail to be promoted within a specified time period may be separated mandatorily from the Service.

Third, employees at the Service are rotated to new positions, usually at new locations, for set periods of time (on the average, every 2 to 3 years). Length of duty, according to the Service's *Personnel Narrative* (U.S. Department of State, 1985, pp. 46–47), depends on seniority[4]; whether the post is located in an unhealthy climate or where medical standards are significantly lower than in the United States, or conditions of civil unrest, terrorism, or international war.

Fourth, and related to the rotational nature of the system, is the stipulation that all members of the Foreign Service and their families must be available to travel worldwide at the time of appointment. This means that FSOs must be willing to accept assignment wherever in the world the Service's needs dictate and so there must be no impediment (such as a medical condition) that precludes such assignment.

The *Personnel Narrative* explained the relationship among the aforementioned factors as follows: "This need for constant rotation is a major determinant of many of the personnel practices of the Foreign Service, including promotions through selection boards rather than by selection for new positions at a higher level, a centralized assignment process, and a single worldwide bargaining unit for purposes of labor management relations" (U.S. Department of State, 1985, p. 10).

Finally, the Service is a "bottom entry career-based system." This means that most people enter at the most junior ranks through a nationwide examination process—which, for FSOs, includes both written and oral components. Although the 1946 and 1980 Acts provided for some outside entry to middle or senior ranks,

---

[3]Much of the subsequent sections of this chapter that deal with the Foreign Service is taken from that *Personnel Narrative*. It is interesting to note use of the generic male pronoun "he" therein, as on p. 66: "In cases where it is immediately possible to give the employee an extension of *his* current assignment or a second tour in *his* proposed new function, this will be done" (emphasis added).

[4]Until tenured and promoted to mid-level status, Foreign Service personnel are limited to 2-year assignments. Mid- and senior-level officers generally serve in domestic and overseas posts from 2 to 5 years.

the Congress still intends for most entry into the FSO corps to take place at the bottom through the exam process (U.S. Department of State, 1985, p. 12).

Job Assignment

One problematic aspect of that system remains in job assignment. Until 1975, assignment panels regularly were constituted to place both specialists in communication and generalists within the four major areas of employment, called "cones." This system, which the Department considered to work in principle (U.S. Department of State, 1985, pp. 49–50), resulted in complaints that officers abroad, in particular, found it difficult to compete for new positions because they were unaware of vacancies.

Now, vacancies are announced in advance to all personnel, who "bid" on desired positions at their transfer time. Now too, ostensibly, every employee has the opportunity to compete for available vacancies, helped by assignment officers and career development officers trying to match the best-qualified person to each position in, according to the *Personnel Narrative* (U.S. Department of State, 1985), "a manner as responsive as possible to the employee's career development and professional aspirations and to accommodate the needs of the Service" (p. 51).

Employees may bid on positions not more than two classes above (or below) their current grade. Assignment to a position above one's personal grade is known as a "stretch." This is considered a desirable assignment, because employees believe they enhance their chances for promotion if they perform well in the stretch assignment. (Stretches also may be dictated by the Service's needs when, for example, the best qualified FSO available has a lower personal grade than the job itself.)

Promotion

The Foreign Service's performance evaluation system is at the heart of its promotion system, according to the *Personnel Narrative* (p. 79). Selection boards review employees not only for promotions but for (limited) career extensions, for within-class increases in salary, and for low ranking (which could lead to separation). The official personnel document argues that an important safeguard for employees lies in the constraint that selection boards may base their judgments only on an individual's official performance file. Nothing may be placed in this file without the employee's knowledge. He or she has an opportunity to review and, if necessary, correct the record through grievance procedures provided in chapter 11 of the Foreign Service Act of 1980. Along the way, periodic written appraisals and counseling help ensure that employees have feedback about their strengths and weaknesses.

Officers on the selection board—chosen on the basis of their reputation for fairness and objectivity—are expected to become familiar with the performance of

each employee up for review. They are required to confirm the work's requirements and then determine the performance and potential of the employee. They
also must comment on the relations between the employee and his or her supervisor. Inadmissible (as specified in 3 FAM 527) in any part of the subsequent
report are direct or indirect remarks about race, color, religion, or sex and marital
status or plans, spouse or family (including references to social activities or the
ability of a member of the family to represent the United States).

According to the *Personnel Narrative* (p. 86), reviewing officers should comment on the following: (a) employees' commitment to the principles of fair treatment and equality of opportunity in their dealings with everyone, (b) their
awareness of EEO as a foundation for good management, and (c) the role of
affirmative action in contributing toward the Department's EEO goals and objectives. Since 1980, selection boards have been required to include women and
minority representatives.[5]

Several promotion principles have special bearing on the topic of this paper,
women in the Foreign Service involved with development communication. Criteria
for promotion, for example, include the ability to understand and deal with people
of other countries, to communicate accurately (both verbally and in writing), and to
supervise the work of subordinates and negotiate effectively.[6]

Special Initiatives for Women

The *Personnel Narrative* provided important and relatively current statistical data
on the status of women in the Foreign Service. It begins with the Service's basic
personnel principles, dating back to its creation by the Rogers Act of 1924 when
separate diplomatic and consular services were consolidated. Its modern structure
and most operating principles were developed and implemented with the Foreign
Service Act of 1946.

Most recently, the Act of 1980 updated that structure to accommodate what it
called "the evolution of American society in intervening years" (U.S. Department
of State, 1985, p. 8). Part of that evolution, of course, resulted from the influx of
women and minorities in the Service. In fact, the 1980 Act emphasized the
importance of affirmative action. A number of EEO-related provisions support its
mandate that the Foreign Service be "representative of the American people." It

---

[5]This provision of the Foreign Service Act of 1980 has served merely to codify the preexisting
practice of including such members on selection boards (U.S. Department of State, 1985).

[6]However, time-in-class also is a factor before an employee is eligible for consideration for promotion. This seniority factor has come to be regarded as a "tie breaker," performance appraisal being equal
between candidates in the competitive—rather than administrative—type of FS promotion (U.S.
Department of State, 1985, p. 96). Keep in mind, though, that competitive promotion (based on a
comparison of performance records of employees of the same rank or function or both) is the primary
mode of promotion for the Service.

prohibited racial and sexual discrimination (Section 105), established a recruiting effort aimed at women and minorities (also Section 105), required an annual EEO report to Congress that includes affirmation action plans (again, Section 105), and required that a substantial number of minorities and women be appointed to selection boards (Section 602).[7]

The Department's personnel document also alludes to the need for "men and women from all backgrounds—Americans of all racial and ethnic origins and from all regions of the country" (U.S. Department of State, 1985, p. 21). Recruiting is directed toward universities that the Service considers likely to produce good candidates, especially women or minorities, who are interested in and prepared for a career in the FS (U.S. Department of State, 1985, p. 22).[8] (Journalism is one undergraduate major sought by the Department.)

As recently as 2 years ago, though, women accounted for only 934 or about 23% of the Service's 4,009 career full-time officers. Minorities, both men and women, comprise 13% of the Service. As further evidence of the uniqueness of the Foreign Service's personnel policy, compare these figures with the U.S. Office of Personnel Management's government-wide percentages: male 53.7%, female 46.3%, and minority, 31.9%. By the end of 1988, 23% of all FSOs were women, as opposed to 4% in 1970. Further, these women have been distributed more evenly throughout the four cones than in previous years (Fitzgerald, 1989, p. 27).

Encouragingly, the percentage of women in the FS as a whole did double between 1975 and 1984, from 9% to about 18%. Most of these officers remain concentrated at the junior and mid levels, as one would expect with a bottom-entry system. Almost 30% of today's junior officers are women, compared with less than 19% in 1975. In 1985, only 3% of the senior officers were women. Today about 40 women, or 6% of the total, occupy senior FS jobs.[9]

With more women entering the FS has come the issue of spousal employment. Known as "tandems," couples employed by the Service comprise 8.5% of the Service's work force (582 employees as of July 1984, according to the *Personnel Narrative*). Members of these married couples may work for any of the U.S. foreign affairs agencies, such as State, AID, USIA, Commerce, or Agriculture. In recognition of the significance of the increasing number of married FS employees, the Department "makes every reasonable effort to assign both members of a working couple to the same post in positions appropriate to their class levels and

---

[7]The Department's *Personnel Narrative*, (U.S. Department of State, 1985, p. 77) points out that, as with the representation of minorities and women on selection boards, many of these mandates simply codify activities and programs that the Department already had undertaken.

[8]Since at least the 1970s, the Department of State has targeted its recruitment efforts at increasing the number of women and minorities competing for entry-level appointments in the Foreign Service (U.S. Department of State, 1985, p. 71).

[9]Whitman (Gamarekian, 1989) called this "a glacial case of progress" and said it is not likely to improve "for a while yet."

qualifications" (3 FAM 141.6a, U.S. Department of State, 1985, p. 53). This policy has the dual purpose of, first, meeting personnel requirements and, second, assuring equity for the career interests of individual FSOs insofar as the overriding needs of the Service permit.

FOREIGN SERVICE WORKERS IN COMMUNICATION

The Foreign Service's extensive *Personnel Narrative* explained that the FS is comprised of both generalists and specialists, those who perform widely disparate support and technical functions. About half of all employees are specialists and half are generalists, mainly Foreign Service Officers.

Generalists

The work of all generalists encompasses communication (T. Whitman, personal communication, September 11, 1989). FSOs performing the traditional diplomatic functions engage in information activities that include political and economic reporting and analysis, representation of official U.S. views to foreign govern-ments, and negotiation with foreign governments (U.S. Department of State, 1985, p. 1). This last function is especially critical, because as the personnel document explained, "The Foreign Service abroad is also responsible for maintain-ing the best possible relations with the governments to which accredited, and with persuading and influencing host governments to adopt policies amenable to the United States" (pp. 5–6). These responsibilities are confounded by virtue of the work's being conducted in foreign languages and within foreign cultures, "always with the possibility of a miscommunication which could severely affect the national interest" (p. 6).

FSOs, although generalists, are assigned to one of four broad occupational groups called "cones." They are administrative, consular, economic, and political. Assignment begins with the time of entry into the Service and is based on: (a) performance on the written exam, (b) an oral assessment, and (c) academic and work experience. Subsequent assignment to a position in one of the other three areas is known as an "out-of-cone" assignment and is relatively rare.

Some interfunctional positions require knowledge and experience drawn from more than one cone or can be filled by an outstanding officer from any cone. An example of an interfunctional position related to public relations is the program officer in the Bureau of Public Affairs. All such positions are called "International Relations Office—General."

Each of the four cones involves communication. *Administrative* officers are most directly responsible for communication and information systems. However, *consular* officers work more closely with members of a public, as a rule, than do

FSOs in the other cones. *Economic* officers serve as liaisons in Washington with other U.S. agencies. Because FSOs in the economic cone serve as liaisons with other government agencies, their potential is particularly powerful in terms of development communication. They also are responsible for gathering and interpreting data, presenting U.S. economic positions to foreign officials, and negotiating agreements. A large part of their work involves staying in touch with the foreign business community while maintaining ties with American businesses.

Finally, *political* officers spend their time analyzing and reporting on political matters that affect U.S. interests. Other communicative aspects of their work involve conveying United States government views on political issues to foreign officials; negotiating agreements with them; and maintaining close ties with political and labor leaders, other diplomats, and other opinion leaders in the host country. In Washington, they communicate extensively with other governmental agencies and with foreign embassies.

Much of the work of FSOs in the political cone could be considered diplomacy, rather than public relations per se. However, as Tran (1987) pointed out, communication has become integral to diplomacy.[10] The purpose of diplomacy, according to Tran, is to reach agreement and to resolve conflicts within a framework of policy. He equated diplomacy, or the conduct of official business by trained personnel representing governments, with a communication act or communication process between governments. If one accepts Tran's argument, then the question becomes one of determining the relationship between communication and public relations. To answer, consider the definition offered by J. Grunig and Hunt (1984): Public relations is the management of communication between an organization and its relevant publics.

Specialists

Specialists, who have narrower careers than do the generalist FSOs described in the preceding section, serve exclusively in their respective functions. The *Personnel Narrative* (p. 15) offered the examples of political and consular functions staffed by FSOs who also are expected to work in areas such as medicine, security, and *communication*. The communication specialist, unlike the generalist, serves as a technician rather than as a manager.

Although the all-important *Personnel Narrative* emphasized that the different personnel categories are not intended to convey differences of status or worth, the lawsuit established otherwise. Personnel in the consular and political cones may serve at the same rank and with the same salary, yet the former may be stamping visas whereas the latter make policy.

---

[10]Cohen (1986) argued that media diplomacy exists as a special type of diplomacy.

THE LAWSUIT

In 1971, a State Department employee in the Foreign Service won the first sex discrimination suit filed against the Department. Alison Palmer's success encouraged her to file suit again, 5 years later, in a complaint that took another 13 years and some $150,000 of her own money to resolve.[11] In the 1976 *Palmer v. Baker* case, however, her victory went beyond personal compensation to encompass another 600 female Foreign Service workers who did not opt out of the suit.[12] Implications of the outcome of 13 years of litigation in this class action suit also extend to many more women—and men—seeking to enter the Foreign Service.

When the case first came to trial in May 1985, a District of Columbia Federal District judge ruled against the plaintiffs. Apparently, the testimony of several senior female FSOs for the defense was persuasive.[13] These witnesses all agreed that the Department was discriminatory "in the old days" but that it had made adequate progress over time. (Apparently these women believed that it would be useful for recruiting rather than discouraging more women if the Department were to win the case.)

The judge tended to put more stock in this anecdotal testimony from "success stories" within the Service than in the statistics that also were provided as evidence for the plaintiffs, which, according to T. Whitman (personal communication, September 11, 1989), is typical in such trials. Five weeks of testimony from statistical experts established, for example, that:

- The preponderance of men in prestigious jobs could not have occurred by chance (but must have resulted from discrimination).

- In the past 11 years, nine women out of 586 assignments had been appointed deputy chiefs of mission (DCM)—which could occur randomly once in 2,500 times.

- Women in the political cone were assigned to the consular cone so much more frequently than men that the odds of its happening were one in 100 million.

---

[11]The court awarded legal fees of $1.7 million to Palmer's attorneys in the firm Terris, Edgecombe, Hecker, and Wayne. $330,000 has been paid to date. The rest is the subject of further litigation.

[12]Background information on the lawsuit comes primarily from two lengthy newspaper accounts (Gamarekian, 1989; Havemann, 1989), an article in the insiders' *Foreign Service Journal* (Fitzgerald, 1989), and personal interviews with the U.S. Department of State, Bureau of Personnel, Office of Policy and Coordination, employee most involved with the case: Torrey Whitman (personal communications, August 7, 1989 & September 11, 1989). According to Whitman, the news and journal coverage are accurate. (Indeed, no discrepancies could be found in the facts described in all four sources.)

[13]One of the witnesses for the defense, Rozanne L. Ridgway, retired in June 1989 as one of the Department's highest-ranking women. The former assistant secretary for European and Canadian affairs pointed to "many important instances of discrimination" in her career, yet she said she saw no pattern of organized and conscious discrimination (Gamarekian, 1989).

Characteristics of the judge himself, according to T. Whitman (personal communication, September 11, 1989), also played a role in the decision. Whitman described Judge John Lewis Smith as "a Virginia gentleman, nearly 80, who was a product of another generation and was a most conservative judge." The Department's bottom-line defense, however, was the fact that women do get promoted in the Foreign Service.[14]

Then, after a successful appeal to a liberal panel of judges in 1987,[15] the case was sent back to D.C.'s District Court. There, Chief Judge Aubrey E. Robinson, Jr. found what he called a "definite pattern of discrimination" (Fitzgerald, 1989, p. 22) in all of the areas charged except one, promotion. Initially, he gave the parties involved a chance to agree or to settle on remedies. When they failed to do so by January 1989, Robinson issued a remedial order for corrective action to the Department of State.

The Department has appealed parts of the order.[16] (It argues not with the basic findings of discrimination but for scaling back the remedies.) In the meantime, the Department has had to acknowledge that it discriminated against women in the Foreign Service in hiring, conal designation, stretch and DCM assignments, performance evaluation reports, and superior honor awards.

Immediate Results of the Suit

At this time, the Foreign Service is (a) responding to claims, as ordered, (b) preparing its arguments for the appeal, and (c) beginning tentative discussions of a settlement. The Department has sent forms to women, inviting them to cite what they consider instances of discrimination in past honors, performance evaluations, or assignments. As soon as 3 months after Judge Robinson's decision, the Department had begun reviewing about 225 returned claims. (Another 85 of the eligible women indicated that they would not make a claim.) After Departmental review of the universe of 601 claimants and of individual claims filed, the total number of women whose claims have been deemed valid equals 150, or about one fourth of the members of the class action.

Just under 10% of the women involved filed a claim in every major category of the suit: about 60 in evaluation, 60 who wanted to change their cone or occupational designation (primarily into the political area), and 60 who sought belated awards or recognition. (This totals more than the 150 women, because of some overlap; plaintiffs could ask for redress in more than one area of discrimination.)

---

[14]While the case was being appealed, the Supreme Court applied the *Connecticut v. Teal* case in ruling that a system is not adequate in spite of such an outcome.

[15]The judges remanded the case on error, convinced that Judge Smith had stated his opinion too extremely when he praised the Department for making "every reasonable effort to remove any vestiges of sexual discrimination" (Havemann, 1989, p. A1).

[16]The plaintiffs, too, have filed notice of appeal. They are challenging Judge Smith's 1987 ruling of no discrimination, claiming a reversible error.

The number went from 601 initially deemed eligible for redress as women who had entered the Foreign Service by May 1985 to the 150 who filed claims for several reasons. T. Whitman (personal communication, September 11, 1989) surmised that because about half of the members of that class are fairly junior (4 to 8 years of experience), they had not been on board long enough to experience significant bias. Indeed, a much larger proportion of women who had been in the Service for 15 to 20 years filed claims. Their experience may go back to the days when women were forced to resign when they got married. As a result, according to Whitman (personal communication, September 11, 1989), they had "a legitimate beef and stored-up antagonism over many years."

Some women who failed to file claims undoubtedly decided for tactical reasons not to rock the boat, as Whitman (personal communication, September 11, 1989) put it. For one thing, "not rocking the boat" is an attitude embedded in the FS. Also, the penalty for alienating peers is heavy. Whitman reminded this author that peer evaluation is everything and of the selection-out mechanism.

One immediate effect of the decision, related to hiring, was that the Department cancelled its 4-hour, multiple-choice Foreign Service Exam for 1989. (In a related court decision, that test was deemed discriminatory because men pass its mandatory background section in general management nearly twice as often as do women. Women, on the other hand, score slightly higher on the English expression test.) The exam was found not only to fail women at disproportionate rates but even to discriminate against women who passed, because they were more likely to have low or marginal scores. Thus men, typically with higher scores, tended to place at the top of the register and women at the bottom because the written exam score alone accounted for 25% of the candidate's ranking (the oral assessment constituted 50% and the remaining 25% resulted from the candidate's resume, work record, autobiographical statement, and any evidence gathered during the security clearance process). The next written exam will be administered in the spring of 1990, giving the Department time to analyze and determine what skills, knowledge, and abilities an FSO must possess for his or her first or second tour—not for a senior position some 20 years off.

The entire examination phase of the hiring process is problematic. More than 17,000 took the exam yearly, yet only about 250 ended up with appointments (U.S. Department of State, 1985, pp. 21–22).[17] Now, the exam is being revised. Whitman, quoted in an interview published in the Foreign Service Journal, said: "We don't know why the scoring patterns are the way the are. We don't feel that we can satisfy ourselves or a court of law that these score patterns really mean that men are going to be better Foreign Service officers than women. What that means is we need to redesign the exam" (Fitzgerald, 1989, p. 24).

In the meantime, the 300 to 400 women who (between 1985 and 1987) failed

---

[17]Further, about one third of the current FSOs have not taken the exam; instead, they were "lateraled in" through some conversion process (Fitzgerald, 1989, p. 26).

sections found to be discriminatory will be allowed to return for an oral assessment, which represents the second step of the Service's traditional selection process. As the Court said: "In the absence of tremendously convincing evidence from you guys, we don't believe that the women are less able. We believe it's more likely that you're asking the wrong questions" (Fitzgerald, 1989, p. 24).

In fact, the Department's entire hiring and personnel procedure is under scrutiny. The Court ordered the Department and the law firm retained by the plaintiffs to each nominate an independent expert in personnel to conduct the review. Whitman (personal communication, September 11, 1989) believed that the most important effect of the remedial order was subjecting the Department to this external investigation. On July 31, 1989, the Department filed its first 6-month report to the Court and to the plaintiffs. At any future point when the statistics show significant disparity, the plaintiffs would have instant access to remedy; they would not have to file suit for the next 5 years. Even at that point, there is likely to be an agreement to continue the scrutiny.

Whitman (personal communication, September 11, 1989) explained that the institution of State has begun to restructure to make sure its female employees make gains. This restructuring, in his opinion, will have the effect of changing behavior. Attitudes, in his view, ultimately will change. Already, the lawsuit has resulted in tremendous changes in the stakes and incentives for managers of the Department. According to Whitman, both the Bush administration in general and Secretary of State Baker in particular are keen on avoiding any "black marks" against them in terms of the status of women and minorities. Baker has made it plain to his Department that it needs to do better in this area. As a result, Whitman said, the men "out there in the field" have more reason to listen to the court order. He contended that the order, plus Baker's support for it, has resulted in a significant change of attitude. The argument that remains, however, is how much more systemic change in the structure of personnel practices is necessary.

Of course, long-term employees of the Department such as Whitman had seen a change in attitudes toward women and minorities even before the remedial order. Whitman (personal communication, September 11, 1989) said, for example, that when he joined in 1975 the key to the selection process was an interview with three people. As he explained, "They sized me up after an hour and a half; so this process seemed designed to give you a new generation like the previous generation."

Again, this excessively subjective interview process by men who claimed to be "fair minded" was scrapped well before the 1989 order. In its place was put a more objective process that still had its opponents. However, Whitman (personal communication, September 11, 1989) contended that that process has been accepted and does result in more women and minorities being hired. Once hired, though, women seem to be systematically undervalued. This was established during the court case, for instance, in terms of women's lower performance "potential" ratings in annual reviews.

In addition to cancelling the examination and overhauling its hiring processes in general, the Department has solicited from the 601 women involved in the suit any evidence of inequities in their past assignments. One charge in the suit was that women had been "pigeon-holed" into administrative and consular cones rather than the economic and political, which are considered fast-track jobs that can lead to policy-making roles. According to Garrison, one of the original plaintiffs, "[t]here was a subtle subculture at work" in such assignments (Gamarekian, 1989).

Indeed, as of December 1989, 41% of the men in the FS were political officers and 16.2% were consular officers. By contrast, 22.9% of the women in the Service held political positions, whereas 36.9% held consular positions. Whitman (Fitzgerald, 1989, pp. 23–24) explained that this happened at least in part because conal designations are based on scores on the functional field portion of the written test. Some 90% of the men but only 60% to 70% of the women passed the political exam. Further, disproportionately few women received stretch assignments and disproportionately many received downstretches (those below one's personal rank).

Within months after the resolution of the case, several job transfers already had been granted. However, according to Wagner, an attorney for the plaintiffs, "One unfortunate aspect is that so much time has passed that some of the women who suffered the worst discrimination can no longer get any relief" (Gamarekian, 1989, p. B5).

The important position of deputy chief of mission, in particular, seemed to elude women disproportionately. Ridgway (Gamarekian, 1989) explained that many ambassadors do not want a woman to be in the Number 2 spot in the embassy. Further, she contended that the Department does nothing to help keep qualified women in the forefront as a pool for when that kind of post opens up. As a result, only 9 of the 135 DCM positions are held by women although 320 women have enough rank to compete for such jobs.

Surprisingly few claims related to DCM jobs ultimately were filed. Only 25 women took advantage of what was considered to be the most valuable part of the lawsuit. Whitman (personal communication, September 11, 1989) explained, though, that conventional wisdom says one not only must hold such a position but succeed at it. Unsuccessful performance as a DCM means not only that the FSO has little chance of achieving more senior ranks but may, in fact, result in being selected out of the Service. Being a DCM is prestigious but it makes one vulnerable. According to Whitman, many DCMs fail at the job. He called it the point at which many people go from being good individuals to poor managers.[18]

Thus fear of failure, compounded with the criterion that one get along with the ambassador (most of whom are men in their 50s who, according to Whitman [personal communication, September 11, 1989], are political appointees who do not think much of FSOs to begin with), may have inhibited many of the women

---

[18]Because most posts are too small to require DCMs, few FSOs get managerial experience.

eligible to claim discrimination in assignment to a DCM position. As Whitman explained, claimants may understand that ambassadors would be especially resentful of being forced to work one-on-one with a woman as a result of the suit.

Whitman (personal communication, September 11, 1989), who acknowledged that disparities exist in the DCM situation, also pointed out that women are no more likely to fail than men in the managerial aspects of their job. As a result, the Department already has initiated 1-month, crash DCM training courses, which are mandatory for all. In the planning stage is a procedure for getting more Departmental control over how both ambassadors and DCMs are selected. Right now, ambassadors are appointed by the president and confirmed by the Senate. The ambassador then selects his or her DCM, most often from career FSOs suggested by the Department. The new plan will attempt to make selections of ambassadors earlier on, allowing more time to fit individuals (ambassador with DCM) on a case-by-case basis.

Further, the Department is working toward the acceleration of the DCM assignment process. Whitman (personal communication, September 11, 1989) explained that his office is responsible for assigning 1,500 to 1,600 FSOs yearly to new jobs. About half of these employees think they should be DCMs (if nothing else, such an attitude shows ambition). Now, however, people bid on summer jobs in November—giving the Department 9 months of lead time. The process gets bogged down, in Whitman's words, because, of the total 135 DCM jobs, only about 30 or 40 open yearly.[19]

Long-Term Effects of the Suit

The acid test of the lawsuit, according to Whitman (personal communication, September 11, 1989), lies 4 years from now. At that time, he asked, will more women have made it into the senior Foreign Service? By then, an appreciable number of women will have worked in the Service for at least 20 years so they should be good prospects for senior positions. If they fail to achieve top-level assignments, such as DCMs, then—at least in Whitman's view—discrimination will persist.

Whitman (personal communication, September 11, 1989) indicated that plaintiffs are legitimately concerned about their continuing progress within the Service, given what he called the "deplorable hiring practices and history of the Department." He considered the data over the last 4 years, in particular, to be encouraging. The number of women hired and promoted recently, in his opinion, continues to be "in synch" with the affirmative action goals of the Department and with the influx of women into the work force in general.

---

[19]Whitman (personal communication, September 11, 1989) said that about 15% of the people qualified for a DCM slot this year are women. He predicted that three or four of these women will be selected, "or we will have more trouble."

Finally, Whitman (personal communication, September 11, 1989) pointed out that this case is not the only litigation of its kind in which the Department is involved. Another, related affirmative action suit is in the discovery stage. Unlike Palmer's second suit, this is not a class action but a group of 20 Black FSOs— women and men—suing as individuals. They are alleging discrimination of the same kinds and during the same time period as in *Palmer v. Baker* (1976). Whitman predicted that they will have even a more powerful case related to their promotion and tenure in the Department. He explained that although the Department has done much over the last 20 years to hire Blacks, critics would say that it has not done enough to help them succeed.[20]

MODELS OF PUBLIC RELATIONS

One of J. Grunig's (1984) models of public relations, the two-way symmetrical, seems to hold great promise for minorities and women in development communication—both women who do the communication as part of their work in the Foreign Service and women in the Third World countries where Foreign Service Officers are assigned. In fact, after his initial depiction of all four models, J. Grunig (1987) decided two-way symmetrical public relations represents the most ethical (and efficacious) model for all types of organizations. However, the models themselves beg further research and analysis.

As a first step, one must have a grasp of each of the models as currently conceived. *Press agentry* or *publicity*, the earliest of the models, can be characterized as "promotional wizardry." Its leading historical figure, the promotional wizard himself, is P. T. Barnum. The purpose of this model, dating from about 1850, is propaganda. The organization's goal is control or domination of the environment. Public relations contributes to this goal through advocacy or promotion.

J. Grunig (1984) credited Ivy Lee, an early 20th-century practitioner, with initiating the second stage of public relations practice in this country. Lee conducted public relations as a "journalist in residence," responsible for disseminating truthful information. In fact, the purpose of the *public information* model is the dissemination of information. It helps the organization achieve its goal of adaption to or cooperation with the larger environment through this one-way flow of accurate information—an approach to public relations that was developed largely through Lee's impetus during the first two decades of this century. Presumably, much of the economic reporting of the Foreign Service—as well as its charge of representing U.S. views abroad—would fall under this rubric.

---

[20]Further, Blacks claim they have been overassigned to posts in Africa.

J. Grunig (1984) described the two two-way models of public relations, *asymmetrical* and *symmetrical*, as dating from 1920 and 1960, respectively. The historical figures credited with their development include Edward L. Bernays and a host of public relations educators and researchers. Scientific persuasion is the purpose of the imbalanced model. The organizational goal is environmental control or domination, and public relations contributes through advocacy of the organization's position.

The final stage in the evolution of public relations practice, symmetrical, is more balanced than its asymmetrical counterpart. Although it, too, builds on the work of Bernays and other leaders of the profession, it values mutual understanding to a greater degree. Public relations practitioners embracing this model serve more as mediators than as advocates. Much of the work of the Foreign Service could be accomplished using either of the two-way models. Negotiating with foreign governments or businesses could be approached either from a manipulative, dominating stance or from a communal, adaptive stance.

Despite the historical progression inherent in the models, all continue to exist in actual practice—either as discrete approaches to doing public relations, as mindsets of practitioners, as values held by the organization's dominant coalition, or in mixed forms that may be more situational than static (L. Grunig, in press).

Reardon and Rogers (1988) discussed the benefits and disadvantages of such categorization as the models of public relations—whatever they may represent. On the one hand, categorizing experience helps predict future events and imposes a degree of order on one's environment. This is only useful, they contended, as long as the categories remain efficacious. Too often, though, categories are retained even after events have challenged their utility. One further danger they warned against is the disunifying distortion or unnatural distinction that can result from categorization.

As it is, the models of public relations have approached cultural norms in public relations research and, to a lesser extent, education. Few papers accepted for presentation at contemporary research conferences in the field fail to include at least a peripheral mention of the models.

Rather than paying slavish homage to the established categorization of these four models, feminist scholars might want to continue developing the models. In so doing, they might discover two, four, or more types of public relations typically practiced. Questioning the assumption of a linear progression inherent in the models seems especially useful in predicting the new role that women will play in the Foreign Service as a result of their successful lawsuit.

Even without the much-needed historical research on the model of public relations that female pioneers in both public relations per se and in the Foreign Service practiced, we have a compelling argument to consider not a linear progression but a curvilinear one. Rakow (1989) began to develop this line of reasoning as follows:

Public relations has developed, at least in part, as a response to clashes between [the] two ideologies of individualism and community, of competition and cooperation, of private interest and public good, of hierarchy and egalitarianism, of power over others to collaborative decision-making, of masculinity and femininity. From this vantage point, we can now begin to characterize the feminization of public relations in different terms, *perhaps as the return of the repressed or the swing to an ideology of cooperation and community.* (p. 10, emphasis added)

Such questioning and challenges are not inconsistent with the field. As Kuhn (1970) pointed out, overt disagreement characterizes the social sciences (unlike natural science).

WOMEN AS COMMUNICATORS

Regardless of whether feminists such as Rakow ultimately reconceptualize J. Grunig's (1984) models of public relations, the models' gender implications already are implicit. As Wetherell (1989) found, femininity (whether possessed by women or by men) facilitates the practice of two-way, balanced communication—but only weakly. In actuality, more men than women seem to practice this symmetrical kind of public relations. Why? Wetherell suggested that far more men (and masculine people) than women (or feminine people) are in the managerial role—the role that correlates with the practice of symmetrical communication. She explained what she perceived as a departure from what the literature on gender would suggest as follows: "The two-way symmetric model is a 'big-picture' model; it looks beyond the effects of the program on the environment in which the organization exists. Women have not been socialized to look at the big picture" (p. 199). Wetherell added this important caveat as well: "It could be, however, that if more women and feminine people become managers, the two-way symmetric model will be practiced more frequently" (p. 200).

Broom (1982) first reported that women tend to outnumber men in the technician role, whereas men predominate in the managerial roles of expert prescriber, communication facilitator, and problem-solving process facilitator. His work and that of colleagues in roles research concluded that "advancement in the field [of public relations] is clearly a function of gender and role in the professional workplace" (Broom & Dozier, 1985, p. 55). Consistent with findings about women's status in the recent court case against the State Department, Scrimger (1985) determined that the status of female public relations practitioners in Canada is viewed as inferior to that of males. Consistent with the Broom and Dozier studies, Scrimger also found that fewer women function as managers.

Now, for the first time in the Foreign Service, women may have an equal chance of being accepted and promoted into managerial positions. And for the first time, according to the personnel specialist at the Department of State most involved with the lawsuit (Whitman, personal communication, September 11, 1989), they would not feel forced to conform to existing approaches to public relations. Even then, though, women may be constrained from practicing the kind of public relations or communication they would choose because of their own lack of self-confidence (Turner, 1989). As the IABC Foundation study termed the "Velvet Ghetto" suggested, women are more likely than men to perceive themselves as technicians rather than as managers (Cline et al., 1986).

A large measure of the work that Foreign Service Officers do is managerial, rather than technical. It relates to negotiation—both with economic and political agencies in Washington and with business and governments abroad. The literature of negotiation and conflict management shows that gender plays a role. Greenhalgh and Gilkey (1986) found that mediators with feminine sex-role orientation tend to approach negotiation as part of a long-term relationship between parties, whereas those with a masculine orientation have an episodic, short-term, win-lose approach. Feminine negotiators, they contended, seek outcomes involving mutual gains; masculine negotiators tend to be rigid and uncompromising in their bid to conquer.

Yelsma and Brown (1985) also found that in situations of conflict management—typical in the work of a Foreign Service officer in developing countries—women use more "accommodative strategies." They take on a "peacekeeper" role, they express more support and solidarity, and they use more facilitative behaviors. Yelsma and Brown characterized women as compromising during confrontations; whereas, in their view, men are more competitive and both verbally and physically aggressive.

Thus we see that any discussion of negotiation and conflict-management styles should take into account the sex-role socialization of the communicators as an initial step in predicting how problems might be solved in overseas missions. This is not to argue that women exhibit greater moral virtues than do their male colleagues. Generalizing about men's and women's styles of management always is risky. In fact, any discussion of "essential differences" between men and women is problematic. Meta-analyses of the literature consistently show greater similarities between sexes than within a sex. However, masculinity and femininity or the gendered socialization inherent in our Western culture seems to be an important determinant of how one would approach diplomatic, political, and moral issues (L. Grunig, in press).

The feminization of the field of journalism has important implications for the way all communicative tasks are carried out, according to Beasley and Theus (1988). Their data indicated that women "place greater emphasis on creativity, interpersonal interaction, societal values, and writing skills than do men. Greater presence of these characteristics in the female journalism population may change the nature of . . . public relations, perhaps for the better" (Theus, 1985, p. 49).

In fact, Bates (1983)—writing in the trade press—attributed the influx of women into public relations to the perception that women candidates have higher levels of education and writing skills. He predicted that the field would grow to take advantage of women's "unique experience" in dealing with human and institutional problems outside the limits of what he called "the traditional male power structure" (p. 7). Employers, in his opinion, would hire women because they sense women have better instincts for public relations, "a different sensitivity to the communication needs of people and institutions, and therefore are better suited to practice the kind of public relations needed in the 1980s and beyond" (p. 7).

Joseph (1985) agreed. He cited numerous public relations practitioners who believe women not only are superior writers but will raise the profession's level of performance through their sensitivity, creativity, perceptiveness, ethics, and superiority at face-to-face communication.

Experts in business management also contend that women are especially well suited to meet the international communication challenges of the next decade. In a fascinating study of North American women serving as expatriate managers, Jelinek and Adler (1988) reported that traditional U.S. approaches to doing business abroad seem "risky" today. Instead, they suggested that "alliances, cooperative efforts, joint ventures, and even business-as-usual carried out across cultural lines can be facilitated by skills traditionally thought of as 'female'" (p. 19). Jelinek and Adler explained that because relational skills are more highly developed among women than men, women represent an underutilized resource. Indeed, the women they studied emphasized that personal relationships are especially important in what they termed "slow clock cultures," often found in developing countries.

Throughout the world in the 21st century, traits associated with women may come to be relied on more and more. As social psychologist Bernard (1976) speculated, the basis of society in the cybernetic age will be an "information net," the effective function of which calls for an honest, cooperative society and greater acceptance of what might be defined as female characteristics.

These characteristics, or traits, cluster into two major constellations that define femininity in the psychological literature. *Communal traits*, according to Bakan (1966), have to do with a woman's others-centered nature and her self-perception as part of a larger collectivity of selves. *Expressive traits*, as conceived by Parsons and Bales (1955), are distinguished from the communal only as they describe a woman's communication style. Taken together, all these traits and skills point to what is known and suspected about the value women bring to a communicative role.

Women enjoyed only a modest introduction into the Department of State and, over time, they have continued to face barriers there—in areas that include hiring, assignment to less-than-coveted positions, and separation from the Foreign Service because of marriage. Even so, women have played an active role in the Service for decades. Since the late 1960s, in particular, the State Department has made efforts to attract, to hire, to retain, and to promote female FSOs. Only after 13 years of exhausting and expensive litigation, however, may women truly have the power to exercise their ability and their interests.

Optimism toward this end must be tempered. Cases of collective protest in the academy and elsewhere have shown that the more authority women seek, the greater the discrimination they experience (Abel, 1981; Epstein, 1970; Rothschild, 1978). Also, as Mary Francis Berry, former member of the U.S. Civil Rights Commission, pointed out, "The clear message [from the Supreme Court] is that they oppose the implementation of plans for women and minorities if it works to the disadvantage of some white male" (Raspberry, 1989, p. A23). She contended that the conservative majority seems unfamiliar with the realities of racism and sexism.

COMMUNICATION IN DEVELOPING COUNTRIES

Another reason for guarded optimism is that much remains to be learned about public relations on a global scale. Discussion during a recent conference on international communication identified several important questions, three of which relate directly to the subject of this paper. Participants from the United States and West Germany attending the Herbert Quandt Foundation conference in Philadelphia during fall 1988 asked:

1. What are the opportunities for women to do cross-cultural public relations?
2. What is the role of public relations in facilitating international dialogue?
3. How is public relations practiced by U.S. organizations operating abroad?

The much-needed research on women's impact on public relations worldwide cannot be dismissed, according to Howe (1984). She pointed out that in developing countries, "the need for accurate information on which to base decisions that affect millions of persons, half of whom are inevitably women, makes . . . research on women—hardly a luxury" (p. 283). Further, as former President Jimmy Carter (1989) said, one important responsibility for scholars in research universities is to concentrate on issues of the third world.

Primarily anecdotal, rather than empirical, evidence suggests that both universities and governmental agencies in the United States need to change their development efforts to become more cooperative and collaborative. By rejecting the technical for the collaborative, Pesson (1989) predicted that "cooperation will be the watchword in the advanced developing countries." Such collaborative efforts will be mutually beneficial to the United States and to the developing world, in Pesson's view.

In the meantime, however, the field of development communication itself is relatively new and, according to a report of the Academy for Educational Development (Clift, 1988), it remains shrouded in mystique. However, at least some planners and policymakers consider women the "key" to communication in developing countries (Clift, 1988).

So we do know that exchanging information between the United States and other countries, especially developing nations, is important (Steeves, 1989). Further, we understand that the typical model is one-way and top-down, with information emanating from government and other aid agencies. The problem, according to Steeves, is that this approach may be responsible for misunderstanding recipients' real needs for information. She pointed out that recipients most likely to be missed are women, disadvantaged minorities, and the poor. A social science analyst for the U.S. Agency for International Development, speaking recently to a group of university students, agreed that programs in underdeveloped countries typically fail to consider women as an integral part of those nations. Carlson (Harrison, 1989) contended that "gender as an economic factor is routinely and systematically ignored in planning development problems (p. 3).

This problem persists despite the 1973 Percy Amendment to the U.S. Foreign Assistant Act that requires all U.S.-funded projects explicitly to address women's needs. In actuality, Steeves (1989) argued, there is little evidence that such policies are effectively implemented or evaluated.

Of course, the designers of such policies may be at odds with women's goals for their own communication programs or approaches. As Rakow (1989) pointed out, "In some organizations, upper management may have had the goal of using public relations to make the organization palatable to outsiders while public relations practitioners in the same organization may have seen themselves as genuinely reconciling differing interests for the good of the whole" (p. 11). Within the Foreign Service, this difference of purpose may represent a real constraint for female communicators who envision a mutually adaptive, cooperative style over the one-way, top-down, directive approach that seemingly has characterized much previous work of the Service in developing countries.

Whitman (personal communication, September 11, 1989) estimated that about one quarter of the women who filed legitimate claims in the sex discrimination suit against the Foreign Service are directly involved in communication at overseas posts. He also predicted that it will be 5 to 20 years before the Service becomes a truly equitable workplace for its female FSOs. He further expected that at that point, women would indeed practice a different brand of communication in precisely the ways the literature suggests: more two-way, interactive, and adaptive and less persuasive and domineering.

IMPLICATIONS AND CONCLUSIONS

The successful *Palmer v. Baker* (1976) suit may be just one of a number of discrimination complaints facing or soon to confront governmental agencies involved in communication and relations with foreign governments, businesses, and peoples. Understanding the dynamics of asymmetrical gender relations in the Foreign Service, described earlier, should lead to concern about the chances of women and minorities to achieve equitable positions and posts without the imposition of a remedial court order.

Earlier parts of this chapter have suggested the implications of women being evaluated fairly and placed in more stretch, DCM assignments within all four cones. In that way, they would be in a position to do what they do well: relating to and communicating with those of different countries and cultures in a symmetrical way. Perhaps for the first time, women have been relieved of some of the constraints under which they operated in a man's organization—the Foreign Service.

The abbreviated history of women in the Foreign Service presented here shows that female FSOs have made significant progress in the last 20 years. The Department of State has taken affirmative action to abolish sex discrimination there in an effort to increase the numbers of female and minority employees, chiefly through:

1. Stepping up efforts to recruit women and minorities.
2. Reviewing the written placement examination for its objectivity and relevancy for entry-level positions.
3. Eliminating, in some cases, the written exam.
4. Granting lateral entry rather than relying exclusively on a bottom-entry system.
5. Allowing married women to remain in the Service.
6. Reinstating women who had left because of the restriction against married women FSOs.
7. Accommodating tandem spouses in overseas assignments.
8. Considering EEO principles as a factor in performance appraisals.
9. Appointing more women and minorities to selection boards.

During those same two decades, the Department also has tried to enhance women's position in the Foreign Service. Toward this end, it has:

1. Instituted a mid-level hiring program to increase the pool of women and minorities qualified for senior positions.
2. Enforced the same protocols for women and minorities as for white men abroad, despite any negative reaction from the host mission.
3. Publicized job vacancies well in advance.
4. Protected employees' rights and reduced subjectivity in reviews by selection boards.

Despite these efforts at increasing both the representation and status of women and minorities, the outcome of the lawsuit was dramatic evidence of the Department's failure to do so. Now, however, with the remedial order and an external review of the Department's compliance, female FSOs should have a chance to practice both managerial and technical roles in communication at home and abroad.

This brief look backward to women in the Foreign Service has provided an historical perspective on women's emergence into that field. However, rather than pursuing "contribution history,"[21] or fitting women such as Margaret Hanna, Lucille Atcherson, or even Alison Palmer into an already existing picture of the Foreign Service, we should examine how less notable women have labored in posts abroad and how the increasing number of female FSOs given the opportunity to do so will contribute in their own way to communication overseas—especially in developing countries.

What would become apparent from any historical analysis, however, it that women in the Foreign Service have been neither entirely victims of its history nor mistresses of their own fate. The paper's brief glimpse of women's early years in the Department and the ensuing decades of affirmative action and EEO rulings is consistent with Cott's (1977) rejection of stereotypes that deny women's active role in history.

The task of all feminist scholarship, however, is to take topics such as communication or public relations that are traditionally associated with the public sphere and thus with men and reconceptualize them so they include women (DuBois, Kelly, Kennedy, Korsmeyer, & Robinson, 1985). Given worldwide social, economic, and political changes and the court-imposed transformation within the State Department, such reassessment seems only reasonable.

Rethinking the way communication will be accomplished when more female FSOs are the communicators must not be what feminist philosophers have called "unabashedly utopian" (DuBois et al., 1985, p. 83). Instead, we should operate on what we know and the implications of that knowledge. For example, we have established that generalists and specialists alike in the Foreign Service are involved in communication.

The importance of women doing this vital work in developing countries lies in the prediction that they will practice a more two-way, symmetrical model of public relations than do their male counterparts—at least if they can transcend the routine assignments of their cones and ascend to the managerial level. At that point, they may go on to influence the priorities of their organizations and those of the groups with which they interact. Finally, we might speculate that male FSOs will be affected positively by the model of their female counterparts and also will be able to take advantage of any refinements in the Foreign Service's management-training program and opportunities.

At this stage, though, shortly after the resolution of the sex discrimination suit

---

[21]Historian Gerda Lerner (1975) has written extensively about the problems of this orientation in general. This author has detailed the troublesome aspects of contribution history related to public relations, in particular (L. Grunig, 1989).

against the Department of State, any such theorizing is more speculative than conclusive. Rather than coming to closure, the importance of such discussion lies in its potential to expand our understanding of women's roles in the Foreign Service in general and in public relations capacities there in particular.

Relegating talented women to routine tasks in relatively insignificant positions within the Foreign Service wastes a vital asset of the Service. Instead, by coming to appreciate what women can and do contribute to organizational effectiveness through their orientation to communication, an organization such as the Foreign Service and its constituencies abroad both stand to benefit. In addition, the organization just may avoid the costly court-ordered relief the State Department recently experienced.

REFERENCES

Abel, E. (1981). Collective protest and the meritocracy: Faculty women and sex discrimination lawsuits. *Feminist Studies, 7*(3), 505–538.

Bakan, D. (1966). *The duality of human existence: Isolation and communion in Western man.* Boston: Beacon.

Bates, D. (1983). A concern: Will women inherit the profession? *Public Relations Journal, 39*(7), 6 7.

Beasley, M. H., & Theus, K. T. (1988). *The new majority: A look at what the preponderance of women in journalism education means to the schools and to the professions.* Lanham, MD: University Press of America.

Bernard, J. (1976). Sex differences: An overview. In A. G. Kaplan & J. P. Bean (Eds.), *Beyond sex-role stereotypes: Readings toward a psychology of androgyny* (pp. 10–26). Boston: Little, Brown.

Broom, G. M. (1982). A comparison of sex roles in public relations. *Public Relations Review, 8,* 17–22.

Broom, G. M., & Dozier, D. M. (1985, August). *Determinants and consequences of public relations roles.* Paper presented at the meeting of the Association for Education in Journalism and Mass Communication, Memphis, TN.

Carter, J. (1989, June 7). Universities can be of greatest benefit by concentrating on the Third World. *Chronicle of Higher Education,* p. B3.

Clift, E. (1988, July). *Diffusion and development: Women, media and primary health care in the Third World.* Paper presented at the meeting of the Association for Education in Journalism and Mass Communication, Portland, OR.

Cline, C. G., Masel-Walters, L., Toth, E. L., Turk, J. V., Smith, H. T., & Johnson, N. (1986). *The velvet ghetto: The impact of the increasing percentage of women in public relations and organizational communication.* San Francisco: IABC Foundation.

Cohen, Y. (1986). Media diplomacy: The foreign office in the mass communication age. London: Frank Cass.

Cott, N. (1977). *The bonds of womanhood, 1820–1860: Woman's sphere in New England, 1780–1835.* New Haven: Yale University Press.

Dubois, E. C., Kelly, G. P., Kennedy, E. L., Korsmeyer, C. W., & Robinson, L.

S. (1985). *Feminist scholarship: Kindling in the groves of academe.* Urbana: University of Illinois Press.

Epstein, C. F. (1970). *Woman's place: Options and limits in professional careers.* Berkeley: University of California Press.

Fitzgerald, E. L. (1989, June). Court orders end to sex discrimination. *Foreign Service Journal,* pp. 22–27.

Gamarekian, B. (1989, July 28). Women gain, but slowly, in the foreign service. *New York Times,* p. B5.

Greenhalgh, L., & Gilkey, R. W. (1986). Our game, your rules: Developing effective negotiating approaches. In L. L. Moore (Ed.), *Not as far as you think* (pp. 135–148). Lexington, MA: Heath.

Grunig, J. E. (1984). Organizations, environments, and models of public relations. *Public Relations Research and Education, 1,* 6–29.

Grunig, J. E. (1987, May). *Symmetrical presuppositions as a framework for public relations theory.* Paper presented at the Conference on Applications of Communication to Public Relations, Illinois State University, Normal.

Grunig, J. E., & Grunig, L. A. (1989). Toward a theory of the public relations behavior of organizations: Review of a program of research. *Public Relations Research Annual, 1,* 27–63.

Grunig, J. E., & Hunt, T. (1984). *Managing public relations.* New York: Holt, Rinehart & Winston.

Grunig, L. A. (1989, August). *Toward a feminist transformation of public relations education and practice.* Paper presented at the meeting of the Public Relations Division, Association for Education in Journalism and Mass Communication, Washington, DC.

Grunig, L. A. (in press). Toward the philosophy of public relations. In E. L. Toth & R. L. Heath (Eds.), *Rhetorical and critical approaches to public relations.* Hillsdale, NJ: Lawrence Erlbaum Associates.

Harrison, A. (1989, February 8). Programs deny role of women. *Diamondback,* p. 3.

Havemann, J. (1989, April 20). State dept. acknowledges sex bias: Women hindered in foreign service. *Washington Post,* pp. A1, A20.

Howe, F. (1984). *Myths of coeducation: Selected essays, 1964–1983.* Bloomington: Indiana University Press.

Jelinek, M., & Adler, N. J. (1988). Women: World-class managers for global competition. *Academy of Management Executives, 2*(1), 11–19 (Abstract No. 11783).

Joseph, T. (1985, Winter). The women are coming, the women are coming: Results of a survey. *Public Relations Quarterly,* pp. 21–22.

Kuhn, T. (1970). *The structure of scientific revolutions* (2nd ed). Chicago: University of Chicago Press.

Lerner, G. (1975). Placing women in history: Definitions and challenges. *Feminist Studies, 3,* 5–14.

Palmer v. Baker III, 905 F.2d 1544 (D.C. Cir. 1990). (Case filed in 1976).

Parsons, T., & Bales, R. F. (1955). *Family, socialization and interaction process.* New York: Free Press.

Pesson, L. (1989). Thoughts from the executive director: An expanded and changing role for U.S. universities. *BIFAD Briefs, 12*(3), 2.

Rakow, L. F. (1989, May). *From the feminization of public relations to the promise of feminism.* Paper presented at the meeting of the Public Relations Interest Group, International Communication Association, San Francisco.

Raspberry, W. (1989, June 14). Ruling in favor of White males. *Washington Post*, p. A23.

Reardon, K. K., & Rogers, E. M. (1988). Interpersonal versus mass media communication: A false dichotomy. *Human Communication Research, 15*(2), 284–303.

Rothschild, C. S. (1978). Women and work: Policy implications and prospects. In S. Harkess & A. Stromberg (Eds.), *Working women* (p. 429). Palo Alto, CA: Mayfield.

Scrimger, J. (1985). Profile: Women in Canadian public relations. *Public Relations Review, 11*, 38–47.

Steeves, H. L. (1989, August). *Women and extension communication in rural development: The case of sub-Saharan Africa.* Working draft presented at the seminar on Gender Issues and Public Relations, Association for Education in Journalism and Mass Communication, Washington, DC.

Theus, K. T. (1985). Gender shifts in journalism and public relations. *Public Relations Review, 11*(1), 42–50.

Tran, V. D. (1987). *Communication and diplomacy in a changing world.* Norwood, NJ: Ablex.

Turner, J. A. (1989, February 15). In math ability, differences between sexes disappearing. *Chronicle of Higher Education*, p. A10.

U.S. Department of State. (1985). *Personnel narrative* (rev. ed.). Washington, DC: Author.

Wetherell, B. L. (1989). *The effect of gender, masculinity, and femininity on the practice of and preference for the models of public relations.* Unpublished master's thesis, University of Maryland, College Park.

Women make their mark in diplomacy. (1989, September–October). *Update from State*, p. 3.

Yelsma, P., & Brown, C. T. (1985). Gender roles, biological sex, and predispositions to conflict management. *Sex Roles, 12*(7–8), 731–747.

Chapter 5

The Limits of Symmetry: A Game Theory Approach to Symmetric and Asymmetric Public Relations

Priscilla Murphy
Drexel University

Recent public relations research has given a great deal of attention to the proper relationship between the communicator and the audience. Should the audience be persuaded to concur with an organization's beliefs? Or is the organization's central purpose to respond to the public interest? When the two sides fail to agree, what is the proper mechanism for resolving the discrepancies?

Such questions concerning the balance of influence between an organization and its constituencies have been fed by a number of different perspectives: historical, sociological, ethical, and so on. All tend toward the same general goal: giving the public a more significant role in public relations. However, few papers have tried to define specifically what the balance of influence would consist of or what its ramifications might be. This chapter attempts to specify these issues more precisely by applying theory borrowed from decision science: that is, the theory of games. Game theory shares important attributes with communication theory-based approaches to public relations. Therefore, the logic, procedures, and insights of game theorists can be used to synthesize various communication theories about the organization–audience relationship, to refine current definitions of organization–audience interaction, and to suggest practical and ethical problems, as well as benefits, associated with the influence issue. In particular, this chapter examines some of the premises and effects of asymmetric and symmetric models by recasting them in terms of the theory of games.

When originally set forth in von Neumann and Morgenstern's *Theory of Games and Economic Behavior* (1944), game theory was viewed as a set of concepts and procedures for modeling economic markets. However, applications for the new field quickly developed in disciplines as various as political science (Schelling, 1980), biology (Axelrod, 1984), business (Luce & Raiffa, 1957; Raiffa, 1982), and ethics (Colman, 1982). The common element in all these applications was game theory's aptitude for conceptualizing and modeling social situations involving conflict and choice. This same facility could prove fruitful in analyzing public relations situations that involve conflicts of interest.

Public relations is already full of imported theories from other disciplines. What is the value of using game theory to critique public relations theory? First and foremost, the central concerns of game theory are the same as those of public relations. Like public relations, the theory of games focuses on the mediation of conflict, the establishment of an equilibrium among conflicting parties, the functions of power and domination, and questions of fairness and ethics. In fact, if we set the writings of game theorists next to those of current public relations scholars, we find striking similarities.

The basic premise of game theory is that social relationships can be modeled as games of strategy. Game theorists model strategic conflicts by considering the parties involved as players in a game. Thus, one player may be a public relations practitioner acting on behalf of his or her organization, whereas the other player represents a target public such as the media, an employee group, a special-interest lobby, and so on. Each player has certain preferences and dislikes; each has to select plays or strategies for reaching a preferred outcome, given the other player's probable strategies. Strategic decisions can often be selected by formal mathematical analysis to equitably balance the needs of everyone involved and resolve conflicting interests.

Communication scholars share the notion that a central—perhaps the definitive—task of public relations is the mediation of conflict. Hence, Ehling (1985) asserted that "cooperation and conflict exhaust the ways in which one individual can affect the expected relative values of another" (p. 12), and he defined a "public relations situation" specifically as "a choice situation" characterized by "decisions. . . about continuation or discontinuation of actual or potential conflicts and about the communicative means to be used in conflict resolution" (p. 16).

Ehling's (1985) view of public relations as the application of scientific decision-making techniques to the mediation of conflict strikingly resembles Lucas's (1972) classic definition of the theory of games:

> Game theory is a collection of mathematical models formulated to study decision making in situations involving conflict and cooperation. It recognizes that conflict arises naturally when various participants have different preferences and that such problems can be studied quantitatively rather than as a mere illness or abnormality which should be cured or rectified. Game theory attempts to abstract those elements which are common and essential to many different competitive situations and to study them by means of the scientific method. It is concerned with finding optimal

solutions or stable outcomes when various decision makers have conflicting objectives in mind. (p. 3)

In game theory, a strategy is never considered in isolation: The point is to
model which action is best given the probable moves of the other player. Game
theorists use the term *games of strategy* in a very particular sense: They are situations in which the best course of action for each player depends on what the other
players do. Indeed, some theorists have suggested that the term *game theory* is a
misnomer: They have suggested instead "the theory of interdependent decision-
making" (Colman, 1982; Schelling, 1980).

Thus, mutual adaptation lies at the root of all game theory: "To study the
strategy of conflict is to take the view that most conflict situations are essentially
bargaining situations. They are situations in which the ability of one participant to
gain his ends is dependent to an important degree on the choices or decisions that
the other participant will make" (Schelling, 1980, pp. 4–5).

In giving central place to the interdependence of the parties' interests, game
theory shares another premise of public relations research: an emphasis on
reflexivity, or the ability of players to adjust their behavior according to other
players' expectations. Such reflexivity develops as a kind of bargaining dialogue: In
public relation terms, the various parties adapt their roles to meet (or preempt) the
perceived positions of the other parties involved. Such mutual adaptation is similar
to Ehling's (1985) definition of public relations as conflict and cooperation prem-
ised on "communication as conversation" in which sender and receiver have
"reciprocal, dyadic roles. You can't have one without the other. . . .The roles of
sender and receiver are acquired in a mutual cooperative endeavor that entails the
joining of the acts of message presentation with message reception" (p. 8).

Game theorists accord equal centrality to sender–receiver reflexivity. Indeed,
the entire point of strategic play is for the players to properly estimate the other's
position. Thus, Schelling (1980) described game behavior as "trying to guess what
the other will guess one's self to guess the other to guess, and so on ad infinitum"
(p. 93). In this respect, game theorists approach the reflexive role taking of symbolic interactionism, which Culbertson (1989) compared to "a TV set tuned into a
program on which the camera is pointed at the set, which in turn contains a smaller
picture of the same set, which in turn contains a smaller picture of that picture, and
so on in an infinite regress" (p. 6). Like Ehling (1985), Culbertson pointed out
that such reflexivity—a positioning of one's stance according to one's perceptions
of another's perceptions of one—is a defining component of organizational–audience interaction in public relations.

Game theorists also propose a continuum of conflict–cooperation that is central
to current public relations scholarship. Conflict and cooperation are themselves
interdependent and one cannot change one without affecting the other. Again, here
is Ehling (in press):

> Cooperation and conflict . . . may be conceptualized as states located at the opposite ends of a single continuum so that it becomes meaningful to think of cooperation and conflict as being opposites but also expressible in degrees. As one moves away from, say, the cooperation end-point, the movement is toward conflict so that the degree of cooperation decreases as the degree of conflict increases and vice versa.

Ehling's continuum describes what some scholars view as an alternate definition of game theory: "the theory of incomplete antagonism" (Schelling, 1980). Hence, in game theory the task is generally not to do away with conflict altogether, but to bring conflict and cooperation into fruitful balance. A game theorist takes conflict for granted, but, as Schelling pointed out, "this does not deny that there are common as well as conflicting interests among the participants. . . .For this reason, 'winning' is not winning relative to one's adversary. It means gaining relative to one's own value system; and this may be done by bargaining, by mutual accommodation, and by the avoidance of mutually damaging behavior" (pp. 4–5). Indeed, Schelling warned against trying to abolish conflict altogether: "Viewing conflict behavior as a bargaining process is useful in keeping us from becoming exclusively preoccupied either with the conflict or the common interest" (p. 5). This carefully maintained balance between conflict and cooperation is one area in which the theory of games may be used to temper conceptions of purely symmetric public relations behavior.

Thus game theorists and public relations scholars are substantially in accord concerning the theoretical underpinnings of their fields. Both predicate their assumptions on establishing an equilibrium between the interests of two or more parties involved in some degree of conflict. Both focus on the interdependence of cooperation and conflict. Both assert that successful conflict resolution must involve dyadic communication and bargaining behavior, rather than imposition of one side's beliefs on the other. Both make reflexivity an essential part of the bargaining process.

At the root of all these shared concepts is the question with which this paper began: What is the proper relationship between an organization and its constituent publics? In communication scholarship, this issue has been defined in terms of *symmetric* and *asymmetric* behavior. Because it shares so many other premises with communication scholarship, game theory may help to further refine our concepts of symmetric and asymmetric behavior as well as to examine the implications of such behavior.

J. Grunig (1989) contrasted two sets of public relations worldviews, or presuppositions: asymmetric and symmetric. He characterized asymmetric presuppositions as the "dominant mindset" in current public relations, which "defines public relations as the manipulation of public behavior for the benefit of the manipulated publics as well as the sponsoring organizations" (pp. 18–19). These asymmetric presuppositions "have suggested attitude and behavior change, means of persuasive communication, diffusion of innovations, and the effects of media campaigns as relevant problems for public relations research" (Grunig, 1989, p. 34).

In contrast, Grunig (1989) defined a symmetric approach as having "effects that a neutral observer would describe as benefitting both organization and publics. Organizations practicing *two-way symmetric* public relations use bargaining, negotiating, and strategies of conflict resolution to bring about symbiotic changes in the ideas, attitudes, and behaviors of both the organization and its publics" (p. 29). Although the Grunig models do not propose strict historical evolution, there is some implication that true two-way symmetric communication is a highly evolved state that should supplant one-way models as organizations mature.

Similar conclusions were reached by Marvin Olasky (1989), who developed a thesis in terms of historical evolution. In this connection, Olasky applied Thomas Kuhn's (1962) theory of scientific revolutions to the evolution of public relations beliefs. He argued that public relations practitioners have condemned themselves to be viewed as "low-life liars" (Olasky, 1989, p. 87) by clinging to an outmoded paradigm used to justify "special pleading, primary responsibility to employer, and lack of concern for objectivity"—the negative side of a mindset developed by Edward Bernays in the 1920s (Olasky, 1989, p. 93). The Bernays paradigm defined the public relations role as persuasion, as the "engineering of consent" among a malleable public. Translated into unscrupulous communication practices, such a paradigm now looks both ethically untenable and ineffective, as the public has learned to receive this type of PR effort with suspicion. Nonetheless, Olasky argued that even where there is lip service to two-way communication with the public, lingering allegiance to the Bernays paradigm still reflects "a desire to use mass psychology to gain organizational goals" (p. 94)—essentially a one-way relationship that disregards audience input.

Ron Pearson (1989a) also contrasted asymmetric and symmetric presuppositions, not from a historical standpoint but on an ethical basis. Like J. Grunig (1989), Pearson based his argument upon the concept of symmetry. He defined the Grunig model of two-way symmetric communication as "characterized by source and receiver who cannot be distinguished as such, but are equal participants in a communication process that seeks mutual understanding and balanced, two-way effects" (p. 71). In Pearson's terms, this is ethical communication: "equal freedom among participants to initiate and maintain discourse, to challenge or explain, freedom from manipulation, and equality with respect to power" (p. 73).

Pearson viewed such ethical dialogue as governed by communication rules or constraints that all parties understand, and that all should be able to question and change. Thus, he concluded: "A communication environment that promotes dialogue will be marked by mutual understanding among communicators about the actual communication rules in place and mutual satisfaction with these rules. Most importantly, however, one would expect a dialogic communication environment to be marked by accurate understanding of and satisfaction with mechanisms for criticizing and changing rules" (p. 84).

Altogether there seems to be a great deal of sense to the model of two-way symmetric communication, with its emphasis on give-and-take, fairness, and ground rules. Yet most of those who strongly advocate it also point out that symmetric communication is exceedingly rare in actual practice. Thus J. Grunig (1989) noted that "few organizations practice the two-way symmetric model be-cause their worldview of public relations does not include that model and they seldom have public relations personnel with the expertise to practice it" (p. 31). Olasky (1989) noted a similar dearth of symmetric practice and ascribed it to the greed-based reluctance of PR practitioners to change their presuppositions: "the public relations occupation was too profitable for its beneficiaries to accept the reformation and reconstruction that paradigm changes require" (p. 94).

Proof of not only the existence, but also the efficacy, of true symmetric commu-nication has been hard to acquire. Indirect support has come in somewhat negative terms. For example, Turk's (1986) study of government agency influence on news stories showed that an asymmetric "persuasive press agentry/publicity model" was less-than-effective in fostering dissemination of agency viewpoints by the media, and implied that symmetric behavior by the agencies might have been more effective. Similarly, L. Grunig's (1986) study of organizations' relationships with activist groups noted that none of the organizations used symmetric communica-tion during crises with their opponents, and none of the asymmetric modes they did use effectively reduced conflict: By implication, symmetric behavior might have been more successful in reducing conflict. Overall, studies of the predictors and effects of asymmetric and symmetric models have emerged as normative, reflecting what organizations should do, rather than predictive of actual organiza-tional behavior (Grunig & Grunig, 1989).

So, in two-way symmetric communication we have an attractive model for an effective, ethical relationship between senders and receivers that is elusive in practice. Is it true that those who fail to practice this mode are merely, as Olasky (1989) judged it, "their own worst enemies" (p. 94)? Or that, as the Grunigs (Grunig & Grunig, 1989) theorized, practitioners lack sufficient power and exper-tise to enforce the practice of symmetric communication within their organiza-tions? In other words, are the practitioners being ineffective, or is there something about the models that does not fully describe what is going on in public relations practice?

This paper proposes that real-life symmetric behavior might be easier to locate if the symmetric model were slightly redefined. One way of doing this is to examine some of the premises and effects of asymmetric and symmetric models in the light of the closely related theory of games. The logic and insights of game theory may serve both to critique the symmetric–asymmetric models and suggest ways in which they might be refined.

As a starting point we can recast symmetric–asymmetric communication behav-iors into game theory terms. In this respect, asymmetric models resemble zero-sum games, whereas two-way symmetric communication resembles games of pure cooperation.

Grunig and Hunt (1984) originally distinguished three disparate types of non-symmetric communication: press agentry (propagandistic and untruthful), public information (journalistically objective but avoids the negative), and asymmetric two-way communication (uses scientific methods to persuade). More recently, Grunig (1989) grouped all three models together under the rubric of an asymmetric worldview characterized by presuppositions that "an organization knows best" and that "the public would benefit by cooperating with the organization" (p. 32). He noted that common metaphors for such a worldview were the notion of "selling" the public a bill of goods and waging a "war" of ideas (Grunig, 1989, p. 32). The underlying concept is that the organization need not change its attitudes, values, or actions; the public relations task is to gain compliance from the public.

Such notions have much in common with the class of games known as zero-sum. Strictly speaking, a zero-sum game is defined as "one in which the payoffs to the players in any outcome add up to zero; what one player gains, the other must necessarily lose" (Colman, 1982, p. 47). Such games of pure opposition are predicated on a wholly asymmetric worldview: "Since one player can gain only at the expense of the other, there are no prospects of mutually profitable collaboration, and models of two-person zero-sum conflicts are therefore described as *strictly competitive games*" (Colman, 1982, p. 47). There is no room for bargaining, mutual adaptation, or compromise; there is a clear-cut winner and loser. Monopoly, poker, and tag are familiar examples of zero-sum games.

Public relations practitioners are not oblivious to the zero-sum worldview: For instance, the former corporate communications director of Union Carbide characterized public affairs as "a 'win–lose' situation. . . a zero-sum game in which no one wins except at the expense of the other" (Lewis, 1984, pp. 32, 55). Even when it does not directly apply the language of game theory, asymmetric public relations uses presuppositions similar to zero-sum game theory. For example, Ciervo (1975) wrote that "mainstream practitioners engage in the engineering of consent that helps to mold public opinion to the profitable interest of the client at the expense of the public good" (p. 12). Lazarus (1963) wrote that the goal of public relations practitioners should be "to make money—for their management, their clients and themselves" (p. 4). The attitude has much in common with the zero-sum universe in which gains are transferred from the losing player to the winning player: "a closed system within which nothing of value to the players is created or destroyed; utilities merely change 'hands' when the game is played" (Colman, 1982, p. 47).

There is also a more profound behavioral connection between the zero-sum approach and the asymmetric worldview. J. Grunig (1989) described an asymmetric worldview as "the manipulation of public behavior" that focuses, among other things, on "attitude and behavior change, [and] means of persuasive communication" (p. 34). Public relations practitioners who specialize in conflict resolution use the zero-sum terminology of game theory to describe the same focus on persuasion: "The 'win–lose' (called 'zero-sum') bargaining situation [is] a common negotiation mode in business-to-business transactions. (It simply means 'one for me is one less for you.' Such bargaining is power- or persuasion-based, with little attention paid to the other parties' wants, needs, or desires.)" (Gossen & Sharp, 1987, p. 35).

Pavlik (1989) also emphasized the role of power—especially economic power—in comparing asymmetric corporate strategies to zero-sum games, pointing out that until recently, zero-sum behavior was "both rational and highly advantageous economically, at least in the short run," because poorly organized public-interest groups provided "little incentive for the organization to engage in compromise" (p. 9). However, Pavlik also proposed that corporate communications strategy has of necessity become more symmetrical, as activist groups have managed to attach economic penalties to zero-sum behavior.

Indeed, most interactions between an organization and its publics are not inherently zero sum. In their role as boundary spanners, public relations practitioners have opportunities to orchestrate the needs of their organization and its constituencies so that both sides can live with the outcome. In current terminology such an approach is known as symmetric.

Symmetric communication as defined by J. Grunig (1989) and others shares important features with a class of games called *games of pure cooperation, pure coordination,* or *pure common-interest.* According to Pearson (1989a), the Grunig model of two-way symmetric communication is "characterized by source and receiver who cannot be distinguished as such, but are equal participants in a communication process that seeks mutual understanding and balanced, two-way effects" (p. 71). Let us compare this definition with Raiffa's (1982) game-theory-based definition of "fully cooperative partners": "Such negotiators might have different needs, values, and opinions, but they are completely open with one another; they expect total honesty, full disclosure, no strategic posturing. They think of themselves as a cohesive entity" (p. 18).

The same common interest informs Colman's (1982) definition of pure coordination games: "It is in every player's interest to try to anticipate the others' choices and obtain a mutually beneficial outcome, and they all know that the other players are similarly motivated. . . A consequence of this is that there is no conflict of interest between the players; their sole objective is to coordinate their strategies in such a way as to obtain an outcome that they all prefer" (p. 31). To illustrate a coordination game, Colman used the analogy of a couple who have gotten separated at a crowded shopping mall and need to guess at each others' likely reasoning in order to figure out how to find each other. Schelling (1980) compared the relationship between players in coordination games to charades, arguing that the primary interest of such games comes from the ways players devise to communicate, in order to align their interests accurately.

On the face of it, it should be simple to achieve agreement between players whose greatest desire is to coordinate. But in public relations practice, such coordination is extremely hard to achieve. In real life it is difficult to envisage "a source and receiver who cannot be distinguished as such" (Pearson, 1989a, p. 71). Even when two-way communication exists, the organization and its publics have different agendas, want different side-payments, retain some conflicts of interest. Purely cooperative behavior is seldom found in the real world. It is generally tainted with elements of conflict.

In fact, game theorists themselves are hard pressed to find real-life games of pure coordination. Their difficulties are not unlike those cited by the Grunigs (L. Grunig, 1986; Grunig & Grunig, 1989) and others in finding organizations that practice true two-way symmetric communication. Indeed Raiffa (1982) argued that fully cooperative behavior is not a productive focus for a book on real-life negotiation: It "would be true, for instance, of a happily married couple or some fortunate business partners. Only occasionally do teams of scientific advisers or faculties of universities fall into this category" (p. 18). We have to ask, then, whether the purely symmetrical model accurately represents organizational behavior. This may explain why researchers have so seldom found it in practice, and in turn this suggests that a pure symmetric model may not be the most accurate one possible to describe organizational behavior.

With its appeal to fairness, equality, and mutual understanding, the symmetrical model is clearly attractive. Yet from a game-theory standpoint, its ethical implications are much murkier. Game theorists point out that games of pure coordination lack obvious rational solutions (unlike their antitheses, zero-sum games of pure conflict, where the minimax solution is provably superior). Instead, games of pure cooperation are generally solved by chance or by custom. This is because such games hinge on the congruence between players' perceptions of each others' interests: "The best choice for either [player] depends on what he expects the other to do, knowing that the other is similarly guided, so that each is aware that each must try to guess what the second guesses the first will guess the second to guess and so on, in the familiar spiral of reciprocal expectations" (Schelling, 1980, pp. 86–87). The net effect of these "infinitely reflexive expectations" (Schelling, 1980, p. 70) is a convergence, not of desired outcomes, but of expectations. As a result, the pure cooperation game degenerates into self-fulfilling prophecy: "What is most directly perceived as inevitable is not the final result but the *expectation* of it, which, in turn, makes the result inevitable" (Schelling, 1980, p. 91).

Although it begins with all good will, this self-fulfilling prophecy does not lead to efficient outcomes. For example, game theorists often cite studies by Schelling (1971a, 1971b) and Grodzins (1957) that indicate spontaneous segregation of multiracial communities into exclusively White and Black areas is inevitable, even if people prefer to live in a mixed community. A similar game theory example of miscarried coordination is the Battle of the Sexes. Here, a husband and wife must decide whether to go to a sports event (husband's preference) or the ballet (wife's preference). Each would prefer to go with the other person, not alone. Altruistic efforts to coordinate with the other person lead to an outcome that benefits no one: The wife goes alone to the sports event, and the husband alone to the ballet. O. Henry (1914) used the same model in his short story, *Gift of the Magi*, in which a devoted wife sells her long hair to buy her husband a watch chain—while her husband sells his watch to buy her combs for her hair.

These pure common-interest games are essentially coorientation situations gone awry. Coorientation studies, like common-interest games, have uncovered situations where misdefined expectations lead to undesirable outcomes. For example, coorientation studies of journalist/public relations values (e.g., Kopenhaver, Martinson, & Ryan, 1984) often reveal actual shared values, whereas each side thinks the other has antithetical values—and this convergence of expectations only feeds traditional antagonism.

Thus, despite the clear attractiveness of the symmetric communication model, game theory suggests that in practice, such attempts at convergence can lead to inefficient outcomes (journalist/PR antagonism) or even morally objectionable outcomes (racial segregation).

This ethical uncertainty is further increased when we look at the broader implications of reflexive behavior from a game theory standpoint. As we have seen, coordination—or fully symmetric behavior—is predicated on both parties' attempts to bring themselves into line with perceived interests of the other. Often the only way to do so is to search for predictable patterns and customs:

> The "coordination" of expectations . . . involve[s] nothing more nor less than intuitively perceived mutual expectations. . . . Players have to understand each other, to discover patterns of individual behavior that make each player's actions predictable to the other; they have to test each other for a shared sense of pattern or regularity and to exploit clichés, conventions, and impromptu codes. (Schelling, 1980, pp. 71, 84–85)

Attempts to coordinate, therefore, encourage players to fix upon the status quo. Schelling (1980), for example, observed that "the coordination game probably lies behind the stability of institutions and traditions. . . . Among the possible sets of rules that might govern a conflict, tradition points to the particular set that everyone can expect everyone else to be conscious of as a conspicuous candidate for adoption; it wins by default" (p. 91).

In its purest form, then, symmetry tends to discourage innovation and encourage custom and tradition, even when both sides in a conflict would prefer to break with the status quo. In this respect, game theory brings to the fore misgivings of certain coorientation theorists who question the desirability of excessive congruence. As Chaffee and McLeod (1968) put it, "A pluralistic society needs a communication system that can bridge social gaps in the transmission of information (i.e., in effecting Understanding and Accuracy) without an attendant pressure toward Congruency or Agreement" (p. 669). And Culbertson (1989) pointed out, "It is . . . clear that level of congruency between own and other's view can create PR problems. Perfect (the highest possible) congruency allows for no difference between self and other. . . . *Ethnocentrism* or *egocentrism* results" (p. 19). Thus, the pressure to reach consensus—to coordinate expectations—may lead to inefficient outcomes that are less desirable than the conflict they were meant to resolve.

Given the practical and ethical problems inherent in pure symmetry, it may be helpful to refine the concept of symmetric communication along less rigorous lines that include shades of behavior along a continuum ranging from conflict to cooperation.

Models that build in such refinement are provided in the theory of games.

Game theorists envisage a spectrum of games ranging from pure conflict at one extreme (the zero-sum game) to pure cooperation (two-way symmetry) at the other (see Colman, 1982, p. 32). This spectrum is schematized in Fig. 5.1. Game theorists posit that behavioral situations are generally best modelled by games that occupy the broad middle range of the spectrum. These are termed *mixed-motive* games, to capture the fact that "the interests of the players are neither strictly coincident nor strictly opposed" (Colman, 1982, pp. 10–11). Each side retains a strong sense of its own interests, yet each is motivated to cooperate in a limited fashion in order to attain at least some resolution of the conflict.

The task in a mixed-motive game is to find an equilibrium. Game theorists define the equilibrium as a balance between the players' interests such that neither player would have any cause to regret his action given what the other player chose to do. True equilibria offer stable solutions to conflict because they lock in benefits and penalties so that neither side could defect from the agreement without causing the other player to also defect, thereby hurting each player's cause. In this sense, mixed-motive equilibria do reduce conflict; they support the hypothesis that "asymetrical public relations would increase (and symmetrical public relations would decrease) the amount, intensity, and duration of . . . conflict" (Grunig & Grunig, 1989, p. 58).

Mixed-motive equilibria do not necessarily exhibit rigid symmetry in the sense of a pure common-interest game, "a source and receiver who cannot be distinguished as such" (Pearson, 1989a, p. 71). They avoid the blending of perspectives implied by symmetry and aim instead for a skillful balancing of communality with conflict. In a coorientation context, mixed-motive games do not aspire to agreement and congruence but rather to understanding and accuracy, which preserve distinctions between viewpoints (Chaffee & McLeod, 1968).

This balance is often an uneasy and precarious one, arrived at by a kind of bargaining dialogue between an organization and its constituent publics. The speed and skill with which the balance is achieved generally marks the difference between what outsiders perceive as good and bad PR: The quicker the resolution, the less damage the organization's image sustains.

Most public relations situations are located somewhere along the continuum of mixed-motive games, with some falling toward the zero-sum/conflict extreme and

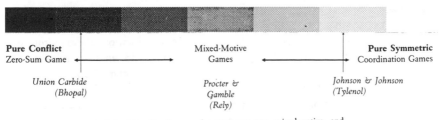

Pure Conflict
Zero-Sum Game

Mixed-Motive
Games

Pure Symmetric
Coordination Games

Union Carbide
(Bhopal)

Procter &
Gamble
(Rely)

Johnson & Johnson
(Tylenol)

FIG. 5.1. Continuum of games: zero-sum, mixed-motive, and coordination.

others, toward the symmetry/cooperation extreme. The 1982 Tylenol tragedy, for example, comes very close to being a cooperative game. Within hours of the first deaths, Johnson & Johnson (J&J) adopted an open information policy, teaming up with the media to publicize the crisis and recall consumers' Tylenol supplies. The various groups involved behaved as "fully cooperative partners," in the sense that they "might have different needs, values, and opinions, but they [were] completely open with one another" (Raiffa, 1982); "their sole objective [was] to coordinate their strategies in such a way as to obtain an outcome that they all [preferred]" (Schelling, 1980). J&J's strategy quickly reduced conflict, and laid the ground-work for the subsequent rebound in Tylenol's market share.

Still, the Tylenol tragedy was not a purely cooperative game in the sense that Pearson (1989a) defined symmetric communication, as a dialogue in which "competing interests can be transformed" (p. 70) into a new stance in which the separate participants' agendas "cannot be distinguished as such" (p. 71). In addition to concerns about social welfare, J&J was trying to protect its product and its bottom line; the news media were concerned not only with providing a public service, but with producing a sensational news coup. Thus the Tylenol crisis is a mixed-motive game in which everyone involved—corporation, media, consumers, law-enforce-ment groups—was motivated to cooperate in order to maximize quite different agendas for each.

Union Carbide's response to the 1984 Bhopal tragedy lies at the other extreme of the mixed-motive continuum. The company entered the conflict with a hard-line denial of responsibility; this approach initiated a 4-year bargaining process leading to a $470 million settlement agreement. The company's initial approach has been viewed as an unsuccessful zero-sum strategy (Pavlik, 1989). Still, Union Carbide's subsequent bargaining behavior suggests, not so much a zero-sum approach that failed to function as planned, but a mixed-motive negotiating strategy that sacri-ficed immediate image to longer-term financial considerations.

In the middle of the mixed-motive spectrum lies Procter & Gamble's (P&G) response to the 1980 Rely tampon crisis. Like Union Carbide, P&G's initial reaction to Rely's alleged connection with toxic shock syndrome was hard-line denial. However, after 4 months of scientific testing bore out the connection, the company changed its approach to something very close to J&J's cooperative strat-egy, initiating product recalls, educational advertising, and an open media relations policy.

All three companies' strategies fall at different points on the mixed-motive spectrum; all three show the dynamics of influence in a situation where neither side has enough power to impose its most desired outcome, and where consensus must be developed by repeated discussion. These bargaining games unfold with one player making an offer and the other player countering with a different offer. In the course of bargaining players are forced to seek compromises, so that each round brings them closer to agreement. The game ends when the two sides cannot improve their lot simultaneously without damaging the other player: Each is locked in place by the other's demands. Such behavior typifies the mixed-motive game, a balance between elements of cooperation and conflict that both sides will accept in order to obtain some resolution.

A definition of public relations as a mixed-motive game helps reconcile the divergent symmetric versus asymmetric—bargaining versus persuasion—models. By splitting public relations communication behavior into only two modes, we tend to polarize undesirable behavior in one (asymmetric) and desirable behavior in the other (symmetric). Mixed-motive games provide a broad third category that describes behavior as most public relations people experience it in the world of practice: a sliding scale of cooperation and competition in which organizational needs must of necessity be balanced against constituents' needs, but never lose their primacy. Researchers have discovered that most organizations appear to practice a blend of three asymmetric, as well as symmetric, communication styles (See Grunig & Grunig, 1989, pp. 56–57). It is possible that what organizations actually practice are a spectrum of mixed-motive games; this may be why no clear-cut boundaries are apparent among the strictly defined asymmetric and symmetric models.

In fact, mixed-motive games sound very much like what Ehling (in press) described as the central focus of public relations: to adjust cooperation and conflict on a sliding scale "so that the degree of cooperation decreases as the degree of conflict increases and vice versa." Raiffa (1982) called parties in such relationships:

> . . . *cooperative antagonists*. Such disputants realize that they have differences of interests; they would like to find a compromise, but they fully expect that all parties will be primarily worried about their own interests. They do not have malevolent intentions, but neither are they altruistically inclined. They are slightly distrustful of one another; each expects the others to try to make a good case for their own side and to indulge in strategic posturing. They are not confident that the others will be truthful, but they would like to be truthful themselves, within bounds. They expect that power will be used gracefully, that all parties will abide by the law, and that all joint agreements will be honored. (p. 18)

This balance-of-influence view is not only eminently realistic but also ethical. The mixed-motive model of public relations brings together the seeming conflict between asymmetric (pure competition) and symmetric (pure common interest) models, in that it preserves the central importance of one's own interests, yet acknowledges the power of opposing viewpoints. Mixed-motive players will try to gain as much advantage as possible given their power; they will yield points proportional to the power of their opposition. However, they will not give in to opponents simply because the opponents are there to be heard. Such a mixed-motive model helps to solve what has been called "public relations' central ethical dilemma . . . a tension between partisan [organizational loyalty] and mutual [public interest] values" (Pearson, 1989b, p. 59).

In this respect the mixed-motive game is ethical in keeping with current views of the term, as questions are decided strictly on their own merits: "The aim of practical [ethical] discourse is to come to a rationally motivated agreement about problematic rightness claims, an agreement that is not a product of external or internal constraints on discussion but soley [sic] of the weight of evidence and argument" (McCarthy, 1982, quoted by Pearson, 1989a, p. 73).

IMPLICATIONS

The theory of games—especially, redefining symmetric behavior as mixed-motive behavior—offers a number of benefits to public relations researchers and practitioners.

First, the theory of games avoids polarization between asymmetric and symmetric classes of behavior, with their correlates of conflict versus cooperation, poor ethics versus sound ethics, conservatism versus liberalism, and so on. Game theory is the science of conflict resolution; but in constantly urging symmetric compromise, it never ignores the asymmetric centrality of self-interest or the usefulness of maintaining tension among competing interests. Game theory, then, offers an inclusive model to unify dichotomies in public relations thinking.

Second, the theory of games can be useful in further clarifying and testing assumptions about what public relations communication ought to be. In public relations research the concept of symmetry builds in the notion that "conflict should be resolved through negotiation, communication, and compromise" (Grunig, 1989, p. 39). However, public relations scholars are still on the threshold of empirically analyzing the process of effective conflict resolution through negotiation. Game theory can provide theoretical models and precise empirical means to test them. At the theoretical end, game theory offers precise definitions of conflict, of cooperation, of the relations between players. At the applied end, it supplies specific procedures for solving games, for specifying facts, for quantifying values, and so forth. This paper has focused purely on the theoretical end, but it should be noted that game theory-based procedures have been used to solve such applied public relations problems as the timing of news dissemination, the amount and type of information disclosed to reporters, and cost/benefit analysis of PR programs (see Ehling, in press; Murphy, 1987, 1989).

Third, viewing public relations as a mixed-motive game permits us a richer view of conflict and cooperation than that allowed by strict prescriptions for symmetry. For example, symmetric views of public relations emphasize the reduction of conflict and give highest value to concord. In contrast, mixed-motive games raise the issue that conflict is productive and positive; its lack is destabilizing and dangerous. Raiffa (1982), for example, argued that one should try to maximize disagreement at the beginning of a negotiation, because parties that start farther apart have a greater area between them to negotiate. Similarly, lab experiments indicate partners arrive at mutually beneficial solutions only after choosing a few alternatives that damage both. As one game theorist put it, "this suggests a possible strategic basis to the common belief in the criminal underworld that two people cannot develop a relationship of mutual trust until they have once quarrelled or fought with each other" (Colman, 1982, p. 41). And Schelling (1980) argued that ostensibly unattractive behavior such as threats may assure mutual benefit by discouraging even more destructive behavior: "Concepts like deterrence, limited war, and disarmament, as well as negotiation, are concerned with the common interest and mutual dependence that can exist between participants in a conflict" (p. 5).

Organizations in conflict with their constituent publics show a similar pattern of mutual damage that leads to balance and compromise. They customarily enter crises of disagreement by adopting a zero-sum, hard-line approach, and through public debate, generally in the media, begin to trade concessions with their constituent groups. In game theory terms, they maximize preliminary disagreement in order to maximize bargaining possibilities later. Hence, Union Carbide's initial abrogation of responsibility for the Bhopal deaths was followed by 4 years of bargaining—corporate claims and interest-group counterclaims—on the pages of newspapers: bargaining that finally established among the conflicting claims a balance that the various participants appeared able to accept. Was the outcome ethical? Certainly in relation to its 1984 stance, Union Carbide's recompense for the Bhopal victims represents a better balance between the parties; from the corporation's point of view, maximizing disagreement at the outset allowed laborious study of the events surrounding the disaster. The company would probably argue that prolonging the conflict allowed, as McCarthy stated, "a rationally motivated agreement about problematic rightness claims, . . . [solely on] the weight of evidence and argument" (Pearson, 1989a, p. 73). In that respect the outcome was ethical.

Although this tough pragmatism may appear repugnant, it does have value. Without proper acknowledgment of the role of conflict and self-interest, the concept of symmetry partakes of what game theorists call the "maximax" approach to the world: that is, choosing one's own best outcome, regardless of the other players' positions. According to Colman (1982), "the maximax principle amounts to angling for the most favorable outcome of the game while blissfully ignoring the less favourable outcomes which are possible. It is an ultra-optimistic approach . . . since it is implicitly based on a hopeful anticipation of the highest conceivable payoff" (pp. 24–25). No matter how attractive this viewpoint may be, in practice it must be tempered by the chastened realizations of game theorists:

> We tend to identify peace, stability, and the quiescence of conflict with notions like trust, good faith, and mutual respect. To the extent that this point of view actually encourages trust and respect it is good. But where trust and good faith do not exist and cannot be made to by our acting as though they did, we may wish to solicit

advice from the underworld, or from ancient despotisms, on how to make agreements work. . . . It seems likely that a well-developed theory of strategy could throw light on the efficacy of some of those old devices, suggest the circumstances to which they apply, and discover modern equivalents that, though offensive to our taste, may be desperately needed in the regulation of conflict. (Schelling, 1980, p. 20)

REFERENCES

Axelrod, R. (1984). *The evolution of cooperation.* New York: Basic.

Chaffee, S. H., & McLeod, J. M. (1968). Sensitization in panel design: A coorientational experiment. *Journalism Quarterly, 45*(4), 661–669.

Ciervo, A. (1975). The poor image of the image makers. *Public Relations Journal, 31*(7), 11–13.

Colman, A. M. (1982). *Game theory and experimental games: The study of strategic interaction.* Oxford: Pergamon.

Culbertson, H. M. (1989). Breadth of perspective: An important concept for public relations. *Public Relations Research Annual, 1,* 3–25.

Ehling, W. P. (1985). Application of decision theory in the construction of a theory of public relations management, II. *Public Relations Research & Education, 2*(1), 4–22.

Ehling, W. P. (in press). Estimating the value of public relations and communication to an organization. In J. E. Grunig (Ed.), *In search of excellence in public relations and organizational communication.* Hillsdale, NJ: Lawrence Erlbaum Associates.

Gossen, R., & Sharp, K. (1987). How to manage dispute resolution. *Public Relations Journal, 43,* 35–38.

Grodzins, M. (1957). Metropolitan segregation. *Scientific American, 1957*(4), 33–41.

Grunig, J. E. (1989). Symmetrical presuppositions as a framework for public relations theory. In C. Botan & V. Hazleton (Eds.), *Public Relations Theory* (pp. 17–44). Hillsdale, NJ: Lawrence Erlbaum Associates.

Grunig, J. E., & Grunig, L. A. (1989). Toward a theory of the public relations behavior of organizations: Review of a program of research. *Public Relations Research Annual, 1,* 27–63.

Grunig, J. E., & Hunt, T. (1984). *Managing public relations.* New York: Holt, Rinehart & Winston.

Grunig, L. S. (1986, August). *Activism and organizational response: Contemporary cases of collective behavior.* Paper presented at the meeting of the Association for Education in Journalism and Mass Communication, Norman, OK.

Henry, O. (1914). The gift of the magi. In *The four million.* New York: Doubleday.

Kopenhaver, L. L., Martinson, D. L., & Ryan, M. (1984). How public relations practitioners and editors in Florida view each other. *Journalism Quarterly, 61,* 680–865, 884.

Kuhn, T. (1962). *The structure of scientific revolutions.* Chicago: University of Chicago Press.

Lazarus, A. J. (1963). Who says public relations is intangible? *Public Relations Journal, 19* (9), 4–6.

Lewis, M. C. (1984). Policy planning. In B. Cantor & C. Burger (Eds.), *Inside public relations: Experts in action* (pp. 31–56). New York: Longman.

Lucas, W. F. (1972). An overview of the mathematical theory of games. *Management Science, 18*(5), 3–19.

Luce, D. R., & Raiffa, H. (1957). *Games and decisions.* New York: Wiley.

McCarthy, T. (1982). *The critical theory of Jurgen Habermas.* Cambridge, MA: MIT Press.

Murphy, P. (1987). Using games as a model for crisis communications. *Public Relations Review, 13*(4), 19–28.

Murphy, P. (1989). Game theory: A new paradigm for the public relations process. In C. Botan & V. Hazleton (Eds.), *Public Relations Theory* (pp. 173–192). Hillsdale, NJ: Lawrence Erlbaum Associates.

Olasky, M. N. (1989). The aborted debate within public relations: An approach through Kuhn's paradigm. *Public Relations Research Annual, 1,* 87–95.

Pavlik, J. V. (1989, May). *The concept of symmetry in the education of public relations practitioners.* Paper presented at the annual conference of the International Communication Association, San Francisco, CA.

Pearson, R. (1989a). Beyond ethical relativism in public relations: Coorientation, rules, and the idea of communication symmetry. *Public Relations Research Annual, 1,* 67–86.

Pearson, R. (1989b). Albert J. Sullivan's theory of public relations ethics. *Public Relations Review, 15*(2), 52–62.

Raiffa, H. (1982). *The art and science of negotiation.* Cambridge, MA: Harvard University Press.

Schelling, T. C. (1971a). Dynamic models of segregation. *Journal of Mathematical Sociology, 1,* 143–186.

Schelling, T. C. (1971b). On the ecology of micromotives. *The Public Interest, 25,* 61–98.

Schelling, T. C. (1980). *The strategy of conflict.* Cambridge, MA: Harvard University Press.

Turk, J. V. (1986). Information subsidies and media content: A study of public relations influence on the news. *Journalism Monographs, 100.*

von Neumann, J., & Morgenstern, O. (1944). *The theory of games and economic behavior.* Princeton, NJ: Princeton University Press.

Chapter 6

Organizational Ideology, Structure, and Communication Efficacy: A Causal Analysis

Kathryn T. Theus
Rutgers University

During the past decade, scholars from the fields of organizational communication and public relations have exhibited interest in the strategies organizations utilize in communicating with outside publics. Although the strategies themselves have been described (Grunig & Hunt, 1984), less is known about the efficacy of such strategies (Gandy, 1982; Grunig & Grunig, 1989; Turk, 1986). For example, media relations specialists have tried to identify the best approaches to take with journalists when organizational issues become public. A key concern focuses on whether the organization's communication system should be tightly controlled or whether management should give reporters access to organizational leaders and information.

Answers to such questions may hinge on organizational characteristics that influence the communication system, such as work arrangements and organizational values. Traditional organizational sociologists have studied the influence of organizational structures on communication (Hage & Aiken, 1968; Hage, Aiken, & Marrett, 1971; Perrow, 1967; Pfeffer & Salanick, 1978) and have looked at the impact of cultures on structures (Collins & Moore, 1970; Miller & Dorge, 1986; Miller, Kets de Vries, & Toulouse, 1982). Research has suggested that bureaucratic structures tend to constrain information flow through one-way, top-down communication. Such systems would make it difficult for journalists to gain access. Smaller decentralized, differentiated organizations with highly educated experts tend to use multilevel, multichannel communication to exchange information and to increase innovation. Theoretically, such systems would be more open.

This study differs from others in that it identifies the simultaneous effects of structure and culture on organizational communication behaviors with news media, which ultimately (through news reports) affect public perceptions of an organization. Specifically, it considers the impact of organizational structure and values (ideology) on openness of communication with journalists and how that openness (or lack of it) contributes to either congruence or discrepancy between journalists and organizational sources on the representation of organizational issues in the news.

Such interchanges or exchanges between sources and journalists have customarily been examined from the perspective of the reporter (Blumler & Gurevitch, 1981; Fishman, 1977; Gans, 1979; Gitlin, 1980; Lipsky, 1970) but fewer researchers (Gandy, 1982; Theus, 1988a, 1988b; Turk, 1986) have studied the exchange from the perspective of the source organization. It stands to reason that source organizations may have important impacts on the stories journalists write, but for reasons only partly related to the organizational issues of interest to journalists. This study demonstrates that work arrangements and cultural values supportive of open communication with news media result in exchanges that are more efficacious for the organization.

ORGANIZATIONAL STRUCTURE, CULTURE, AND COMMUNICATION

Organizational form has long been considered an important influence on organizational outputs. Much of the thinking that has emerged from the contingency model (Lawrence & Lorsch, 1967) has dealt directly with this issue. The basic notion is that there are multiple organizational forms that are most likely to be successful, depending on the situation the organization is confronting. One of the major tasks of top management is to determine what the most appropriate organizational form is for various situations. It is not uncommon to find business firms in rapidly changing technological fields, for example, that have no formal tables of organization and organizational charts because the organization is in a constant change mode (Hall, 1982).

The literature has recognized that organizational goals and objectives, which drive the adaptation process, must also affect a substantial part of organizational arrangements. If policy statements affect the activities of organizational members as they function in their roles, they can also lead to structural changes that will reinforce this mode of operation (Katz & Kahn, 1966).

Recent studies of the influence of organizational culture on organizational behavior have generally focused on dimensions of culture as process, for example, shared values, politics, social transactions, legends, and rituals (Siramesh & Grunig, 1988), but have neglected the joint impact with structure on organizational actions.

Early work on culture suggested a conservative to liberal framework derived from the structural dimension, technology; but Perrow (1967) suggested that technology predicted other structural dimensions better than it did culture. Although Perrow did not find consistent evidence to support his thesis, he suggested that the conservative or authoritarian end of the value continuum more often coincided with bureaucratic structures and the liberal end of the continuum more often coincided with differentiated structures.

Deal and Kennedy (1982) indicated that "core values" espoused by an organization determine everything from "what products get manufactured to how workers are treated" (p. 31). Structure, presumably, falls under the category of everything. Along a similar vein, a study by Miller and Dorge (1986) showed that the chief executive officer's (CEO) need for achievement (a guiding vision) and the organization's size had the strongest relationships to structural constructs. Technology and uncertainty had little impact on structure. CEOs that had a need for achievement had more impact in small struggling firms than in large firms. This outcome is not in conflict with findings relating to structural influences on communication systems; for example, smallness and innovative goals are compatible with multilevel communication styles leading to change, even in the face of administrative control.

Characteristics of organizational structures have been shown to impede or enable the flow of information within organizations and externally to organizational constituents. Generally, large bureaucratic organizations feature greater centralization and stratification and less complex knowledge bases. These structures tend to constrain information flow through one-way, top-down communication systems (Hage, 1980; Hage & Aiken, 1968). Such organizations gain efficiency through coordination and control of subordinates rather than through the introduction of new ideas. Thus, bureaucratic structures often stifle innovation, lower morale, and constrain feedback (Hage, 1980).

On the other hand, smaller decentralized, destratified, and differentiated organizations with highly educated or skilled experts tend to use multilevel, multichannel communication to exchange information and to increase innovation (Blau, 1972; Hage, 1980; Hall, 1982).

Organizational dependence on an outside source for resources, even if that resource is a community's good will, also serves as a powerful determinant of communications, transactions, and consensus building (Aiken & Hage, 1968; Aldrich, 1979; Emery, Marek, & Trist, 1965; Hage, 1980; Thompson, 1967). When one organization is able to control the definition and interpretation of another organization's activity, that entity may be said to have the power to establish organizational legitimacy (Pfeffer & Salanick, 1978) and may call into question organizational credibility. Media are often regarded as having such power (Mintzberg, 1983).

Environmental uncertainty also increases communication (Van de Ven & Walker, 1984). Innovative organizations characteristically experience a great deal of uncertainty in the environment and communicate to coordinate external rela-tionships, especially in the presence of high capital investment and technical demand (Thompson, 1967). Differentiated, decentralized, innovative organiza-tions may be more open to journalists than those from traditional, centralized organizations because the ideology of the former values opens communication as a means of coordination (Pfeffer & Salanick, 1978).

HYPOTHESES

The current study, in identifying the likelihood of disagreements or discrepant outcomes between organizations and reporters on the salience, selection, and in-terpretation (accuracy, framing, and emphasis) of news reports, examines the com-munication of an organization as a causal system with established relationships among the organization's structure, ideology, and communication behavior.

This study then, postulates several hypotheses:

1. Hypothesis 1: The more differentiated the organization's structure, the great-er the organizational openness.
2. Hypothesis 2: The more value placed on openness by organizational ide-ology, the greater the organizational openness.
3. Hypothesis 3: The greater the organizational openness, the less the discrep-ancy in reporting (and the greater the communication efficacy).

Operationalization

Organizational Structure. This term derives from Weber's (1946) definition, which referred to how work is organized. Work arrangements determine the amount and quality of products produced or services provided. Weber felt that a strict hierarchy of authority and a reliance on rules would facilitate greater efficien-cy. His has been characterized as a bureaucratic or mechanical model.

Burns and Stalker (1961) on the other hand envisioned a differentiated or organic organizational form held in tension with its external environment, and constantly adapting to feedback in a cybernetic system. Their emphasis, rather than on centralization of and loyalty to vertically stratified authority, focused on work arrangements that value technical skill, response to markets, innovation, and product development. Organic organizations, they found, usually have de-centralized network structures of control and authority, with communication sys-tems consisting of information and advice, which aid in greater adjustment to and redefinition of task.

Thus, measures of organizational structure used in this study were designed to show the relationship between the organic and mechanical model. They included: centralization (degree of centralization of power in making strategic decisions), stratification (degree of differentiation in pay, power, or prestige), and complexity (concentration of skilled specialists) (see Hage, 1980).

Organizational Ideology.   Otherwise defined as the importance of overarching organizational values, this notion was very much a part of the structural-functional perspective in the 1950s (Blau, 1955; Gouldner, 1954), but during the 1960s, many lost sight of this essential ingredient for understanding organizational behavior. It was Perrow (1967), referenced earlier, who most effectively brought back a goal or value perspective, especially the notion of the derivation and character of organizational goals, even though he did so in the context of technology. Structural functionalism argues that the origin of values, such as organizational objectives, lies in structure.

The other view is that values have an independent origin, and one that lies in other aspects of collective attitudes (Child, 1977; Warner, 1977). Little work has been done on the origins of values held by dominant coalitions in organizations and the degree of control these perspectives exert over organizational norms, or whether organizational leaders become socialized to preexistent organizational ideologies.

Organizational ideology in this study was assessed by determining the relative importance of a range of economic and social value orientations to the organization, such as willingness to disclose organizational perspectives to publics and to incorporate new perspectives into the organizational information system, reducing costs, profitmaking, efficiency, social responsibility, and organizational growth.

Organizational Openness.   Mechanisms for coordination and control in organizations were described by Perrow (1967) as falling along a continuum of cultural expectations (goals and objectives, plans and programs), communication arrangements (volume, formalization, direction, and special arrangements; e.g., committee structures), and incentive structures (rewards, peer approval, sanctions, task visibility, and attitude conformity). Although most of the organizational literature emphasizes internal organizational arrangements and attributes, the implications for organizational communication across organizational boundaries are pronounced.

For example, Grunig and Hunt (1984) have focused on interorganizational communication through a study of public relations practices. They found that such boundary spanning communication has generally taken four forms: publicity (press agentry, promotion), public information (dissemination of information), two-way asymmetric communication (persuasion based on research to gain a strategic advantage over publics), and two-way symmetric communication (dialogue based on research to reach mutual understanding on issues of concern to the organization and publics).

Because the literature suggests that organic organizations rely on cybernetic principles and feedback to help them adapt to environmental contingencies, these organizations should be more likely to stress two-way boundary spanning communication approaches, particularly symmetric communication for organizational communication. An organization that relies on symmetric feedback to adjust, but not exclusively to press its own advantage, may be described as open.

Mechanical organizations, subject to more stable routines and environmental expectations, should emphasize publicity and public information to a greater degree. These organizations, precisely because their structures are more centralized and stratified, should be more likely to exercise control over communication outcomes through nondisclosure, limited disclosure, or message manipulation—closed forms of communication.

To assess the degree of organizational openness in this study, measures focused on the organizations' customary use of publicity, public information, two-way asymmetric, and two-way symmetric communication with media. Measures of symmetric communication emerged as predictive for the model. (A concept included in an early form of the model, openness of communication on the specific issue, was later dropped because of slight redundancy between its measures and those used to gauge organizational openness.)

Discrepancy. This concept was defined as the degree of noncorrespondence in views on the coverage of organizational issues in news reports between organizational communicators (as represented in surveys and interviews) and reporters (as represented in content analysis of articles and interviews). The dimensions of discrepancy in reporting centered on issue salience, selection of information, accuracy of information, framing of the organization and issue in the news report, and emphasis on specific elements contained therein.

METHOD

In order to study the impact of structure and organizational ideology on organizational communication, and to ascertain the efficacy of that communication behavior with reporters, a random sample of articles focusing on nonelective organizations was drawn from seven Maryland, Delaware, and District of Columbia newspapers. Organizations mentioned in these articles were identified and the CEO or public relations manager was sent a questionnaire designed to identify organizational structures, values, communication philosophies, communication behaviors with media, generally, and on the issue that stimulated the news report; and to identify perceptions of the news report as compared with the organization's own understanding of the issue. Of 237 organizations surveyed, 155 returned questionnaires for a 64.5% response rate.

Simultaneously, the articles were content-analyzed by independent coders to assess the tone of articles and the values implied in them. In addition, field interviews were conducted with eight pairs of reporters and organizational representatives to explore cases of high and low discrepancy on the salience, selection, and interpretation of the issues, as well as on organizational credibility, legitimacy, and interorganizational dependency.

The scaling procedure for the survey, although somewhat complicated for respondents, was chosen to maximize correlations in standard statistical programs and in LISREL analyses (Joreskog & Sorbom, 1983). Most questions used a zero to infinity scale with 100 identified as the average on all items (thereby giving respondents a unit of measure by which to estimate their own positions). A zero indicated total absence of an attribute, whereas multiples of 100 indicated proportions of an attribute greater or lesser than "average." A percentage scale was used on one section of the questionnaire and demographics were generally evaluated as categorical variables.

A LISREL structural equation analysis was used to estimate the parameters of a model proposed in Fig. 6.1. LISREL uses the maximum likelihood method to estimate model parameters. The data set used for this analysis came from the survey exclusively; however, it should be noted that the outcome of the LISREL

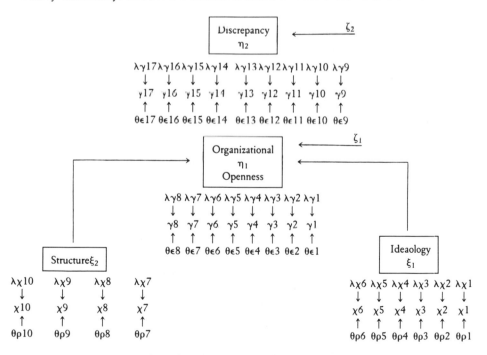

FIG. 6.1. Measurement and theoretical model.

analysis reported here complemented canonical correlations utilizing both survey data and data from the content analysis of news articles.

In preliminary analyses a review of the statistics revealed variables with somewhat less than normal distributions of cases; thus, variables were transformed into logarithms or square roots of their original values in order to normalize distributions. Only 5 of 98 variables fell outside a range of skewness of +2 or −2. Care was taken in the interpretation of results when these variables were used in analyses.

The LISREL Analyses

The general linear model is a comprehensive scheme for representing all elements and relationships of a theory in a single structure. It permits the modeling of theoretical, derived, and empirical concepts. The model provides a direct measure of the degree to which theoretical constructs are related, the extent of errors in equations and variables, and the relationships between constructs and operationalizations. LISREL further allows the researcher to determine how good one's model is and to diagnose incorrect specifications of cause and effect by providing a test statistic for the entire model.

The LISREL model consists of two parts: the measurement model and the structural equation mode. The measurement model specifies how the latent variables or hypothetical constructs are measured through observed variables. The structural equation model specifies the causal relationships among the latent variables and is used to describe the causal effects and the amount of unexplained variance. The program calculates measures of Goodness of Fit (GIF), which show the fitting function of the data to the specified model.

The model that follows in Figure 6.1 indicates the theoretical model [Xi (ξ) exogenous theoretical variables and Eta (η) endogenous theoretical variables] and the measurement model consisting of empirical measures of observed variables (x for exogenous measures and y for endogenous measures). Theoretical concepts studied included organization ideology and complexity of organizational structure (exogenous variables), and organizational openness, openness of organizational behavior, and discrepancy (endogenous variables).

Specifically, symmetric communication was assessed by the extent to which organizational communicators provided information to help media understand the organization, provided all information journalists asked for, and provided accurate information to media. Ideology was assessed as indicated in Table 6.1.

Discrepancy was measured by the extent to which:

1. The issue in the news article was significant to top managers (salience).

2. They believed the issue was reported completely (selection).

3. They wanted the issue reported as completely as it was (selection).

4. The story was reported accurately (accuracy).

5. The reporter had not formed an opinion before writing the story (frame).

6. The article did not reflect that previously reached opinion (frame).

7. The reporter did not overemphasize or exaggerate information in the story (emphasis).

8. Top managers would not have emphasized something different in the story (emphasis).

Complexity was identified as the extent to which:

1. Employees had no specialized skill and little or no higher education.

2. Employees had at least a college degree.

3. Employees had a graduate degree.

4. Organizational work was done at remote locations.

In first iterations of the model, variables for centralization and stratification of organizational structure were included, but because these attenuated the *t* values of other structural variables, they were excluded in subsequent models.

FINDINGS

Tables 6.1 and 6.2 contain both the maximum likelihood estimates and the standardized solutions, as suggested by McPhee and Babrow (1987). Tables also contain *t* values, reflecting the presence of nonzero parameters with significance levels greater than 1.96.

Goodness of fit indicators showed that the data fit the model moderately well. Estimates of the path coefficients supported the theoretical model and were consistent with the canonical correlational analysis. Value structures do seem to influence the communication of the organization. With a *t* value of 1.62, complexity did not achieve a great enough level of significance to assume a nonzero influence on openness. However, organizational ideology contributes significantly to organizational openness. Finally, *t* values indicate open communication is negatively related to discrepant communication.

As a check on the maximum likelihood (ML) estimates, unweighted least squares (ULS) estimates were run because these estimators are less sensitive to outliers causing nonnormality or skew in the data. The ULS Coefficient of Determination and the Root Mean Square Residual were very similar to ML indices; however, ULS improved the goodness of fit estimators substantially, suggesting that the presence of outliers attenuated ML estimators. Even though ML estimators are robust under conditions of nonnormality (Bagozzi, 1980), Joreskog

TABLE 6.1
LISREL Estimates for the Measurement Model

	Maximum Likelihood Estimate		Standard Solution		T-Value	
Endogenous Variables						
Orgaizational Openness	Eta1	Eta2	Eta1	Eta2	Eta1	Eta2
Symmetric Comm. 1 (LY 1,1)	1.00	.00	.68	.00	.00	.00
Symmetric Comm. 2 (LY 2,1)	1.13	.00	.77	.00	8.83	.00
Symmetric Comm. 3 (LY 3,1)	.43	.00	.29	.00	3.48	.00
Symmetric Comm. 4 (LY 4,1)	1.13	.00	.77	.00	8.82	.00
Open on This Issue (LY 5,1)	.48	−1.33	.32	−.43	4.08	−3.40
Organization Is Good (LY 6,1)	.93	.00	.64	.00	7.39	.00
Organization is Source (LY 7,1)	.64	−1.24	.44	−.40	5.51	−3.02
Organization is Open (LY 8,1)	1.42	.15	.96	.05	10.13	.91
Discrepancy						
Salilence 1 (LY 9,2)	.00	1.00	.00	.32	.00	.00
Salience 2 (LY 10,2)	.00	1.24	.00	.40	.00	2.91
Selection 1 (LY 11,2)	.00	1.67	.00	.54	.00	3.25
Selection 2 (LY 12,2)	.00	1.91	.00	.62	.00	3.36
Accuracy 1 (LY 13,2)	.00	1.68	.00	.55	.00	3.25
Framing 1 (LY 14,2)	.00	1.30	.00	.42	.00	2.97
Framing 2 (LY 15,2)	.00	1.21	.00	.39	.00	2.88
Emphasis 1 (LY 16,2)	.00	1.27	.00	.48	.00	2.94
Emphasis 2 (LY 17,2)	.00	1.48	.00	.48	.00	3.12
Exogenous Variables						
Organizational Ideology						
Openness (LX 1,1)	1.00	.00	.00	.00	.00	.00
Reduce Cost (LX 2,1)	2.74	.00	.84	.00	3.59	.00
Make Profit (LX 3,1)	1.24	−.35	.38	−.28	2.95	−3.26
Efficiency (LX 4,1)	2.67	.00	.82	.00	3.58	.00
Socially Responsible (LX 5,1)	1.83	.00	.56	.00	3.33	.00
Growth (LX 6,1)	1.27	.00	.00	.39	2.94	.00
Organizational Structure						
Complexity 1 (LX 7,2)	.00	1.00	.00	.78	.00	.00
Complexity 2 (LX 8,2)	.00	.94	.00	.74	7.74	.00
Complexity 3 (LX 9,2)	.00	.94	.00	.73	7.70	.00
Complexity 4 (LX 10,2)	.00	.19	.00	.15	1.63	.00

TABLE 6.2
ULS Estimates for the Measurement Model

	Maximum Likelihood Estimate		Standard Solution	
Endogenous Variables				
Organizational Openness	Eta1	Eta2	Eta1	Eta2
Symmetric Comm. 1 (LY 1,1)	1.00	.00	.71	.00
Symmetric Comm. 2 (LY 2,1)	1.02	.00	.73	.00
Symmetric Comm. 3 (LY 3,1)	.48	.00	.34	.00
Symmetric Comm. 4 (LY 4,1)	1.03	.00	.73	.00
Open on This Issue (LY 5,1)	.56	−1.03	.40	−.35
Organization Is Good (LY 6,1)	.95	.00	.67	.00
Organization is Source (LY 7,1)	.70	−.96	.49	−.33
Organization is Open (LY 8,1)	1.36	.28	.97	.09
Discrepancy				
Salience 1 (LY 9,2)	.00	1.00	.00	.34
Salience 2 (LY 10,2)	.00	1.38	.00	.47
Selection 1 (LY 11,2)	.00	1.70	.00	.57
Selection 2 (LY 12,2)	.00	1.77	.00	.60
Accuracy 1 (LY 13,2)	.00	1.57	.00	.53
Framing 1 (LY 14,2)	.00	1.21	.00	.41
Framing 2 (LY 15,2)	.00	1.02	.00	.34
Emphasis 1 (LY 16,2)	.00	1.29	.00	.44
Emphasis 2 (LY 17,2)	.00	1.51	.00	.51
Exogenous Variables				
Organizational Ideology				
Openness (LX 1,1)	1.00	.00	.36	.00
Reduce Cost (LX 2,1)	2.30	.00	.82	.00
Make Profit (LX 3,1)	1.20	−.37	.41	−.27
Efficiency (LX 4,1)	2.20	.00	.78	.00
Socially Responsible (LX 5,1)	1.42	.00	.51	.00
Growth (LX 6,1)	1.29	.00	.46	.00
Organizational Structure				
Complexity 1 (LX 7,2)	.00	1.00	.00	.74
Complexity 2 (LX 8,2)	.00	.94	.00	.69
Complexity 3 (LX 9,2)	.00	1.09	.00	.81
Complexity 4 (LX 10,2)	.00	.23	.00	.17

and Sorbom (1983) suggested use of ULS when the determinant is very small relative to the magnitude of the diagonal elements in the correlation matrix. Because the determinant for this matrix was .006242635, the ULS indicators should be the preferred estimators. These will be utilized when interpreting results.

Table 6.2 shows the ULS measurement model and Table 6.3 shows a comparison between ML and ULS estimators and their standardized counterparts. In the ULS analysis, path coefficients increased. Figure 6.2 shows the model using both sets of standardized path coefficients. (ULS coefficients are enclosed in parentheses.) When data were displayed as *q*-plots using ML and ULS estimation methods, both plots indicated linearity and moderate fits to the data. In inspecting the goodness of fit measures between the original model and the modified model, few changes occurred among the indicators of fit, confirming, generally, the stability of the model and the theoretical relationships hypothesized.

TABLE 6.3
LISREL ML and ULS Estimates for the Theoretical Model

Structural Coefficients	ML Estimate	Standard Solution	ULS Estimate	Standard Solution
Beta Matrix[a]				
Eta 2,1	−.13	−.28	−.15	−.32
Gamma Matrix[b]				
Eta 1, Xi 1	1.41	.64	1.27	.64
Eta 1, Xi 2	.11	.13	.24	.25
Phi Matrix[c]				
Xi1, Xi 1	.09	1.00	.13	1.00
Xi2, Xi 1	−.04	−.16	−.04	−.15
Xi2, Xi 2	.61	1.00	.55	1.00
Psi Matrix[d]				
Eta 1	.28	.61	.29	.58
Eta 2	.10	.92	.10	.90

Goodness of Fit	ML Solution	ULS Solution
Coefficient of Determination	.40	.42
Goodness of Fit Index	.66	.83
Adjusted Goodness of Fit Index	.60	.80
Root Mean Square Residual	.12	.12

[a]Coefficients correspond to direct paths between Organizational Openness and Discrepancy. [b]Coefficients correspond to direct paths between Organizational Openness and Ideology, and Organizational Openness and Structure. [c]Covariance matrix of Structure and Complexity (unconstrained). [d]Covariance matrix of Discrepancy and Organizational Openness (constrained).

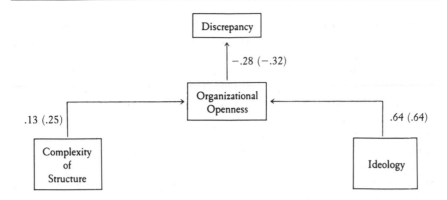

FIG. 6.2. Theoretical model.

Taken as a whole, these analyses suggest the following about the proposed hypotheses:

1. Hypothesis 1: Structure was not shown to have a significant and measurable impact on communication in organizations, and thus the hypothesis was not supported.
2. Hypothesis 2: Organizational ideology does influence organizational communication, and especially the extent of organization openness. Hypothesis 2 was supported.
3. Hypothesis 3: Finally, organizational openness was shown to be negatively related to discrepancy in communication with news media, as suspected.

SUMMARY

The larger study of which this analysis is a part indicates that organizations either proactively seek to subsidize news by "placing" information with journalists, or reactively respond to inquiry from journalists along a continuum of openness to closedness. Organizational values and structures and the adeptness of organizational communicators serve as mechanisms to drive this communication behavior (Theus, 1988b).

However, in the LISREL analysis reported here, structure dropped out, suggesting a much more important role for organizational culture as a determinant of communication. The LISREL analysis also showed that openness in communication serves as an antidote for discrepancy, its primary strength derived from organizational values supportive of openness. Closed communication increases discrepancy and open communication decreases it. Although it is generally thought that organic or differentiated organizations are more likely to be open than mechanical or highly bureaucratic organizations, the strength of the relationship in the LISREL analysis, as measured by the *t* value, fell just below the 1.96 significance level required to indicate a nonzero path.

The relationship between ideology and structure was not tested in the LISREL analysis. But other analyses (Theus, 1988b) suggest that centralization and stratification provide neutral environments for the development of capitalistic organizational values—profit, competition, reducing costs, and efficiency. Yet these same values may be negatively associated with measures of complexity in an organic organization. Its typically horizontal span of control and emphasis on research and development often engage the organization in high-risk expenditures of both time and organizational assets. Emphases on efficiency and profit, in particular, tend to discourage such risk taking.

On the other hand, values such as organizational openness and organizational survival follow logically from the design of organic organizations. Lateral structure, designed to increase innovation, employs communication horizontally across positions. With outlays for research dominating the organization's fiscal arrangements, and with payoffs of profits not yet secure, organizational survival emerges high on the organizational agenda.

Path coefficients in the LISREL analysis indicated that organizational values have a strong direct effect on organizational openness. Values contributing to openness include accountability to the public and service. Organizations embracing openness in this analysis were likely to provide accurate but not necessarily complete information to journalists. Generally, organizational values fostered no incentives for communicators to provide management with journalists' perspectives.

The strong negative path between organizational openness and discrepancy in the LISREL analysis showed that open communication addresses problems of discrepancy in reporting. The analysis showed that strategic withholding of information from media by communicators may result in an organization's finding fewer criticisms of the articles covering its kind of organization. That is to say, if the organization has seized the issue and defined it, it may not be necessary to provide all information relevant to that issue.

But the consequences of withholding too much organizational information may be dire. The negative path, then, should sensitize organizational designers that communication efficacy is related to organizational values. Organizations valuing public accountability experience less discrepancy in their communication with journalists, in part because they may exercise the opportunity to provide accurate and somewhat complete information, framed and emphasized in ways the organization feels are justified.

The antagonism organizations feel toward media may actually stem from organizations' failure to participate in the development of the frames journalists impose on them in news reports. Even if organizations frame themselves as primarily concerned with service and accountability to the public, they may utilize closed communication strategies because of excessive concern over lost profits, loss of a competitive edge, or loss of efficiency—and these are the very frames journalists perceive and emphasize in the stories focusing on public accountability that they write about closed organizations.

By finding that open communication produces less discrepancy than more controlled communication, this study contradicts much of the conventional wisdom in public relations—especially the conventional wisdom of top management that discourages open communication with media. The finding is important, both as advice to practitioners and as support in their wars with managements, who want them to control information. Symmetrical communication is most effective in reducing discrepancy. Likewise, a culture of openness leads to congruent communication, as well as to organic structure.

Thus, organizational culture is a significant pillar upon which communication efficacy rests. Nevertheless, attention should be given to differences in measures of structure to explain why the influence of structure appears as significant in some studies and drops out in others. Additional work may also identify more precisely the differing value orientations or ideologies that lead to differing communication strategies (sorted by organizational type) and whether those values pervade the organizational system or reside primarily in the dominant coalition.

If structure really has little or no impact on communication, it would be appropriate to assess the impact ideology has on structure that may account for the attenuation of its effects. Future analyses should consider the effects of structure, ideology and open communication on organizational credibility and legitimacy, particularly in the light of persuasion studies that suggest that compliance-gaining strategies used in public relations usually involve mixed (cooperative and competitive) motives (Murphy, this volume; Reardon, Sussman, & Flay 1989). Indications of this study suggest that cooperative techniques are more efficacious, even though some information may be withheld strategically. Future studies may identify the appropriate balance between cooperative and competitive strategies. Such information could provide organizational managers with a normative basis for practicing public relations with media and external constituencies.

REFERENCES

Aiken, M. & Hage, J. (1968). Organization interdependence and intraorganizational structure. *American Sociological Review, 33,* 912–930.

Aldrich, H. (1979). *Organizations and environments.* Englewood Cliffs, NJ: Prentice-Hall.

Bagozzi, R. P. (1980). *Causal models in marketing.* New York: Wiley.

Blau, P. (1955). *The dynamics of bureaucracy.* (1955). Chicago: University of Chicago Press.

Blau, P. (1972). Interdependence and hierarchy in organizations. *Social Science Research, 1,* 1–24.

Blumler, J. G., & Gurevitch, M. (1981). Politicians and the press: An essay on role relationships. In D. Nimmo & C. Saunders (Eds.), *A handbook of political communication* (pp. 467–493). Beverly Hills, CA: Sage.

Burns, T., & Stalker, G. M. (1961). *The management of innovation.* London: Travistock.

Child, J. (1977). *Organization: A guide to problems and practice.* London: Harper & Row.

Collins, O., & Moore, D. (1970). *The organization makers.* New York: Appleton–Century–Crofts.

Deal, T. E., & Kennedy, A. E. (1982). *Corporate culture: The rites and rituals of corporate life.* Reading, MA: Addison-Wesley.

Emery, F., Marek, J., & Trist, E. L. (1965). The causal texture of organizational environments. *Human Relations, 18,* 21–32.

Fishman, M. (1977). Manufacturing the news: The social organization of media news production. Unpublished doctoral dissertation. University of California, Santa Barbara.

Gandy, O. (1982). *Beyond agenda setting: Information subsidies and public policy.* Norwood, NJ: Ablex.

Gans, H. (1979). *Deciding what's news: A study of CBS Evening News, NBC Nightly News, Newsweek and Time.* New York: Vintage Books.

Gitlin, T. (1980). *The whole world is watching.* Berkeley: University of California Press.

Gouldner, A. (1954). *Patterns of industrial bureaucracy.* New York: Free Press.

Grunig, J. E., & Grunig, L. A. (1989). Toward a theory of public relations behavior of organizations: Review of a program of research. In J. E. Grunig & L. A. Grunig (Eds.), *Public relations research annual* (Vol. 1, pp. 27–63). Hillsdale, NJ: Lawrence Erlbaum Associates.

Grunig, J. E., & Hunt, T. (1984). *Managing public relations.* New York: Holt, Rinehart & Winston.

Hage, J. (1980). *Theories of organizations.* New York: Wiley.

Hage, J., & Aiken, M. (1968). Relationship of centralization to other structural properties. *Administrative Science Quarterly, 12,* 72–91.

Hage, J., Aiken, M., & Marrett, C. (1971). Organization structure and communication. *American Sociological Review, 36,* 860–871.

Hall, R. (1982). *Organizations: Structure and process.* Englewood Cliffs, NJ: Prentice-Hall.

Joreskog, K. G., & Sorbom, D. (1983). *LISREL: Analysis of linear structural relationships by the maximum likelihood method.* (Versions V & VI). Uppsala: University of Uppsala, Sweden.

Katz, D., & Kahn, R. L. (1966). *The social psychology of organizations.* New York: Wiley.

Lawrence, P., & Lorsch, J. (1967). Differentiation and integration in complex organizations. *Administrative Science Quarterly, 12,* 1–47.

Lipsky, M. (1970). *Protest in city politics.* Chicago: Rand McNally.

McPhee, R. C., & Babrow, A. (1987). Causal modeling in communication research: Use, disuse and misuse. *Communication Monographs, 54,* 344–366.

Miller, D., & Dorge, C. (1986). Psychological and traditional determinants of structure. *Administrative Science Quarterly, 31,* 539–560.

Miller, D., Kets de Vries, M., & Toulouse, J. M. (1982). Top executive locus of control and its relationship to strategy-making, structure and environment. *Academy of Management Journal, 25,* 237–253.

Mintzberg, H. (1983). *Power in and around organizations*. Englewood Cliffs, NJ: Prentice-Hall.

Perrow, C. (1967). A framework for the comparative analysis of organizations. *American Sociological Review, 32*, 194–209.

Pfeffer, J., & Salanick, G. (1978). *The external control of organizations*. New York: Harper & Row.

Reardon, K., Sussman, S., & Flay, B. (1989). Are we marketing the right message: can kids "just say 'no'" to smoking? *Communication Monographs, 56*, 307–324.

Siramesh, K., & Grunig, J. (1988). *Culture, communication and public relations*. Paper presented at the meeting of the Educator Academy of IABC, Anaheim, CA.

Theus, K. (1988a). Organizational response to media reporting. *Public Relations Review, 14*, 45–57.

Theus, K. (1988b). *Discrepancy: Organizational response to media reporting*. Unpublished doctoral dissertation, University of Maryland, College Park.

Thompson, J. (1967). *Organizations in action*. New York: McGraw-Hill.

Turk, J. (1986). Information subsidies and media content: A study of public relations influence on the news. *Journalism Monographs, 100*.

Van de Ven, A. & Walker, G. (1984). The dynamics of interorganizational coordination. *Administrative Science Quarterly, 29*, 598–621.

Warner, M. (Ed.). (1977). *Choice and constraint*. London: Halsted.

Weber, M. (1946). Bureaucracy. In H. H. Gerth & C. Wright Mills (Eds.), *From Max Weber: Essays in Sociology* (pp. 196–244). New York: Oxford University Press.

Chapter 7

Conflict Between Public Relations Agencies and Their Clients: A Game Theory Analysis

J. David Pincus
Lalit Acharya
Edgar P. Trotter
Carrie St. Michel
California State University, Fullerton

Businesses today are increasingly retaining public relations and advertising agencies to perform or supplement many of the tasks traditionally reserved for in-house staff. Unfortunately, the agency–client relationship is frequently short-lived because one of the parties quickly becomes dissatisfied with the other. Beiser (1984) observed, "Clients and [advertising] agencies are a lot like husbands and wives. The relationships are rarely without turmoil and all too often end up in divorce court" (p. 3). Added Hume (1979), "If you judge by the accounts shifts reported weekly, you'd think the divorce rate in the ad industry is accelerating as fast as it seems to be with people" (p. 4). Fractured agency–client relationships are not endemic to advertising agencies: "A similar trend exists in regard to public relations agencies and their clients. As is true with advertising agencies, it is not unusual for client relationships to terminate after a year or less" (St. Michel, 1988, p. 1).

RATIONALE

Knowing why public relations agency–client relationships frequently break down is important for several reasons. First, as public relations grows in size and importance, and as corporate staffs are made leaner in the current wave of downsizings and restructurings, top managers are increasingly seeking specialized counsel from outside firms, now numbering about 7,000 (Wilcox, Ault, & Agee, 1989).

151

Second, organizations' reliance on outside counsel seems to be increasingly more selective and situation-driven, often resulting in short-term project relationships between the client and a number of different public relations agencies. As Maister (1985) observed: "Increasingly, clients are less willing to establish relationships with outside firms (giving them all their public relations work). More and more, they shop around on a transactional basis, trying to find specialists to deal with specific short-term problems" (p. 15).

Therefore, discovering how to create more lasting bonds with clients can be vital in extending project assignments to longer-term relationships.

Third, although the target of much speculation, the subject of agency–client conflict is void of systematic and empirical research. According to DiMingo (1987), "The agency/client relationship is the subject of entirely too much mystique. At the bottom line, it is a hard-headed, results-oriented marriage intended to produce specific, measurable results. Yet, little of the management literature focuses scrutiny on the thin line between success and failure" (p. 144). This exploratory study sought to identify the major source(s) of disruptive conflict in the public relations agency–client relationship within the conceptual framework of game theory.

CONCEPTUAL FRAMEWORK

Understanding why agencies and their clients fail to maintain long-term business relationships requires an appreciation of the varying perspectives of conflict.

The Nature of Conflict

An initial step, according to Frost and Wilmot (1978), is to define the concept of conflict, "one of the most pervasive and confounding of all activities" (p. 1), as: " . . . an expressed struggle between at least two interdependent parties, who perceive incompatible goals, scarce rewards, and interference from the other party in achieving their goals. They are in a position of opposition in conjunction with cooperation" (p. 9).

Some of the terms of the definition apply directly to agency–client relationships. For one, its focus is on expressed rather than hidden conflict: "It is through communication behavior that conflicts are recognized, expressed and experienced" (Frost & Wilmot, 1978, p. 10). Thus, inclusive to the term is not only expression but actual behavior. Echoing this aspect of conflict, Miller (1985) listed 15 warning signs "indicating when an account person is 'on the outside, looking in'" (p. 34). These include, for example, clients not returning phone calls, agency representatives finding out about a major speech in the client institution after the fact, and so forth.

A second aspect of the definition that merits attention is its notion of interpendence where "each person's choices affect the other because conflict is a mutual activity" (Frost & Wilmot, 1978, p. 12). Thus, conflict could arise because of decision choices made by either the agency or client organization. Implicit in the notion of interdependence is that people are bound by common interests and concerns, therefore, "not totally antagonistic to each other" (Kiely & Crary, 1986, p. 39). Despite the frightening regularity with which agency–client partnerships end, Kent (1985) argued that the drive is toward maintaining rather than ending this professional relationship: "Firing an agency far outweighs the annoyance of a troubled relationship" (p. 54). At the same time, problem relationships receiving no special treatment may "stretch the fragile partnerships to the limit" (p. 54). And, although remedies may be available, it is sometimes easier to terminate an "ailing relationship" than to work out a cure (Kent, 1985, p. 54).

Thus, the frequency of breakdowns in a public relations agency–client relationship may indicate the presence of intense and unendurable levels of conflict.

Conflict can be a healthy outlet through which an agency and client can debate, air differences, force recognition of other viewpoints, or otherwise search for common ground. However, when it is left unattended, conflict—inevitable in any human relationship—can "disrupt or drastically alter the existing interdependency" in a relationship (Ehling, 1983, p. 63).

Implications for the agency–client partnership are that both have to work hard and constantly to contain the destructive potential of conflict. DiMingo (1987) suggested that a common mistake public relations agencies make is to stop working to keep an account once they win it: "Too many agencies insist on selling the agency forever—'our people, our places, our resources, our awards.' The agency rule: you've got the client already. Keep the account (and by implication, keep out the conflict) by servicing—understanding and solving its problems—not by selling" (p. 144).

Sources of Conflict

But, what are the main types of relationship-ending conflict? Anecdotal literature in this area identifies three types: (a) technical incompetence by the agency, (b) the tendency of individuals participating in the agency–client relationship to deviate from expected norms of professional conduct, and (c) the inability of participants in the agency–client relationship to strategically exchange and manage information. We use game theory to explain this last aspect of conflict in the agency–client relationship.

Game Theory

Game theory postulates that preferred outcomes can be obtained by strategically negotiating and trading information (Davis, 1983; Heckathorn, 1986; Luce & Raiffa, 1957). Information, properly extracted and used, can reduce the uncertainty necessary for productive decision-making. For game theory to become operative, at least two actors are necessary, each with a goal to achieve. In this study, those actors are the client representative and the agency representative.

Two types of games are identified by this theory. The first, a *zero-sum* game, is a win–lose situation in which, if one player wins, the other must lose. War is an example of a zero-sum game. Clearly such a game model is inappropriate for examining agency–client relationships.

The second type of game—one more appropriate to the agency–client relationship—is the *non-zero-sum* game. This is a win–win situation in which, as Murphy (1985) described it:

> . . . opportunities exist for all players to make the most of the situation by negotiating skillfully so that no one loses and everyone gains an acceptable payoff. In non-zero-sum games, cooperation between players is key because the issue is not "winning" or "losing" per se, but rather negotiating an outcome that will maximally benefit all players. Indeed, a player might cede "points" early on, so as to maximize her own payoff later. . . . (p. 21)

Negotiation is the key term of the non-zero-sum game because of its emphasis on information as a commodity that can be traded strategically for a mutually satisfactory outcome (Murphy, 1985). Information critical to this negotiation process might include what goals are to be pursued in what sequence, the availability of different courses of action, and the determination of the particular subset of actions most conducive to attainment of a desired goal (Ehling, 1983).

Popular literature on agency–client conflict indicates that this strategic process of negotiating and trading information does not occur to the extent that it should. Towers (1987) reported a survey in which 300 communication and marketing managers gave public relations agencies a *D* grade for strategic thinking. Public relations professional John Budd (1988) lamented that "he gets no direct input from agencies unless it is in response to a direct question" (p. 9).

Thus, conflict may arise because of an inability to efficiently play a non-zero-sum game, that is, manage the information in a negotiated decision environment to the optimal advantage of both client and agency.

RESEARCH QUESTIONS

In the absence of prior empirical research, the overriding question asked was: *What are public relations agencies' and their clients' perceptions of the major issues of conflict in their professional relationships?*

Game theory suggests that conflict arises because of an inability of people to strategically trade and use information at different stages of the decision-making process. Clearly, the first step is to identify the precise areas of conflict between public relations agencies and their clients.

Public relations decisions are complex because of the many variables and steps in them. Hence, the game-playing ability of either the agency or client representative could break down at any stage of the public relations programming process. It may be useful to isolate the primary decision points and variables in a prototypical public relations program.

Many public relations scholars have outlined their views on structuring public relations programs (e.g., Cutlip, Center, & Broom, 1985; Newsom & Scott, 1985). Recognizing that one schema may be just as appropriate as another and that each emphasizes different aspects of the public relations programming process, we chose Reilly's (1981) six-part planning approach as a framework for this study. Reilly's six steps are: (a) purpose of plan, (b) goals and objectives, (c) plans, (d) implementation of actions, (e) key target audiences, and (f) cost.

Using Reilly's (1981) six-part public relations decision process as an organizing mechanism, client and agency representatives were asked at which of these six steps, in their opinions, they most severely disagreed with each other.

Answering this question will tell what agency or client representatives individually think is the locus of conflict in the decision-making process. It does not, for example, reveal whether agency and client representatives agree about the types or sources of conflict.

According to Laing, Phillipson, and Lee (1966), consensus is the product of a process they called a "spiral of reciprocal perspectives," involving three levels of perceptions. The first is a *direct perspective* (what the agency or client representative individually perceives is the problem); the second a *metaperspective* (or what the agency representative feels is the client perception of the problem); and, the third a *metametaperspective* (what the agency representative perceives is the client representative's perception of the agency representative's perception of the problem).

People agree with and understand each other to the extent that one person's metaperspective matches another person's direct perspective. By the same token, a mismatch between these two levels of perceptions can cause cognitive imbalance (Heider, 1946) or asymmetry (Newcomb, 1953) in a person, leading to misunderstanding and psychological tension. In his coorientation model, Newcomb further suggested that knowing another person's perspective about or orientation toward an issue can provide clues either person can take to reduce the discrepancy in cognitions and, consequently, tension. Further, it is a necessary precondition for corrective action. Among discrepancy-reducing steps suggested by Newcomb are changing one's own (or conversely, the other person's) attitude or orientation toward the problem.

Based on this theory, McLeod and Chaffee (1973) developed a coorientation model for measuring the degree of symmetry among two parties' (A and B, or, in this case, the client and agency representatives) opinions of their own and each other's views about a common object (X, or, in this case, conflict) of concern or attention. The three elements in the McLeod and Chaffee model are: *agreement*, or the similarity between A's and B's direct perspectives of X; *congruency*, or A's and B's metaperspectives about X; and, *accuracy*, or the degree of actual similarity between A's metaperspective and B's direct perspective of X, and B's metaperspective and A's direct perspective of X.

Because public relations agencies and clients need to know each others' perceptions of where conflict lies in the decision-making process prior to resolving it, the next step is to examine such perceptions. The McLeod and Chaffee (1973) model provides a framework for the research questions that guided this investigation:

1. *To what extent do public relations agencies and their clients agree on the sources of conflict in their professional relationships?*

2. *To what extent are public relations agencies' and their clients' perceptions congruent about the sources of conflict in their professional relationships?*

3. *To what extent do public relations agencies and their clients accurately perceive each others' perceptions of the sources of conflict in their professional relationships?*

METHODOLOGY

Sample

The target population was 25 Los Angeles-based public relations agencies and one or more of their current or prior clients. Because of the inherent sensitivities involved in asking agencies and their clients to disclose information about their relationship, only agencies where one of the researchers was known were asked to participate in the study.

The sample consisted of 30 pairs of agencies and their clients. Of the 25 public relations agencies contacted, 12 agreed to participate. The agencies included in the study ranged in size from a one-person agency with $35,000 in annual billings to a 60-person organization with $5 million in annual billings. Therefore, in order to produce the 30 pairs, some agencies provided information on more than one of their clients. Of the 30 agency–client pairs, 19 represented prior clients, and 11 represented current clients. Agencies refusing to participate in the study indicated that they were uncomfortable divulging information about conflict in their relationships with clients.

Agency representatives were asked to identify one or more current or prior clients who would be appropriate candidates to participate in the study. The only stipulation was that the designated client had to agree to complete a questionnaire.

Of the 30 agency representatives, 4 were presidents, 3 were media relations managers, 7 were account supervisors, and 16 were account executives.

Among the 30 client organizations completing the questionnaires, 16 represented service companies and 14 consumer product companies. Participating client representatives included 3 presidents, 9 marketing/public relations vice presidents, 7 marketing directors, and 11 public relations directors.

Instruments and Data Collection

The guiding data analytic model used in this study was McLeod and Chaffee's (1973) version of coorientation. With this model as a basis, pretested questionnaires were used with the agencies and clients involved in the study. The questionnaires were pretested among six public relations agency executives and two client representatives. These same individuals or organizations were excluded from the actual study. During this pretest phase, feedback was sought on the questionnaire's readability, clarity of terms and instructions, appropriateness of questions and response categories, length of time to complete, and general reactions. This pretest yielded several minor suggestions regarding questionnaire format and the need for a more precise working definition of conflict. Those recommendations were incorporated into the final questionnaire, which was typeset and printed in a brochure format. Each version of the questionnaire comprised three sections: the respondent's (agency or client) views of the sources of conflict, and key demographic data.

More specifically, each party was asked to express its agreement or disagreement on a five-point Likert scale (strongly agree, agree, strongly disagree, disagree, don't know) with a series of statements concerning their perceptions—as well as their evaluation of the other party's perceptions—of areas of conflict in their business relationship. These areas were linked to Reilly's (1981) six-part programming approach described earlier.

The demographic questions differed between agency and client. Agencies were asked the respondent's title, number of employees, annual billings, and duration of association with client. Clients were asked the respondent's title, type of company, annual public relations budget, number of times it had fired a public relations agency in the past 5 years, and duration of the association with the designated agency.

Each agency participating in the research was initially contacted by telephone. Upon agreeing to serve as respondents, they were asked to name one or more former or current clients who might also participate. Those clients were then asked via telephone if they would be willing to complete a short questionnaire about their relationship with the particular public relations agency. All parties were guaranteed anonymity. Once these preliminary commitments were gained, each agency and client was mailed a copy of the appropriate questionnaire and a stamped return envelope. Those who failed to respond within 14 days were reminded by telephone and asked if they needed another copy of the questionnaire.

RESULTS

Individual responses to the questionnaire items were correlated using Pearson product-moment correlation coefficients in the Statistical Package for the Social Sciences. Thus, the scores of each person in the agency were correlated with those of the appropriate counterpart at the client.

With respect to the first research question—the extent to which agencies and their clients *agreed* on the sources of conflict—both parties agreed that three issues were problematic: implementation ($r = .36, p < .05$), audience ($r = .38, p < .05$), and costs ($r = .61, p < .001$) (see Table 7.1). This seems to suggest that agencies and clients are more likely to agree on problems relating to the applied or "hands-on" phases of a public relations program. Conversely, they are less likely to agree on points of conflict during the early, more conceptual phases of a program (purpose, objectives, plan).

The second research question investigated the extent to which agency and client perceptions of the sources of conflict are *congruent*. As noted earlier, congruency is a term used to describe how similar one's beliefs about how others think compares to one's own opinions on a set of issues. Table 7.1 indicates that agency opinions of the sources of conflict and the agency's perceptions of the client's opinions were all significantly correlated.

Although agency representatives were likely to believe that their and their clients' views on sources of conflict were similar, client representatives' views were similar on purpose ($r = .47, p < .01$), objectives ($r = .50, p < .01$), implementation ($r = .44, p < .01$), and audience ($r = .60, p < .001$), but dissimilar on plan and costs. Consequently, agencies appear to be more likely to believe they hold beliefs similar to their clients' about sources of conflict than do their clients. Again, as the agency–client relationship shifts toward the technical phases of a program, agencies and clients seem to be better able to isolate points of conflict.

The third research question explored the extent to which agencies and clients

TABLE 7.1

Pearson Product-Moment Correlation Coefficients for
Public Relations Agency and Client Coorientation Measures

PR Programming Steps	Congruency		Agreement	Accuracy	
	Client	Agency		Client	Agency
Purpose	.47[b]	.55[c]	.19	.05	.54[c]
Objectives	.50[b]	.60[c]	.25	.05	.42[b]
Plan	.07	.55[c]	.06	.51[b]	.46[b]
Implementation	.44[b]	.47[b]	.36[a]	.27	.51[b]
Target audiences	.60[c]	.31[a]	.38[a]	.14	.53[c]
Costs	.16	.55[c]	.61[c]	.08	.70[c]

[a]$p < .05$. [b]$p < .01$. [c]$p < .001$.

accurately identify the other party's perceptions of the issues of conflict. This was done by correlating each party's perceptions of the other party with the other party's actual perceptions. Results indicated statistically significant correlations between agencies' accuracy in predicting clients' perceptions on all six phases of a public relations program. (See Table 7.1.) In contrast, clients' accuracy in predicting agencies' perceptions was limited to only one phase, plan ($r = .51, p < .01$). Clearly, then, agencies appear to be much more "tuned in" to clients' perceptions of conflict than are clients to agencies' perceptions.

DISCUSSION

To summarize, the key findings of this study were:

1. Both agencies and clients tended to agree that common sources of disagreements were with target audiences, implementation procedures, and costs of a public relations program.

2. Neither agencies nor their clients perceived public relations program goals and objectives as sources of conflict.

3. Both agency and client representatives believed they knew and understood the other's perceptions of conflict points in the public relations programming process. Findings showed, however, that agencies were more accurate in their reading of client perceptions of conflict points than were clients in their reading of agency perceptions.

Despite the limitations of a small sample, these findings have a number of theoretical and practical implications.

Theoretical Implications

To best understand what they mean, the findings must be interpreted within the conceptual framework that served as a basis for this study.

Game Theory. The implications of the information exchange notion underlying game theory are evident in our findings. It is interesting to note that both clients and agencies perceived that conflict lies more at the action-oriented phases of the public relations program than at the conceptual phases. This would suggest that agencies and clients are entering into a business arrangement without a shared vision of where they are going. Forming goals and objectives—and linking these to organizational philosophy—is perhaps the most critical step in the agency–client relationship because it provides a baseline platform against which to evaluate program outcomes. According to Management-by-Objectives (MBO) thinking, establishing such a platform is also critical because it sets a clear, mutually agreed upon direction, which then determines the quality and amount of information that needs to be exchanged in order to ensure profitable outcomes.

The absence of such a platform could potentially cause either or both parties to work at odds because of unverified, inaccurate assumptions. Such erroneous assumptions, if present, could exacerbate the potential for conflict that both agencies and clients agree lies in the selection of target audiences, choice of implementation strategy, and the attendant costs. Thus, it would benefit both client and agency to develop a signed "contractual benchmark" of clearly-stated, written goals and objectives upon which to logically build and budget action plans.

The inability of clients to accurately pinpoint agency concerns suggests that client representatives may not be giving agency representatives sufficient information on which to plan a campaign. This may be explained because clients view their relationships with agencies as likely to be short-term. As such, they may believe it to be to their benefit to strategically limit the amount of information they are willing to share (Bok, 1983; Eisenberg, 1984). If so, client organizations may be adopting the more self-serving win–lose game model in which they try to take advantage of a short-term relationship without giving too much away when they ought to be trying to build long-term relationships by playing the more cooperative and productive win–win game.

By the same token, the acknowledged presence of conflict, despite the ability of agency representatives to accurately read clients, would suggest that agencies may be grasping the information provided, but may not be actively seeking more of it. This may be because the agencies, pressed by unending competitive and bottom-line pressures, are trying to get the greatest return as soon as possible from the client before the relationship ends. Again, in game theory parlance, agencies may be playing a short-term and conflict-generating zero-sum game rather than the long-term cooperative win–win game. A win–lose notion suggests an "us" versus "them" mentality, whereby each party tries to take advantage of the other party because neither one believes the relationship will last or is worth investing in.

In essence, both clients and agencies need to develop win–win strategies based on a more open and candid exchange of information if they are to sustain long-term, stable professional relationships.

Public Relations Roles

An area of research that offers further explanation of this study's findings is the body of literature on public relations roles (Acharya, 1985; Broom & Smith, 1979; Smith, 1978). The essence of this research suggests that public relations practitioners play either a communication technician or a broader-based management role or some combination of both, depending on the client's need. Despite public relations professionals' ability to play these multiple roles, clients have historically viewed them in technician terms only.

It is precisely this view by clients that may cause a conflict over expectations between client and agency. Technical communication services may not, in and of themselves, be capable of solving the client's problems. Yet, the client may only expect or allow an agency to play a technician role, even though the agency is capable of offering a wide range of technical and management services. The result may be a client organization that is disappointed in the agency's performance but unable to pinpoint why.

In an effort to limit the potential conflict over client and agency role expectations, then, agencies should at the outset clearly communicate to the client the roles it can and will play at various stages of their relationship. In addition, the client's expectations should be solicited. Without this understanding, damaging conflict is much more likely.

Applied Implications

Findings also indicated that of the three major sources of conflict, program costs are perhaps the most problematic. Cost disagreements may tie back to unclear goals and objectives. If clients do not understand or agree what a program is expected to achieve, then they will not appreciate the cost-benefit ratio underlying it. This issue of accountability has gained importance in recent years as organizations—pressed by fierce competition from abroad—continue to restructure and downsize in an effort to increase productivity and enhance organizational survival.

So what should agencies do? First, they must effectively estimate and budget projects so that their original cost projections are accurate and realistic. In addition, these costs should be a direct outgrowth of the project (and client) goals and objectives. Approaching a client for increased budget midway through a project can precipitate conflict. Second, agencies and clients should agree from the beginning on the total cost, as well as particular costs within various budget categories. And, like the goals and objectives, this agreement should be in writing and agreed to by both parties.

A Future Research Agenda

This chapter attempts to isolate some sources of conflict between a public relations agency and its clients. However, it suffers three limitations, which future researchers should address:

1. The first is that it is based on a small sample, thus weak on generalizability. This calls for larger sample replications.

2. Second, despite using game theory, this study does not have data showing the extent to and the manner in which agencies and their clients exchange information relevant to consensual decision-making. Future investigations should expand the current conflict identification instrument to incorporate such questions. Such

studies could lend themselves to ethnographic methods of investigation such as participant observation.

3. Third, this study explored agency–client conflict based on Reilly's (1981) concept of public relations programming. Other programming scenarios (e.g., Cutlip, Center, & Broom, 1985; Newsom & Scott, 1985) emphasize different aspects of this process. Subsequent research should consider, as well as compare and contrast, all possible sources of conflict.

Addressing these issues will increase our understanding of, and help minimize, debilitating conflict in agency–client relationships.

REFERENCES

Acharya, L. (1985). Public relations environments. *Journalism Quarterly, 62,* 577–584.

Beiser, M. (1984, April). It's time to name names. *Adweek,* p. 3.

Bok, S. (1983). *Secrets: On the ethics of concealment and revelation.* New York: Pantheon.

Broom, G. M., & Smith, G. D. (1979). Testing the practitioner's impact on clients. *Public Relations Review, 5,* 47–59.

Budd, J. (1988, August 29). Is there anybody out there? Agencies should try listening. *PR Week,* p. 9.

Cutlip, S. M., Center, A. H., & Broom, G. M. (1985). *Effective public relations.* Englewood Cliffs, NJ: Prentice-Hall.

Davis, M. D. (1983). *Game theory: A nontechnical introduction.* New York: Basic.

DiMingo, E. (1987, May). Eleven deadly sins in agency/client relationships. *Business Marketing,* pp. 142, 144.

Ehling, W. P. (1983, August). Application of decision theory in the construction of a theory of public relations management. Paper presented to the meeting of the Public Relations Division of the Association for Education in Journalism and Mass Communication, Oregon State University, Corvallis.

Eisenberg, E. M. (1984). Ambiguity as a strategy in organizational communication. *Communication Monographs, 51,* 227–242.

Frost, J. H., & Wilmot, W. W. (1978). *Interpersonal conflict.* Dubuque, IA: Brown.

Heckathorn, D. D. (1986). Game theory and sociology in the 1980s. *Contemporary Sociology, 15,* 206–208.

Heider, F. (1946). Attitudes and cognitive organization. *Journal of Psychology, 21,* 107–112.

Hume, D. (1979). Agency–client marriages can last—happily. *Southern Advertising Markets, 54*(3), 4–5.

Kent, D. (1985, September). When to fire your ad agency: And how to avoid needing to. *Business Marketing,* pp. 54–56.

Kiely, L. S., & Crary, D. R. (1986). Effective mediation: A communication approach to consubstantiality. In J. A. Lemmon (Ed.), *Emerging roles in divorce mediation. Mediation Quarterly, 12,* 37–49.

Laing, R. D., Phillipson, H., & Lee, A. R. (1966). *Interpersonal perception: A theory and method of research.* New York: Springer-Verlag.

Luce, R. D., & Raiffa, H. (1957). *Games and decisions: Introduction and critical survey.* New York: Wiley.

Maister, D. (1985). Firm management. *Public Relations Journal, 41*(8), 15.

McLeod, J., & Chaffee, S. (1973). Interpersonal approaches to communication research. *American Behavioral Scientist, 16,* 471–473.

Miller, R. (1985). How to keep clients: 11 mistakes to avoid. *Public Relations Journal, 41* (6), 36, 34.

Murphy, P. (1985). Using games as models for crisis communications. *Public Relations Review, 13*(4), 19–28.

Newcomb, T. M. (1953). An approach to the study of communicative acts. *Psychological Review, 60,* 393–404.

Newsom, D., & Scott, A. (1985). *This is PR: The realities of public relations.* Belmont, CA: Wadsworth.

Reilly, R. (1981). *Public relations in action.* Englewood Cliffs, NJ: Prentice-Hall.

St. Michel, C. (1988). *The relationship between public relations agencies and their clients: A coorientation analysis.* Unpublished master's thesis, California State University, Fullerton.

Smith, G. D. (1978). *Public relations roles: An empirical study of public relations consulting.* Unpublished master's thesis, University of Wisconsin, Madison.

Towers, A. (1987). How to evaluate and choose a public relations firm. *Public Relations Journal, 43*(2), 33–34.

Wilcox, D., Ault, P., & Agee, W. (1989). *Public relations: Strategies and tactics* (2nd ed.). New York: Harper & Row.

Chapter 8

How Publics, Public Relations, and the Media Shape the Public Opinion Process

James K. Van Leuven
Michael D. Slater
Colorado State University

The literature of public opinion has little explored the changing nature of the interrelationships between publics, organizational communicators, political figures, and the media over the course of the public opinion process. Some authorities have acknowledged that such interrelationships do develop in characteristic ways (Price & Roberts, 1987), and that the audience for an issue may also evolve (Grunig, 1989). These ideas, however, remain nascent. This chapter discusses evolutionary changes in the publics attending to public debate, and how this evolution influences communication from organizations and media coverage. This chapter also emphasizes the role played by organizations, organizational communicators, and public relations practitioners in the public opinion process, a role too often obscured by the relative visibility of the media.

Our central argument is that the changing nature of the publics attending to a developing public issue shapes the communication behavior of organized interests and the mass media. By "nature of publics," we refer to two related issues: the information-seeking and processing strategies characterizing publics addressed at different points in the public opinion process and what Price and Roberts (1987) called "the public's issue-specific 'state of social organization'" (p. 804).

We utilize a communication stage approach to explain the interaction among organizational communicators, publics, and the media at critical points in the opinion formation and mobilization process. Our stages roughly parallel those employed by political scientists (e.g., Nimmo, 1978). The type of stage theory advanced here follows Van Leuven and Ray (1988) in which a five-stage communication model matched issue developments to the nature of the journalistic or newspaper coverage at each stage. Underlying that model was the notion that patterns of media coverage result from running stories appropriate to the publics' information preferences and needs at each stage. Here, we make that assumption explicit by analyzing the changing nature of emerging publics and the consequences for both media and organizational participants in public debate.

Organizational Communicator Roles

Public opinion emerges from the interactions of organizational communicators, the media, and the publics. Organizational communicators include organizational leaders, spokespersons, and public relations practitioners. Price and Roberts (1987) employ the term *political actors*, but here we distinguish organizational communicators from political candidates and public officials.

As shown in Fig. 8.1, the public opinion formation process is instigated by organizational communicators.[1] Once that happens, interested members of the public take notice. They develop impressions of what is happening in public debate that are both (a) based on mass media representations of political events and of developing public response, and (b) filtered through social interaction. They talk to others and may even mobilize their own groups and organizations in response. And, as groups aggregate, consensus and dissensus form around certain dimensions of the issue. Seen this way, the public opinion process is the study of how individuals and groups assemble and use issue-relevant knowledge.

As this process develops, organizational communicators direct their efforts to different audiences at different points in the process. Both the organizational communicator and the journalist adjust communication style and content to different publics according to their changing assessments of the publics' relative importance at each stage. Organizational communicators must match the type and intensity of programming to the capabilities of different publics for achieving different levels of communication and behavioral effect.

Media Roles

The media perform two critical roles in the public opinion process. In their traditional reporting role, they provide running accounts of developing issue dimensions and events prompted by the issue. Second, the media provide both organizational participants and interested publics with a description of how publics are organizing around an issue through a process Price and Roberts (1987) call *polltaking*. Polltaking involves feeding back political response to political actors, organizational communicators, and interested publics by reporting of scientific

---

[1]Similarly, Price & Roberts (1987) saw the issue formation process beginning with political actors making their issues public and by getting them onto the media agenda and, in turn, the public one.

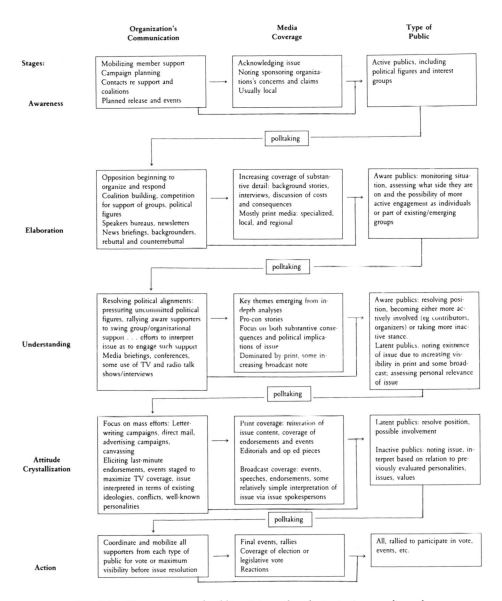

FIG. 8.1.   The emergence of public opinion: roles of organizations, media, and publics.

opinion polls, interpreting emerging trends, and through antecdotal reporting of public response.[2]

Polltaking also triggers the key dynamic in the Price and Roberts (1987) model. As trends are reported, members of both the interested public and political actors (organizational participants including public relations practitioners) revise their perceptions of their own and others' stances. As a result, the power of competing groups and emerging publics accrues not so much in what they do, but in political actors' perceptions of what they might do.[3]

Our conception of media roles in the process focuses on both media type and media content. First, we build on Olien, Donohue, and Tichenor's (1984) media ecology concept in which different types of mass media dominate different phases in the issue's life cycle.

According to this media stages approach, public controversies develop in three more-or-less distinct phases. During an initiation stage, the sponsoring interest group or agency brings the issue to the attention of the media through its own newsletter or a release to the local paper.

Media coverage intensifies at the bureaucratic phase when officials and legislators must confront the issue. The result is acceleration of the topic to a higher and wider level of public awareness, interest, and intensity than it would have reached otherwise, according to studies by the Minnesota group. The regional daily fills the bill with its relatively large newshole and reporting staff.

The public's interest in the issue peaks during what the authors call the legitimized conflict stage. Vocal, polarized positions make good television footage. As well, the open controversy attracts the masses, the passive and previously uninterested members of the public.

Our formulation of the media's role in the process is somewhat more variegated than that suggested by Olien et al. (1984) and Price and Roberts (1987). Although channel effectiveness may well vary by stage, we suggest that the same mass media channel to some extent can adapt the nature of its coverage to meet the communication requirements at each stage as opinion formation processes take hold. Likewise, we do not presume that the mass media are the sole or necessarily the principal providers of information about the issue at all points in the process. Instead, organizational communicators direct many controlled messages to particular publics through speeches, newsletters, position papers, and so forth. Unfortunately, most formulations of the public opinion process fail to account for mediated information coming from other than mass-mediated channels.

---

[2]Glynn (1987) noted a similar dynamic, saying that mass-mediated communication links groups just as interpersonal communication links the individual members of a group by providing a norm with which to compare their own group with others.

[3]Recently, Dearing (1989) demonstrated that early media accounts of the AIDS issue influenced the questions drafted by survey researchers to assess public perception of AIDS. Because the opinion surveys incorporated certain dimensions of the AIDS issue but not others, these same dimensions would be included in subsequent reports of the survey results, thereby reflecting the reciprocal nature of the polltaking function.

Emerging Publics

At the core of this model is the process by which publics emerge as issues develop. As with Dewey (1927), Grunig (1989), and Price and Roberts (1987), we see publics arising around issues that have consequences to them. Price and Roberts called these "interested publics." We argue that the level of interest, involvement, and activity, and characteristic type of social organization of "interested publics" vary in particular ways during the public opinion process.

Grunig's situational theory of publics as explained in Grunig & Hunt (1984) provided the basis for differentiating types of publics. In situational theory, groups are distinguished in terms of how likely they are to attend, process, and respond to communication as a function of different combinations of three variables. His first variable, problem recognition, regards whether individuals stop to think about a situation. The second, constraint recognition, is conceptually similar to the notion of self-efficacy (Bandura, 1986), or the extent to which people feel capable of performing behaviors in response to communication. The third, level of involvement, regards the issue's relevance to the individual and, therefore, whether communication behavior will be active in terms of information seeking and processing. Grunig maintains that the combinations of these variables distinguish publics and indicate appropriate communication strategy for reaching each.

Grunig's research on situation theory (1978) suggested that four types of publics defined by these variables are prevalent in many campaigns. We suggest that these same four types of publics can be viewed as a developmental progression in the public opinion process.

At one extreme are active publics who are high in problem recognition and level of involvement and low in constraint recognition. They get involved early because they make a practice of understanding issue dimensions and the issue's relevance to them, and because they perceive no barriers precluding active engagement. They may favor or oppose the issue, and they are capable of performing a wide range of activities to influence public debate.

Next are the aware publics, which differ from the active publics in terms of higher constraint recognition and lower levels of involvement. They also tend to monitor emergent issues and understand issue complexities, but are not predisposed to act unless relevant issue dimensions are made salient to them. Knowing this, organizational communicators are quick to peg publicity and information campaigns to aware publics.

Latent publics, the third grouping, are relatively low in problem recognition and high in constraint recognition. Public issues do not ordinarily prompt the interest of latent publics until they see the connection with their established interests, social relationships, and values. Their interest in an emergent issue, unless it strikes vitally close to home, tends to be in terms of how the issue is related to already established values and positions rather than in terms of specific dimensions of the new issue. Because they are less well prepared to process the complexities of a new issue, their involvement, when it happens, links to their established social networks and group affiliations rather than to particular pro or con arguments surrounding the issue. Even so, they have some potential for low-level participation in public debate, letter writing, rally attendance, and so forth.

And, at the far extreme are the inactive, least involved members of the public who differ from latent publics in two respects. Although their numbers are large, they tend not to be organized in any meaningful way with respect to the issue at hand. When an issue becomes highly visible, members of inactive publics may take notice but only as the issue relates to their basic values and allegiances. Thus, there is little interest in processing complex information.

THE PUBLIC OPINION MODEL

We turn now to five typical stages in the development of public issues to explain further the interactions among organizational communicators, emerging publics, and the mass media. Any number of stages might have been singled out, but we utilize these five because they reflect the hierarchies of effects most commonly associated with complex and developing issues (Van Leuven, 1989). Figure 8.1 illustrates the changing relationships among publics, organized participants, and the nature of mediated communication. In addition to describing the stages, we illustrate them with examples from a typical school levy campaign.

Awareness Stage

Communication about emergent public issues typically is confined for some time within an interest group or sponsoring organization before it moves onto the public stage. The group may be studying the issue, educating and rallying its own members, and sizing up allies, opponents, and other publics whose stances may not be known. The sponsoring organization may even be drawing up a full-scale public relations program to be launched about the time the issue is made public.

At some point, though, the issue becomes public and this often involves the sponsoring organization trying to place the issue on the media's agenda. Because the media represent one of the sponsoring organization's most critical publics at this stage, care will be given to the manner in which the issue is announced. Often, the issue is announced unintentionally. Editors may scan the group's newsletter or some specialized publication and decide that the issue is worth a separate story.

When the announcement is planned, it comes in the form of a news tip, news release, press conference, or special event such as a rally. Olien et al., 1984 noted that the announcement of community issues is generally reported first in the local weekly press. However, this is not always the case. Issues of obvious moment to a community as a whole may merit attention by regional daily newspapers and television, especially if the sponsoring organization or individual is highly placed or highly visible. The press conference called by a mayor, governor, or president can be very effective at gaining media attention quickly even if not guaranteeing sustained attention. Media content will typically focus on the basics of the issue and on the key players involved in the issue. If the issue is a new one, usually neither the journalist nor the audience is well equipped yet to deal with complex information.

As the initial announcements reach the public, the sponsoring organization's goal is to get the issue on the media agenda, and in so doing, to assess how the issue is perceived. At the same time, the sponsors will be assessing how the media interpreted their presentation and will seek to modify future communication accordingly.

From the organization's vantage point, the most important publics or stakeholders at this early stage are Grunig's active publics. They see the connection of the issue to their collective interests and declare their positions accordingly. These active publics and public figures immediately begin to seek more information. The second principal audience for the announcement are the aware publics who likewise are well able to grasp the story and are in a position to act if only the issue were made sufficiently relevant to their interests.

Consider a local school levy issue. For months, a citizens' committee has been studying the school district's financial needs. Committee membership may even include key individuals who will lead the levy drive. Still, the levy issue is not a public one until the study committee presents its arguments to the school board in a public forum. Now, the issue becomes public as newspaper accounts announce plans for putting the levy issue to the voters.

Elaboration Phase

The issue and its implications are developed more fully during the elaboration stage as political, economic, and social ramifications are learned. Questions are raised within existing community groups, and ad hoc special interest groups or coalitions may form in response.

The organization's public relations plan is set in motion with different levels of programming pegged to different audiences based on their relative importance at this stage. Position papers are distributed, a speaker's bureau may be put in place, and mailings are targeted to specific groups. Stories are planned with various specialized media along with story placement in newsletters and house organs published by key interest groups. Story lines are written to link the target audience, primarily the aware publics, to the issue.

For the most part, the elaboration stage relies on newspaper and specialized publication coverage along with direct mailings. The active and aware publics, who are the primary audiences for newly emergent issues, tend to be prototypical consumers of public affairs news: They are ardent newspaper readers, are seeking additional detail to inform their positions and actions, and are well prepared to understand issue complexities. Newspapers respond with in-depth treatment of the issue including interviews, backgrounders, meeting coverage, and the use of graphics to portray costs and other details. Now that the newspaper has decided to explore the issue's background and explain its ramifications, media content reflects increasing substantive complexity, addressing opposing points of view concerning an issue as well as some of the complexities, ambiguities, consequences, and conflicting interests inherent in the issue. Already media coverage is helping people to sort out how they and others are affected by the issue.

Thus, members of active publics are gathering more knowledge about the issue and its implications for group action. They are hearing the issue being discussed at club and organizational meetings where committees and task forces are typically appointed to investigate further.

Meanwhile a larger circle of aware and potentially active individuals and groups continues to monitor the situation, trying to determine whether or not their participation is called for. These audiences are relatively sophisticated politically and at least somewhat knowledgeable about the content area of the issue. They are trying to make sense out of opposing points, rebuttals, and counterrebuttals.

In the case of the school levy campaign, the elaboration phase is characterized by media reports detailing the new programs, buildings, and salary increases to be made possible by levy passage. Meanwhile, the levy steering committee is confirming appointments to numerous committees assigned particular tasks, for example, campaign financing, doorbell ringing, letter-to-the-editor orchestration, community group endorsements, yard sign planting, and so forth.

Understanding Phase

The issue's political, social, and economic ramifications get synthesized, condensed, and integrated at the understanding stage. Then, as issues are cast as two-sided contests, members of groups begin to take collective stands, and, in turn, to align themselves with other groups to form more organized publics.

Thus, the focus of media attention advances beyond reporting of opposing views toward definition of the consequences and implications of the emergent issue. Media coverage remains largely the domain of newspaper and magazines, given the profile of the interested audience and the complexity of the content. Certain repetitive themes permeate the coverage as explained in analysis pieces and stories summarizing pro and con arguments, clarifying options, explaining consequences, and delineating implications of action and inaction. Media coverage increasingly emphasizes group alignments or the political and social organization around the issue.

Organizational communication expands. Press briefings for the reporting staff are replaced with editorial conferences involving top media leadership and organizational communicators. Media relations efforts begin to target the more latent publics with television talk show appearances and drive-time radio interviews. Video feeds are beamed to the news media to maintain the steady flow of news events about the issue. As well, professional communicators are organizing their publics at the local level, now that the coalition-building task has moved beyond the primary stakeholders to new groups. Grassroots organizing efforts are producing cadres of letter writers and volunteers willing to visit public officials and to become involved in other ways.

We expect the primary audiences for information at this phase to be aware publics, but also latent publics to a lesser extent. Aware publics are processing information in order to resolve their positions. In turn, they may become more involved with the issue in organizational contexts. Latent publics may start to recognize the issue due to increased prominence in the print media and occasional exposure on the broadcast media.

Given that members of latent publics begin to recognize the issue, the next question is whether or not they see the issue as requiring personal involvement. If so, they attend to relevant cues from interpersonal and group communication, organizational ties, and the media reports of the issue's status (poll taking). In considering the issue, members of latent publics focus on adjusting individual stances to those of group leaders and organizational norms. At the same time, the interests of small groups are being reconciled to larger collectivities as group leaders sense the need to establish alliances and reconsider the issue in light of the changing dynamics.

Alignments are now more apparent as issues come to be defined in group rather than individual terms. Groups size up their consensus points with allies and the extent of their differences with opponents. These same groups mobilize, and the sheer numbers of these new and larger coalitions—as reflected in part by poll taking—may change the overall power relationships. It should be clear that many of these alliances are being orchestrated intentionally by organizational communicators rather than forming spontaneously and that polltaking coverage of these alliances is also actively being sought.

The school levy promoters are busy at this stage implicating community groups by making presentations at community organization meetings. The clergy are being called upon to reach members of latent publics who belong to their congregations. The clergy are asked to mention the levy in their church bulletins, to endorse the levy from the pulpit, and even to advertise the levy on church signs and reader boards. Not coincidentally, school art displays and other performances are being staged now and covered by the media so that grandparents and those without children will associate kids they know with the levy appeal.

Attitude Crystallization Stage

The complexion of the process changes considerably now that the primary participants have emerged, and the interests, implications, and consequences have been clarified. Aware publics have had sufficient information to cast their lot with one side or another and to gauge their desired level of active involvement with the issue. Latent publics are now increasingly interested in gaining a basis for making similar decisions.

Even more important is that attention has shifted to a much broader set of relatively passive, uncommitted constituents and audience members. These audience members lack the experience and knowledge to easily process complex information concerning the issue and are probably disinclined to do so. Experimental research findings (Chaiken, 1980; Petty & Cacioppo, 1986; Wu & Shaffer, 1987) indicate that persons who are not highly involved in an issue tend to be less influenced by the content of the arguments about the issue and to be more influenced by peripheral information such as the type of person who provides those arguments. In other words, inactive audience members are probably more attentive to the social cues and their perception of the social organization or alignments around the issue. They are likely to base their own positions on their prior sense of affiliation and shared values with political participants.

As Price (1988) pointed out, the set of affiliations made salient in persuasive messages is an effective means of eliciting support for a given position. Recent research by Salmon and Oshagan (1988) held that the perception of social support and consensus is especially influential in the context of emergent public issues—the topic under consideration here.

Not only is the audience more general but the emerging social organization around the issue makes it easier to cover from a visual standpoint. Television becomes the key medium at this stage with its emphasis on personalities, entertainment, drama, conflict, and simplified presentation of complex issues.

Even more visible, when the sponsoring organization's budget permits, is the start-up of full-scale advertising efforts employing familiar themes, symbols, and supportive social cues, all of which tend to promote decision making in terms of established values and social allegiances.

Besides mounting an advertising campaign, organizational communicators are typically orchestrating support via mass rallies, letter-writing campaigns, media events, stepped-up lobbying efforts to individual politicians, and other symbolic activity.

From the print media's standpoint, political conflict is the dominant issue at this stage of the campaign, and prompts a need to reflect the pro and con sides, to provide a public forum, and sometimes to declare their own position. Hence, more time and space goes to editorials, op-ed pieces, letters to the editor, and guest columns.

Media will serve to feed back to both political actors and the public how various components of the publics are siding on this issue. Content regarding the issue as articulated by participants and reported by the media will tend to be simplistic and to relate issue stances to personalities and to positions on other issues in which sides have already been clearly drawn. The sheer prominence of advertising may overshadow other media activities at this stage.

This attitude crystallization stage probably represents the first instance in which members of the general public have had to confront the levy issue. This happens when the local citizen "bellringer" comes to the door with a brochure and asks for an immediate "yes" commitment. Those who waver are given a follow-up call from the telephone committee. As well, column after column of solicited and unsolicited letters to the editor endorse and oppose the levy. Full page newspaper endorsements list all the names of supporters that can fit the space.

Readiness/Action Phase

Last-minute mustering of support takes many forms in public issue campaigns. Lobbying, negotiation, and other influence activities requiring high-level public relations skills are tested. Because there is so little time to correct misunderstandings, the organizational communicators employ all of their talents in maintaining constant liaison with key publics. Sometimes organizational communicators must motivate desired behaviors such as driving voters to the polls, providing them with marked sample ballots, giving free demonstrations, and so forth. Not surprisingly, a number of highly visual media events may be staged to ensure that the issue makes the evening news.

School levy promoters have seen to it that all yard signs are in place, the telephone calls have been completed, and rides to the polls have been arranged for acknowledged "pro" voters.

For their part, the media cover these activities more or less routinely unless an altogether new issue dimension changes the context of the argument or the emergent social organization around the issue. At the time of decision, media coverage reverts to the surveillance function, for example, election mechanics, brief issue summaries, reports and analyses of the outcomes, and implications for the future.

PREDICTIONS

The model outlined here affords a range of predictions for each of its three principal variables.

Media Content. Obviously, the scenario outlined earlier is a prototype that should describe the evolution of any given issue at best imperfectly. However, several predictions regarding media content may be derived that should hold true over a range of emergent public issues.

First, the substantive complexity of news coverage about the issue—coverage of facts, figures, analysis, and interpretation—should form an inverted U-shape over the course of public debate. The average substantive complexity of coverage will increase to a peak as stories cover opposing views, rebuttals, implications, and consequences. Then, this complexity should decrease as latent and inactive audiences are less willing to process such information, and as media attention shifts to content related to social organization, for example, endorsements, alliances, rallies, and public response to the issue. (See Pavlik & Wackman, 1985, for a detailed discussion of cognitive complexity issues in campaigns.)

Second, media coverage of social organization around the issue should reveal a different pattern. It should build slowly at first and then increase rapidly after complexity of coverage has peaked, and the new primary audience for coverage is mostly concerned with relating the issue to well-known social values and alliances.

In making these predictions, it is difficult, and intriguing, to sort out the influence of increasing television coverage from the influence of decreasing audience cognitive involvement. The argument presented here suggests that television increases its coverage of the issue because the audience has broadened to a relatively mass audience and the appropriate news content has become in consequence simpler, more personalized, and more dramatic—making it better grist for the television news mill. One could argue, conversely, that it is the participation of television that is largely responsible for the broadening of the audience. Similarly, it is probable that the increasing focus on social organization and simplistic argument toward the climax of public debate is also a consequence of organizational communicators molding their argument to the medium, television, that gives them greatest exposure.

It may be most reasonable to suggest that the relationship is indeed a circular one. The effect of television may be simply to exacerbate an existing tendency toward oversimplification inherent in addressing audiences better prepared to process social cues than complex cognitive arguments. If so, our predictions should look somewhat different when television coverage is excluded from the analysis. Substantive complexity of coverage is unlikely to decline nearly so much—although some decline should exist—and the increase in coverage concerning social organization should be somewhat less dramatic.

Publics.   In a more general sense, the model predicts that publics will enter the process in developmental stages based on their likely communication behavior. This would support Price and Roberts (1987) social identification model and the overall implications of Grunig's situational theory, which holds that publics become increasingly more cognitively active and socially organized as problem recognition and issue relevance increase and behavioral constraints subside.

Public Relations Practitioners and Organizational Communicators.   Organizational communicators direct their attention and programming to publics according to the nature of each public's importance at each stage. The initial task of creating awareness among active and aware publics is relatively simple. Although emphasis at the second stage is on making aware publics more knowledgeable of the issue's dimensions, organizational communicators are also mobilizing active publics and creating awareness among latent ones. Public relations or organizational programming at stage three involves reconciling the issue's relevance to established ties held by latent publics, sparking awareness among passive audiences, and bolstering active participation among active and aware publics. Aggressive communication programs are then aimed at inactive audiences whereas separate, sometimes defensive, strategies are designed to maintain existing support among active, aware, and latent publics when the political context of the issue becomes most volatile.

SUMMARY

In some ways, our approach to describing public opinion processes is very similar to those of Dewey (1927), Nimmo (1978), Lang and Lang (1983), Price and Roberts (1987), Glynn (1987), and others. Like them, we emphasize that public opinion comes into being as a social process. Groups move to form coalitions. That is, individuals in those groups process information, discuss the issue with their peers, and may help swing existing or emergent groups into action.

However, we suggest several distinctive points of emphasis. First, the behavior of the public or publics should be understood as top-down as well as bottom-up. Group leadership may operate relatively autonomously, and seek to rally membership support, especially if the issue is central to the group's purpose. Professional communicators, such as public relations practitioners, seek actively to rally such groups into action, perhaps as a consequence of other groups' communication efforts. Group members may become engaged in a public issue and swing the group to some active stance with respect to that issue.

We also argue that public figures, organizational communicators, journalists, and other seasoned veterans of public debate are responsive to differences in the public audience for debate on an issue at various points in the evolution of the issue, and shape communication strategy accordingly. We described predictable patterns in the types of publics attending to public debate, organizational communication behavior, and the role of media over the course of an emergent public issue. In so doing, we also seek to come to terms with the consequences of a relatively recent development in public opinion processes: the impact of television in reaching a mass audience.

Conceptualizing public opinion processes in terms of the changing interrelationships between the publics attending to public debate, the participants in that debate, and the media coverage of that debate may move theory closer to reflecting political reality.

REFERENCES

Bandura, A. (1986). *Social foundations of thought and action.* Englewood Cliffs, NJ: Prentice-Hall.

Chaiken, S. (1980). Heuristic versus systematic information processing and the use of source versus message cues in persuasion. *Journal of Personality and Social Psychology*, *39*, 742–766.

Dearing, J. W. (1989). Setting the polling agenda for the AIDS issue. *Public Opinion Quarterly*, *53*, 309–329.

Dewey, J. (1927). *The public and its problems*. Chicago: Swallow.

Glynn, C. J. (1987). The communication of public opinion. *Journalism Quarterly*, *64*(4), 688–697.

Grunig, J. E. (1978). Defining publics in public relations: The case of a suburban hospital. *Public Relations Review*, *55*, 109–118.

Grunig, J. E., & Hunt, T. (1984). Identifying organizational linkages to publics. In J. E. Grunig & T. Hunt (Eds.), *Managing public relations* (pp. 138–162). New York: Holt, Rinehart & Winston.

Grunig, J. E. (1989). Publics, audiences, and market segments: Models of receivers of campaign messages. In C. T. Salmon (Ed.), *Information campaigns: Managing the process of social change* (pp. 199–225). Newbury Park, CA: Sage.

Lang, G. E., & Lang, K. (1983). *The battle for public opinion*. New York: Columbia University Press.

Nimmo, D. (1978). *Political communication and public opinion in America*. Santa Monica, CA: Goodyear.

Olien, C. N., Donohue, G. A., & Tichenor, P. J. (1984). Media and stages of social conflict. *Journalism Monographs*, *90*.

Pavlik, J. V., & Wackman, D. (1985, November). *Cognitive structure and involvement in a health information campaign*. Paper presented at the annual meeting of the International Communication Association, Honolulu.

Petty, R. E., & Cacioppo, J. T. (1986). *Communication and persuasion: Central and peripheral routes to attitude change*. New York: Springer-Verlag.

Price, V. (1988). On the public aspects of opinion. *Communication Research*, *15*(6), 659–679.

Price, V., & Roberts, D. F. (1987). Public opinion processes. In C. R. Berger & S. H. Chaffee (Eds.), *Handbook of communication science* (pp. 781–816). Newbury Park, CA: Sage.

Salmon, C., & Oshagan, H. (1988, July). *Community size, perceptions of majority opinion and opinion expression*. Paper presented at the meeting of the Public Relations Division, Association for Education in Journalism and Mass Communication, Portland, OR. July 1980.

Van Leuven, J. K. (1989). Theoretical models for public relations campaigns. In C. Botan & V. Hazelton (Eds.), *Communication theory in public relations* (pp. 193–202). Hillsdale, NJ: Lawrence Erlbaum Associates.

Van Leuven, J. K., & Ray, G. W. (1988). Communication stages and public issue coverage. *Newspaper Research Journal*, *9*(4), 71–83.

Wu, C., & Shaffer, D. R. (1987). Susceptibility of persuasive appeals as a function of source credibility and prior experience with the attitude object. *Journal of Personality and Social Psychology*, *52*, 677–688.

Chapter 9

Effects of Involvement on Reactions to Sources of Messages and to Message Clusters

Robert L. Heath
William Douglas
University of Houston

Involvement is an important concept for public relations practitioners and scholars because it can be used to predict persons' willingness to receive a message as well as the likelihood that existing message content will be used to assess each new message. For this reason, involvement plays a prominent role in persuasion as well as media use and effects research. Setting the concept of involvement into perspective, Salmon (1986) observed, "Over the course of the past 40 years, researchers have increasingly recognized the importance of the concept of involvement in consumer and communication research" (p. 244). The relevance of the concept for public relations was made apparent when key pieces of involvement literature, especially the research of Petty and Cacioppo (1981, 1986a), were included in the PRSA Task Force's (1988) corpus of basic literature. And Pavlik (1987) included involvement in his review of public relations research.

In the context of public relations, Grunig (1987, 1989; Grunig & Hunt, 1984) has used the concept of involvement to predict who will become activists. His findings have implications for practitioners. For instance, persons self-interested in an issue are likely to be easy to reach with communication whereas their uninvolved counterparts are not. However, although active publics seek information, they are likely to be difficult to persuade; that is, it is likely to be difficult to change opinions on involving issues (Grunig, 1987). Predicting the likelihood of persons becoming involved in an activist group, Grunig's (1989) situational theory proposed that activism (perhaps all key publics) is fostered when people experience high levels of involvement, recognize problems related to specific issues, and see minimal constraint in regard to taking action on those issues.

Involvement affects a wide range of communication activities. Heath and Douglas (1990) reported that persons who are highly involved on a topic of public policy can externalize (generate) more arguments on the topic, have a greater proportion of arguments supporting their position, seek issues-associated information by utilizing print and television media, talk more frequently about the issue with others, and express more extreme and more supportive opinions on the topic. Once a person becomes involved in an issue, whether for reasons that are supportive of or contrary to the interests of an organization, he or she is more likely to seek and receive information on the issue and is likely to process that information in different ways than a person who is low-involved.

Active and Passive Audiences

This research domain has several implications for public relations practitioners who routinely face the problem of inducing audiences to receive (listen to, tele-view, and read) and be influenced by a message. This problem is compounded because audiences actively seek and receive information on some topics and ignore information on others. Active audiences are easy to reach with a message even if they do not agree with it, but they may resist the information or be reinforced by it depending on their opinion position prior to receiving the message. In this way, public relations practitioners routinely face the task of communicating with an array of audiences, some of which are hostile toward the sponsoring company or organization, whereas other audiences are supportive or indifferent.

This line of reasoning can lead to a two-part taxonomy such as that proposed by Grunig (1987), who distinguished between active and passive publics. The case of the Exxon Valdez oil spill, however, suggests that a two-part taxonomy may be inappropriate. In that instance, three kinds of audience response existed. Persons who were oriented to the environmental side of the Exxon Valdez issue were likely to receive, talk about, and cognitively process information related to the oil spill because of their interest in protecting the environment and their outrage over what appeared to be irresponsible corporate behavior that led to destruction of innocent wildlife and a pristine wilderness. Equally attentive, however, but for different reasons, were persons who had a direct self-interest in Exxon (such as employees, shareholders, or vendors) or persons who are concerned about the viability of current technologies for producing and transporting domestic oil and gas or who desire a strong domestic oil program because it lessens dependence on foreign oil producers. Based upon this supposition, two active populations seem likely to attend to messages about the spill and cleanup but for two different reasons. And the uninvolved population, which Grunig calls passive, would pay minimal attention to details about the spill and its cleanup.

Based on the three-part model, one would predict that opposing-involved audiences would seek, receive, focus on, and cognitively process information during an event—such as the Exxon Valdez spill—but so would supporting-involved audiences. The two groups would be willing communicators and process each new message by comparing it against the existing knowledge (beliefs and information) and the opinion valences (positive and negative) held on that topic. The passive audience is apathetic because it lacks involvement, but could be brought to see that its interest is tied to an issue and thereby become involved and support either the company (or industry) or the activist group position.

A three-part taxonomy divides the active public category into two subcategories: (a) opposing-involved, those who are involved but disagree with the actions of or position taken by a source (such as a company), and (b) those who are supporting-involved because they have an interest in the well-being of the source or have an ideology that supports the actions of the source (such as a company or industry). Opposing-involved audiences are concerned about a company, industry, or governmental agency's actions because they conflict with opinions, perhaps in the form of values, held by the audiences. In contrast, supporting-involved audiences are interested in the policies, actions, or problems of a company or other organization because the opinions held by the audiences express their self-interests. Based on the dynamics of this three-part model, the relationship between involvement and a topic is likely to be curvilinear.

Opposing-involved audiences are typically thought to ignore or distort messages with which they disagree; consequently, practitioners are often tempted to ignore this audience even though thoughtful and informative messages might be effective. Thus it could be supposed that if people are opposing-involved, they should not be targeted with public relations messages, even though ignoring such audiences can be counterproductive when they hold stakes that the company needs. However, having people against the side of the issue sponsored by a company is not irremediable. For instance, Winters (1988) reported that it pays to advertise to a hostile audience. This conclusion is based upon the success of the Chevron Oil Company environmental responsibility, corporate image campaign. That campaign led "unfavorables" to think more favorably (or less unfavorably) about Chevron as an environmentally responsible company and to prefer buying its products to those of its competitors. A study such as this suggests that companies need either (or both) to communicate with people who already experience a high level of issue involvement—whether it initially favors the company or not—or to create involvement by demonstrating how an issue relates to the audience's self-interest. Simply put, public relations practitioners are advised to address issues that are related to an audience's self-interest. The assumption is that if a company has a worthy message to communicate, its chances of being successful are increased if it does so when involvement exists on the part of key audiences, or by increasing levels of involvement. Its effectiveness is increased if it repeatedly tells its story (Saltiel & Woelfel, 1975).

In contrast to opposing-involved audiences, supporting-involved audiences, ones that agree with a company's position because it confirms ideas to which they are predisposed, are willing to receive messages even though they are reinforced and not changed by them. Such audiences could be ignored by managements who believe that communicating with "supporters" is not cost-effective because there is no reason to "convert the converted." Being sensitive to the supporting-involved audience, however, is important because it increases the opportunity to enlarge the size of and motivate grass-roots participation in behalf of the interests advocated by a company. For instance, the American Bankers Association learned through two focus groups that a key segment of the public, persons 40 years and older, could easily be motivated to serve in a grass-roots campaign opposing the Ronald Reagan Administration's proposal to impose a 10% withholding tax upon the tax-paying public's savings accounts and stock portfolios. Because of the level of involvement this issue generated, a campaign sponsored by the American Bankers Association activated a grass-roots audience, which mounted a letter-writing campaign in behalf of the legislative position advocated by the banking, savings and loan, and securities industries and resoundingly defeated the Reagan 10% withholding proposal (Elmendorf, 1988). This analysis suggests that the kind of reaction a person has to the source of a message can be important, and that involvement is one of several factors that influences the likelihood of a person becoming an activist for or against a public policy issue.

Involvement and Cognitive Processes

Involvement research demonstrates that persons apply two cognitive processes to new messages depending on the degree to which they are involved in a topic. Studies on involvement suggest that audiences respond to messages and sources either centrally or peripherally depending on the degree of involvement with the message. High levels of involvement lead people to focus more on messages and less on sources; in contrast, low-involved people attend more to the source of a message and less to its content. This cognitive processing pattern is developmental, becoming more central and less peripheral as involvement increases (Petty & Cacioppo, 1981, 1986a, 1986b). The traditional explanation for this phenomenon is that highly involved people have more message components to use in reacting to an issue or assessing the quality of a new message. In contrast, people with low involvement have fewer messages to be retrieved and used in the critical assessment of new messages. Therefore, low-involved people have more comments to make about message sources who remark—either favorably or unfavorably—on a message. (Favorability is determined by the extent to which the receiver agrees with the source's opinion on the issue.)

People who lack knowledge on an issue tend to rely upon peripheral cues about the source of the message or about the object of discussion such as a company or a product (Wood, Kalgren, & Preisler, 1985). The distinction between central and peripheral cognitions is basic to the research program of Petty, Cacioppo, and their associates (Petty & Cacioppo, 1981, 1986a, 1986b; Petty, Cacioppo, & Schumann, 1983; Petty, Kasmer, Haugtvedt, & Cacioppo, 1987). Persons process information centrally when they have ample information on an issue and use that information to evaluate new messages on the issue. In contrast, peripheral routes are less complex—consist of fewer message components—and are more oriented toward source or cue variables, whether positive or negative. Peripheral routes result when people are low-involved, whereas high involvement prompts people to central cognitive processing. People respond self-interestedly to situational factors (Grunig, 1989) and use information that they can cognitively retrieve to evaluate the messages advocated by sources (Wright, 1973, 1974).

How audiences respond to sources of messages is important. When cognitive processing is easy to moderately difficult, persons tend to rely more upon messages than upon source variables, but when cognitive processing is difficult, they rely more upon source variables (Petty et al., 1987). Motivation and ability to process messages predict whether persons rely upon source or message variables when making a decision. Those who are more peripheral in their message processing rely more upon source variables and less upon message variables, especially when the message requires high levels of processing skills. Petty et al. (1983) reported that when people are low-involved they are more likely to use (positive or negative) source cues to make a decision than they are to use message content. As well as the peripherality of the message (which depends upon the degree of involvement), whether a person relies upon message or source variables depends upon the person's ability and willingness to elaborate on a message (Petty et al., 1987).

Wright (1974) concluded that persons who are low-involved are more critical of sources than are those who are high-involved. Wright (1973) argued that counterargument should be the primary mediator in message acceptance:

[C]ounterarguing may require considerably more effort than either supportive arguing or source derogating. To counterargue, a person must search back through his [or her] belief system for rebuttal evidence to discredit multiple, often unexpected, message arguments. In contrast, generating support arguments should be relatively easier since the message itself makes these salient and immediately accessible. Source derogation should likewise be easier than counterarguing; it requires reaction only to a single cue and the source of an advertising message is easily evaluated. If more effort is required to counterargue, a person's ability to generate counterarguments might be more closely related to his acute motivational state than his ability to generate either support arguments or source derogations. (p. 196)

Consistent with this line of reasoning, Wright (1974) noted that counterargument was more common among women acutely involved with evaluation of advertising information than among those who were less involved. In regard to derogation, "high content involvement" women generated significantly *less* spontaneous source derogation than 'low content involvement' women" (p. 201). Whereas involvement related to counterargument, it did not increase the number of support arguments subjects could produce to bolster their position. Reliance upon counterargument is message driven, whereas derogation is source driven.

Message Clusters

Consonant with involvement theory's division of central and peripheral processes is the assumption that people who are involved with an issue tend to hold as important all of the arguments available in a field of debate regarding the topic. This means that many arguments are germane to any issue. A receiver might not be able to think of (retrieve) the arguments at a given moment, but if an array of those arguments were presented in a single message or over a series of messages, the high-involved person should judge all of the messages as important, whereas the lower-involved person would not. This line of analysis would suggest that each topic has a *message cluster* to which the involved are more sensitive than are the uninvolved.

This line of reasoning maintains the traditional assumptions that high-involved people focus more on message content when assessing a new message whereas low-involved people focus more upon the source of a message. Based upon this set of assumptions, if a company is attempting to discuss key topics with audiences, it must target messages at three major types of audience (opposing-involved, support-ing-involved, and passive), take into consideration an array of topic positions if the audience is highly involved, and present itself (corporate identity) in the most favorable way to achieve or maintain credibility with less involved audiences.

METHODOLOGY

Two studies were conducted to explore the relationship between persons' involve-ment and (a) their reaction to message features and (b) their sensitivity to constitu-ent rhetorical features of messages. In any study of involvement, researchers are encouraged to specify the assumptions they make about involvement because each view of involvement has different implications for research (Salmon, 1986). The view of involvement used in the two studies reported here approximates that described by Salmon "as salience, relevance, future consequences *of a stimulus for an individual*" (p. 256). This approach to involvement focuses on the interaction between stimulus and receiver and is usually operationalized by manipulating the consequences of an issue for an individual (e.g., immediate versus postponed decision making; Krugman, 1965, 1966; Petty et al., 1983; Wright, 1973, 1974, 1980, 1981). In the present analyses, participants reported the importance of an issue to them so that the assessment of involvement was self-generated rather than experimentally induced. As such, involvement was seen to be associated with persons' existing opinions that lead them to seek, focus upon, communicate about, and be receptive to information that can help them reduce uncertainty about an issue.

The two studies reported here are extensions of work completed by Heath and Douglas (1990) who explored persons' reactions to three public policy issues: the move to make English the national language, efforts to create an independent Palestinian state, and the potential divestiture of U.S. companies in South Africa. These issues were selected from a more extensive set that had been pretested to assess the currency of each issue and the extent to which each issue was considered important to the population involved. These particular issues were preferred to others because of their currency and because each was associated with a fairly broad range of importance ratings (taken as a measure of involvement). Variance in ratings is crucial in order to ensure a mix of opinions and to avoid the problem of attenuated correlations that occurs in homogeneous sets.

STUDY ONE: REACTIONS TO THOSE WHO COMMENT ON POLICY ISSUES

Participants

Ninety-one undergraduate students enrolled in communication courses at the University of Houston participated in the first study. Persons were awarded extra credit for their participation, and the study was conducted during regular class meetings.

Procedures

Persons were assigned randomly to respond to a series of questions concerning either English as the national language, an independent Palestinian state, or divestiture of U.S. companies in South Africa. Participants were required to indicate on a series of 7-point bipolar scales (e.g., extremely important/extremely unimportant) the following: (a) how important they considered the issue (a measure of involvement), (b) their support/opposition to the issue, (c) how much they talked to others about the issue, (d) how often they read about the issue, and (e) how often they watched television programs dealing with the issue. Participants were required as well to indicate how they felt about (a) people who supported the issue and (b) people who opposed the issue. These last two items were open-ended and persons were given as much time as they needed to respond. When they had completed these tasks, persons were debriefed.

Coding

Responses to the two open-ended questions (regarding reactions to supporters and opponents of an issue) were given to two judges who were instructed to identify independently the number of attributions (trait-like characterizations; e.g., educated, informed) generated by each participant. In regard to attributions made toward supporters of an issue, the judges agreed in 87 of the 91 cases (agreement ratio, .96), whereas they agreed in 85 of the 91 cases (agreement ratio, .93) concerning attributions made toward opponents of an issue. The judges conferred to resolve instances of disagreement. Of the 10 disagreements, 6 were resolved in favor of judge A and 4 in favor of judge B.

In a second phase of coding, the judges, again acting independently, indicated whether they considered each attribution positive (e.g., caring, responsible), neu-tral (e.g., entitled), or negative (e.g., racist, uninformed). The judges assigned 191 of the 201 attributions generated in Phase 1 to the same category (agreement ratio, .95). As in the first phase of coding, the judges conferred to resolve disagreements; four were resolved in favor of judge A and six in favor of judge B.

From these data, four scores were generated for each participant; the proportion of all attributions about persons who support an issue judged positive (Score 1) and negative (Score 2); the proportion of all attributions about persons who oppose an issue judged positive (Score 3) and negative (Score 4). Proportional scores were developed because previous research (Heath & Douglas, 1990) has shown in-volvement to be related positively to the number of arguments or attributions persons make about an issue. Unlike proportional scores, raw scores are unin-terpretable because, for example, they would not disallow the claim that some persons generated more positive or negative attributions simply as an artifact of having generated more total attributions.

Results

Investigation of the relationship between involvement and support/opposition pro-ceeded through several stages. First, the distribution of support/opposition scores was examined within each of the three issues. This preliminary analysis revealed that, in each case, the distribution was biased toward the support end of the scale. However, because the bias was consistent (i.e., across issues), issue was not included as a factor in subsequent analysis. The second step in this phase of inquiry was to recode support/opposition so that all persons were classified as either opponents (those scoring below the scale mid-point, $n = 14$), neutrals (those at the scale mid-point, $n = 30$), or supporters (those scoring above the scale mid-point, $n = 47$). Support/opposition was then entered as the independent variable in a completely randomized ANOVA in which the dependent variable was per-sons' importance (of issue) ratings. This analysis revealed a significant between-group difference, $F(2,88) = 24.40, p < .001$, eta$^2 = .43$; opponent mean $= 4.21$, neutral mean $= 3.00$, supporter mean $= 5.53$. A subsequent Newman-Keuls test showed that, whereas supporters were significantly more involved than opponents, both supporters and opponents were significantly more involved than neutrals. That is, there was some evidence that the relationship between support/opposition and involvement is curvilinear although, because of the discrepant group sizes, these data must be interpreted cautiously.

First-order partial correlations were computed between persons' involvement in an issue and (a) their three communication scores (frequency of talking, reading,

TABLE 9.1
Partial Correlations of Involvement with Commmunication
and Attribution Scores: Controlling for Support/Opposition

	Amount			People Who	
	of Talking	*of Reading*	*of Televiewing*	*Support Issue*	*Oppose Issue*
Communication Involvement	.58[a]	.49[a]	.46[a]		
Affirming Attributions Involvement				.05	.30[a]
Derogating Attributions Involvement				.22[a]	.20[a]

[a]$p < .05$.

televiewing about an issue) and (b) their four attribution scores (two derogation scores and two affirmation scores). In each case, the effects of support/opposition were removed because that variable is associated with persons' use of the media and their ability to generate arguments on an issue and, as such, may produce confounding effects.

The correlations displayed in Table 9.1 were relatively stable across groups (i.e., issues) and indicate, first, a strong positive relationship between persons' involvement in an issue and the extent to which they seek/exchange information about that issue and second, that persons highly involved in an issue talk more often and teleview and read more frequently about an issue than do persons low in involvement. The conjunction between involvement and persons' affirmation/derogation of others is somewhat weaker but, nonetheless, significant. More specifically, involvement correlated positively with participants' derogation of both supporters and opponents of an issue and with their affirmation of opponents although, when persons' own support/opposition of an issue was controlled, involvement was not a useful predictor of affirmation of issue supporters.

STUDY 2: MESSAGE CLUSTERS

Participants

Forty-two undergraduate students drawn from the same population as those used in the first study participated in the second analysis. Persons were awarded extra credit for their participation and the study was conducted during regular class meetings.

Procedures

This study focused on a single policy issue, the efforts to establish an independent Palestinian state. In the analysis conducted by Heath and Douglas (1990), participants confronted by this issue generated a total of seven arguments in defense of their own policy position: Israeli rights, Palestinian rights, feasibility of this solution, peace in the region, instability in the region, regional history, and justice. Because no single participant used all of these arguments, it was assumed they represented the most that reasonably could be invoked and were treated as a message cluster on the issue.

These seven arguments were presented in summary form to participants in the present analysis who were required to indicate, on a series of 7-point bipolar scales (very important/very unimportant), the importance of each argument when considering the creation of a Palestinian homeland. Participants also indicated on similar scales (a) how important they believed the issue to be, (b) how much the issue affected them personally, and (c) their support/opposition of the issue.

Participants' ratings of importance (of arguments) were used in two ways. First, the separate scores were used to assess whether involvement is associated with the perceived importance of all arguments in a message cluster. Second, the variance of the seven ratings was computed and used as a measure of disparity in order to examine the likelihood that persons high in involvement are comparatively more discriminating about the centrality/peripherality of specific arguments.

Results

As in the first study, the effects of participants' support/opposition to the issue were controlled and first-order partial correlations computed between the involvement variable and (a) the degree to which the issue affected them personally, (b) the importance ratings assigned the separate arguments, and (c) the ratings discrepancy score.

As the correlations shown in Table 9.2 indicate, persons' involvement in the Palestinian issue was not a function of the issue's effect on them personally ($r = +.20$, $p > .05$, power for a moderate effect size $= .60$, one-tailed; Cohen, 1987).

TABLE 9.2
Partial Correlations of Involvement Controlling
for Support/Opposition

		Mean rating
Extent Personally Affected	.20	2.19
Importance of Arguments		
(1) Israeli Rights	.26	5.10
(2) Palestinian Rights	.40[a]	5.55
(3) Feasibility of This Solution	.47[a]	5.00
(4) Peace of the Region	.35[a]	6.33
(5) Stability of the Region	.46[a]	6.05
(6) Regional History	.50[a]	5.07
(7) Justice	.26	6.17
Discrepancy of ratings	−.46[a]	1.03

[a] $p < .05$.

This is not to say that hedonic relevance cannot determine involvement in some issues. Presumably, in local issues and in issues such as the MADD campaign, involvement is often a consequence of some personal investment. Nonetheless, the present data suggest that persons can become involved even though a policy issue is materially irrelevant to them.

Involvement was significantly associated with almost all of the importance (of argument) ratings; only the correlations involving "Israeli rights" and "justice" were not significant ($r = +.26$ in both cases, $p > .05$, power for a moderate effect size $= .60$, one-tailed; Cohen, 1987). In regard to the "justice" issue, this may reflect a ceiling effect in that the argument's average rating (6.17) approached the upper extreme of the scale. However, it should be noted that the issue "peace in the region" had an even higher average rating (6.33) and, yet, was meaningfully related to persons' involvement. There is no evidence that the issue "Israeli rights" was seen as uniformly high in importance (average rating = 5.10) so that the nonsignificant relationship between judgments of its rhetorical importance and involvement is unlikely to have been a methodological artifact.

Notably, involvement was inversely related with the variance of ratings score; that is, highly involved participants judged the separate arguments as more similar in importance than participants low in involvement. This suggests that, as persons become increasingly involved in an issue, they become less discriminating between what may be central and peripheral arguments and tend to see all topic-related arguments as important. Although this may suggest that as persons become more involved in an issue they become less sensitive to the comparative rhetorical significance of specific arguments; it may signal, alternatively, that one aspect of involvement is adoption of a more holistic understanding of issue-related arguments.

DISCUSSION

The present analyses yielded some evidence that the relationship between involvement and persons' support/opposition to an issue is curvilinear. Although participants who supported the stimulus issues used in Study 1 exhibited higher levels of involvement than others (opponents and neutrals), opponents of the various issues displayed higher involvement than neutrals. Because of the comparatively small sample (of opponents) available in the current study, this finding must be interpreted cautiously. Nonetheless, the finding does suggest the usefulness of a tripartite division of audiences and implies that public relations practitioners are likely to encounter audiences that are opposing-involved as well as supporting-involved and neutral. Moreover, each of the audiences may require different types of messages. Whereas opponents of an issue may not be easily persuaded, they are likely to communicate (talk, read, and teleview) about the issue under discussion; thus, they can be reached and may be favorably affected by sustained messages that they interpret to be credible and useful to their opinion position. Those who are supporting-involved may be reinforced by the messages public relations practitioners provide, even leading to grass-roots involvement; for this reason, such audiences should not be taken for granted but should be targeted to receive information that reinforces their support and provides opinions and information that they can use in conversations with others. Neutral audiences—those experiencing low amounts of involvement—need to be addressed in terms of their self-interest or through value positions (altruistic concern) they hold that are relevant to the issue.

A second important issue raised by the current analyses concerns the relationship between involvement and affirmation/derogation of sources. Although previous research has shown that high-involved persons are relatively more likely to rely upon message variables than source variables (Petty et al., 1987) and are more likely and more able to counterargue (Wright, 1974), the present analyses showed that, when attention is directed toward the sources of messages (participants in this research were asked to think about a message source), highly involved persons engage in comparatively higher levels of derogation against both supporters and opponents of public policy (i.e., they respond like low-involved persons). Further, involvement was associated positively with affirmation of opponents of an issue, suggesting that high-involved persons are prepared to think critically, both negatively and positively, about sources of messages even if their final judgments on an issue are content oriented. An important topic for future research is clarification of the way in which audiences, both high- and low-involved, respond to messages. The distinction between message source and message content, although customary among researchers, may not reflect what occurs in the head of some audience members. The current analysis provided some indication that highly involved persons adopt a holistic view in which messenger and message are examined as an integrated set. In contrast, audience members low in involvement appear to be informationally deficient and, hence, more likely to react primarily on the basis of message sources.

One would have expected high-involved persons to be more discerning in their estimation of the importance or relevance of the components of a message cluster. High-involved persons not only read and teleview about issues more often than others but also talk more about those issues. As such, they should be more rehearsed and more sensitive as to the centrality/peripherality of arguments. However, high involvement was characterized by less discrimination between arguments; persons low in involvement showed more variability in their importance ratings than did persons high in involvement. Although this suggests a comparative inability among highly involved persons to distinguish between arguments in a cluster, it is also likely that they are more compelling in public and interpersonal argument because they judge all arguments important and, therefore, are more able to assert their positions on a public policy issue. These findings suggest as well that public relations practitioners may need to demonstrate the relevance of issues for persons who are low-involved, whereas persons who are high-involved are likely to see the relevance.

A final finding from the present study that deserves consideration is the low (and nonsignificant) correlation between involvement and the extent to which persons were personally affected by an issue. Although this correlation was based upon a relatively small sample, statistical power for a moderate effect size was acceptable. The finding is contrary to the assumptions of involvement theory and implies that persons can become involved in issues because of altruistic (i.e., external) concern about others or the world in general. That is, public policy debate may often require more complex levels of reasoning than mere expressions of personal self-interest so that a person's level of involvement may result from values less confining than direct self-interest. In this case, participants perhaps felt strongly about the issue of a Palestinian homeland because of a desire to have peace and to see people enjoy their rights. This could also account for why two of the issues in the message cluster were unrelated to involvement. Altruism appears to be inherent in neither "Israeli rights" nor the generic issue of "justice," especially in deciding the advisability of a Palestinian homeland.

CONCLUSION

Involvement is a powerful predictor of the way in which persons receive and process information. The concept, however, is not without its problems. Research findings such as those reported here as well as the actual behavior of persons who are obtaining and processing information about public policy issues suggest the construct may be confounded with reduction of uncertainty (Berger & Calabrese, 1975), which has been used to explain why and how people seek information. In this context, involvement may be a threshold variable, that is, may affect person's motivation to seek out and/or exchange topic-related information. As Salmon (1986) concluded:

> Despite differences in the actual operationalization of involvement, there seems to be consensus that salience-involvement, the salience of a stimulus for an individual, and interest-involvement, the degree of an individual's interest in a stimulus, play a key role in information processing through activating a heightened state of arousal and/or greater cognitive activity in an interaction between an individual and a stimulus. Involvement—in any form—seems to mediate both the acquisition and processing of information from the environment. Further research is needed to determine more precisely the conditions under which this motivational state is activated and to better understand how information is processed and stored to facilitate retention and recall. (pp. 263–264)

Findings reported here lend support for this call for additional research. In addition to the candidates for further investigation suggested by Salmon, it is likely that others should be included: uncertainty reduction (Berger & Calabrese, 1975), the perceived utility of information (Atkin, 1973; Katz, Gurevitch, & Haas, 1973; Palmgreen & Rayburn, 1985a, 1985b; Rosengren, 1974), and the normatively approved search for and use of information coupled with the expected reward value of that information (Ajzen & Fishbein, 1980; Fishbein & Ajzen, 1975).

ACKNOWLEDGMENTS

The authors acknowledge the assistance of Amy Clawson, Kristin Liles, and Kathy Nathan.

REFERENCES

Ajzen, I., & Fishbein, M. (1980). *Understanding attitudes and predicting social behavior.* Englewood Cliffs: Prentice-Hall.

Atkin, C. K. (1973). Instrumental utilities and information seeking. In P. Clarke (Ed.), *New models for communication research* (pp. 205–239). Newbury Park, CA: Sage.

Berger, C. R., & Calabrese, R. J. (1975). Some explorations in initial interaction and beyond: Toward a developmental theory of interpersonal communication. *Human Communication Research, 1,* 99–112.

Cohen, J. (1987). *Statistical power analysis for the behavioral sciences* (rev. ed.). Hillsdale, NJ: Lawrence Erlbaum Associates.

Elmendorf, F. M. (1988). Generating grass-roots campaigns and public involvement. In R. L. Heath (Ed.), *Strategic issues management: How organizations influence and respond to public interests and policies* (pp. 305–320). San Francisco: Jossey-Bass.

Fishbein, M., & Ajzen, I. (1975). *Belief, attitude, intention, and behavior.* Reading, MA: Addison-Wesley.

Grunig, J. E. (1987). Research in the strategic management of public relations. *International Public Relations Review, 11*(Autumn), 28–32.

Grunig, J. E. (1989). Sierra Club study shows who become activists. *Public Relations Review, 15*(3), 3–24.

Grunig, J. E., & Hunt, T. (1984). *Managing public relations.* New York: Holt, Rinehart & Winston.

Heath, R. L., & Douglas, W. (1990). Involvement: A key variable in people's reaction to public policy issues. In J. E. Grunig & L. A. Grunig (Eds.), *Public Relations Research Annual* (Vol. 2, pp. 193–204). Hillsdale, NJ: Lawrence Erlbaum Associates.

Katz, E., Gurevitch, M., & Haas, H. (1973). On the use of mass media for important things. *American Sociological Review, 38,* 164–181.

Krugman, H. E. (1965). The impact of television advertising: Learning without involvement. *Public Opinion Quarterly, 29,* 349–356.

Krugman, H. E. (1966). The measurement of advertising involvement. *Journal of Advertising Research, 11*(1), 3–9.

Palmgreen, P., & Rayburn, J. D., II. (1985a). A comparison of gratification models of media satisfaction. *Communication Monographs, 52,* 334–346.

Palmgreen, P., & Rayburn, J. D., II. (1985b). An expectancy-value approach to media gratifications. In K. Rosengen, L. Wenner, P. Palmgreen (Eds.), *Media gratifications research: Current perspectives* (pp. 61–72). Newbury Park, CA: Sage.

Pavlik, J. V. (1987). *Public relations: What research tells us.* Newbury Park, CA: Sage.

Petty, R. E., & Cacioppo, J. T. (1981). *Attitudes and persuasion: Classic and contemporary approaches.* Dubuque, IA: Brown.

Petty, R. E., & Cacioppo, J. T. (1986a). *Communication and persuasion: Central and peripheral routes to attitude change.* New York: Springer-Verlag.

Petty, R. E., & Cacioppo, J. T. (1986b). The elaboration likelihood model of persuasion. In L. Berkowitz (Ed.), *Advances in experimental social psychology* (Vol. 19, pp. 123–205). New York: Academic.

Petty, R. E., Cacioppo, J. T., & Schumann, D. (1983). Central and peripheral routes to advertising effectiveness: The moderating role of involvement. *Journal of Consumer Research, 10,* 135–146.

Petty, R. E., Kasmer, J. A., Haugtvedt, C. P., & Cacioppo, J. T. (1987). Source and message factors in persuasion: A reply to Stiff's critique of the elaboration likelihood model. *Communication Monographs, 54,* 233–249.

PRSA Task Force (1988). Public relations body of knowledge task force report. *Public Relations Review, 14*(1), 3–39.

Rosengren, K. E. (1974). Uses and gratifications: A paradigm outlined. In J. G. Blumler & E. Katz (Eds.), *The uses of mass communications* (pp. 269–286). Newbury Park, CA: Sage.

Salmon, C. T. (1986). Perspectives on involvement in consumer and communication research. In B. Dervin & M. J. Voigt (Eds.), *Progress in communication sciences* (Vol. 7, pp. 243–268). Norwood, NJ: Ablex.

Saltiel, J., & Woelfel, J. (1975). Inertia in cognitive processes: The role of accumulated information in attitude change. *Human Communication Research, 1,* 333–344.

Winters, L. C. (1988). Does it pay to advertise to hostile audiences with corporate advertising? *Journal of Advertising Research, 28*(3), 11–18.

Wood, W., Kalgren, C., & Preisler, R. (1985). Access to attitude relevant information in memory as a determinant of persuasion: The role of message attributes. *Journal of Experimental Social Psychology, 21,* 73–85.

Wright, P. L. (1973). The cognitive processes mediating acceptance of advertising. *Journal of Marketing Research, 10,* 53–62.

Wright, P. L. (1974). Analyzing media effects on advertising responses. *Public Opinion Quarterly, 38,* 192–205.

Wright, P. L. (1980). Message-evoked thoughts: Persuasion research using thought verbalizations. *Journal of Consumer Research, 7,* 86–94.

Wright, P. L. (1981). Cognitive responses to mass media advocacy. In R. E. Petty, T. M. Ostrom, & T. C. Brock (Eds.), *Cognitive responses in persuasion* (pp. 263–282). Hillsdale, NJ: Lawrence Erlbaum Associates.

Chapter 10

Communicating with Risk Takers: A Public Relations Perspective

Mary Ann Ferguson
JoAnn Myer Valenti
Geetu Melwani
University of Florida

Many Americans behave in risky ways. In studies of perceived risk by Slovic (1987) and others, use of nuclear power, motor vehicles, handguns, cigarettes, motorcycles, and alcoholic beverages are rated as highly risky activities by both experts and the general population. Yet some 30% of Americans currently smoke in spite of repeated warnings about the dangers of tobacco, over 20% of sexually active unmarried women use no birth control at all, purchases of firearms have increased by more than 30% since 1980, and more than 35% of all persons have more than five drinks in one day. Not only do we take risks with our personal health, our actions often create risks for others who have little control over our risky behavior. In 1985, for example, there were more than 11,000 polluting incidents in and around U.S. waters.

Some might ask, "Who can afford to gamble with their health?" or "Why would anyone take risks with their environment?" Yet, many people take risks with their health and many do not seem averse to living in a risky environment. There are even organizations for those who actively seek adventure through risky behaviors such as spelunking, sky diving, and other athletic or physical activities. Those who enjoy and seek out such adventure may be predisposed to take other risks in their lives, such as infrequent medical checkups or risky sexual behaviors. Others may engage in risky behaviors as a sort of general rebellion. These risk takers may rebel against rules or what appears to impose regulations on their lives. And still another type of risk taker may only act on impulse, engaging in risky behaviors without much thought.

People who are not averse to risk present special problems for the public relations professional who is attempting to promote preventive care, attention to healthful lifestyles, including safety on the job, and other risk avoidance behaviors. What, for example, does the public relations director of the American Lung Association do about that persistent 30% who continue to choose to smoke? And how does the public relations director of an AIDS information agency design messages about safe sex for young people who generally tend to be high risk takers? Or what strategies does the Director of Public Information for the U.S. Environmental Protection Agency enlist to motivate homeowners who may resent being told what to do on their own private property to take measures to protect the water supply from their wells?

We are not, in this research, concerned about that portion of the public that reacts to risk with avoidance behaviors. Rather, we are concerned with reaching a public of risk takers with messages about risks to be avoided; how can we communicate effectively with risk takers when they may be predisposed to ignore messages about risk?

Risk-Taking Predispositions

Our definition of risk taking takes the actor's viewpoint. For a behavior to be defined as taking a risk, the actor must perceive some likelihood of negative consequences—either punishment or loss of a reward. Behavior that later turns out to have negative consequences, but that the actor did not understand was likely to result in punishment, is not in our view risk-taking behavior. We are not suggesting that these behaviors are not actually risky, only that risk taking from an actor's viewpoint only occurs when it is understood that there is some likelihood of an unwanted event as a result of the behavior. Thus, our definition of a risk-taking predisposition is a tendency to engage in behaviors that the actor understands have some likelihood of resulting in a punishment or in the loss of a reward. Although we begin with an assumption that some individuals are not risk aversive and, in fact, may enjoy taking risks, we are not calling these people risk seekers in that we do not believe it is the possible negative consequence that they are always seeking, but rather some other element such as sensation or arousal or the potential reward from taking the risk.

Origins of Risk-Taking Predispositions

There are at least two potential origins for risk-taking predispositions. First, variation in risk-taking tendencies may originate as a preference for or aversion to arousing stimuli. Zuckerman (1988) suggested these preferences stem from biological mechanisms. Zuckerman, Kolin, Price, and Zoob's (1964) Sensation-Seeking Scale is based on an assumption that people differ reliably in their preference for or aversion to arousing stimuli. Generally, those who score high on sensation seeking are more restless when confined to monotonous situations (Zuckerman, Persky, Hopkins, Murtaugh, Basu, & Schilling, 1966).

Zuckerman (1988; Neary & Zuckerman, 1976) postulated a biochemical basis for this preference or aversion. In a summary of the biochemical basis of sensation seeking, Zuckerman reported a positive correlation of testosterone levels with sensation seeking for males. Several studies have examined the role of monoamine oxidase (MAO) and sensation seeking. MAO is an enzyme that, generally speaking, determines the sensitivity of the neural systems it regulates. MAO shows a negative correlation with sensation seeking: "There is a considerable literature linking these monoamine systems to activity, explorativeness, aggressiveness, lack of inhibition, consummatory behavior, sexual behavior, fear or lack of it, and sensitivity to reward and punishment in other species, primarily rodents." (Zuckerman, 1988, p. 185).

Although Fulker, Eysenck, and Zuckerman (1980) reported evidence from identical and fraternal twins for high heritability of sensation seeking, they also concluded that at least one third of the variation in the trait is not inherited. Research indicates that sensation seeking peaks in the late teens and early twenties and declines with age (Zuckerman, 1979).

Sensation Seeking

Validation studies of sensation seeking have found four factors (Ball, Farnill, & Wangeman, 1984; Birenbaum, 1986; Rowland & Franken, 1986; Zuckerman, 1971; Zuckerman, Eysenck, & Eysenck, 1978) associated with the Sensation Seeking Scale:

> *Thrill and Adventure Seeking (TAS):* a desire to seek sensation through physically risky activities that provide unusual sensations and novel experiences, e.g. parachuting and scuba diving.
> *Experience Seeking (ES):* a desire to seek sensation through a non-conforming lifestyle, e.g. travel, music, art, drugs, and unconventional friends.
> *Disinhibition (DIS):* a desire to seek sensation through social stimulation, e.g. parties, social drinking, and variety of sex partners.
> *Boredom Susceptibility (BS):* an aversion to boredom produced by unchanging conditions or persons and a great restlessness when things are the same for any period of time. (Zuckerman, 1988, p. 175)

Zuckerman (Zuckerman et al., 1964) and his research group have found differences for these scales on preferences for visual complexity, music, (Litle & Zuckerman, 1986) and media, as well as age and sex differences. Sensation seekers engage in activities that include parachuting, hang gliding, scuba diving, skiing, mountain climbing, and auto racing (Zuckerman & Neeb, 1980). But not all of those interested in athletic pursuits are sensation seeking; gymnasts and physical education majors are not and runners seem to be lower on the scale than nonrunners.

Those high in sensation seeking prefer visual complexity (Looft & Baranowski, 1971; Zuckerman, Bone, Neary, Mangelsdorff, & Brustman, 1972) and ambiguous surrealistic or impressionistic paintings (Zuckerman & Ulrich, 1983).

High sensation seekers tend to prefer classical or jazz music whereas those low in sensation seeking prefer Muzak. High sensation seekers (who were psychiatric patients) liked all music more than low sensation seekers, but had even greater preference for "grating" music (Watson, Anderson, & Schulte, 1977).

Several media differences have also been reported in the sensation-seeking studies. Sensation seekers (measured with the Change Seeker Index) spend more time listening to music, attend movies more frequently, attend X-rated movies more, read more, read more fiction books (Brown, Ruder, Ruder, & Young, 1974), and have higher levels of curiosity about morbid events or sexual events.

Impulsivity

The Eysencks (Eysenck, 1958; Eysenck & Eysenck, 1969) proposed a two-factor theory of personality: Factor E (extraversion) and Factor N (neuroticism). Factor E includes the subfactors impulsivity and sociability. Eysenck and Eysenck (1977) administered impulsivity scales to over 2,000 subjects and found four subfactors of impulsivity:

1. *Impulsivity in the Narrow Sense (IMPn)*—Items in this factor include: (a) Do you often buy things on impulse? (b) Do you generally do and say things without stopping to think? (c) Are you an impulsive person?

2. *Risk taking*—Includes questions such as: (a) Do you quite enjoy taking risks? (b) Would life with no danger in it be too dull for you? (c) Would you do almost anything for a dare?

3. *Nonplanning*—Includes questions such as: (a) Do you like planning things carefully ahead of time? (b) When buying things, do you usually bother about the guarantee? (c) When you go on a trip, do you like to plan routes and timetables carefully?

4. *Liveliness*—Includes: (a) Do you usually make up your mind quickly? (b) Do you prefer to "sleep on it" before making decisions?

For Eysenck and Eysenck (1978, 1980), impulsiveness and venturesomeness are distinct concepts with the former deriving from Psychoticism and the latter from Extraversion. Eysenck, Pearson, Easting, and Allsopp (1985) reported that venturesomeness and impulsiveness decline with age. Females score higher on impulsiveness; however, males score higher on venturesomeness. Eysenck, et al., 1985 concluded that although impulsiveness and venturesomeness are correlated (reported correlations range from about .10 to .40), they are different concepts.

In a recent validation, Corulla (1988) also found that females score higher than males on the Impulsivity Index. In this study, impulsiveness and venturesomeness are positively correlated (average correlation = .21), but impulsiveness is not correlated with any of the Zuckerman sensation-seeking subscales. Venturesomeness, on the other hand, is positively associated with disinhibition and experience seeking in males, and with thrill and adventure seeking for females. Corulla concluded that sensation seeking and those constructs of interest to the Eysenck research group are not identical and that sensation seeking measures something not measured in the Eysenck Personality Indices.

Uncertainty Orientation and Risk Taking

Another concept we think is similar to our notion of a risk-taking predisposition and that has origins in learning models is uncertainty orientation. Sorrentino and Short (1986) argued that because uncertainty is inherent in any risk situation, the individual difference variable they call uncertainty orientation should be influential in risk-taking situations. Certainty-oriented people do not like ambiguity in their lives. They can be thought of as careful, cautious individuals who avoid unpredictability—low risk takers. Uncertainty-oriented people, on the other hand, like some ambiguity in their lives. They can be characterized as risk takers who thrive on unpredictability.

We assume with Sorrentino (Sorrentino & Short, 1986) that high risk takers, at least those who are uncertainty oriented, may have been rewarded for exploratory or risky behaviors, whereas low risk takers, at least those who are certainty oriented, may not have been rewarded or may even have been punished for these behaviors.

In a research program begun recently by the authors (Ferguson & Valenti, 1988; Valenti & Ferguson, 1988a, 1988b), we focus on risk-taking predispositions rather than on the origins of the behaviors, such as uncertainty orientation or sensation seeking. Our focus on behavioral tendencies comes from an assumption that risk-taking behavior has several potential origins and although the origins will help to understand why the behavior occurs, the behavioral tendencies are of particular interest to communicators.

This early work led us to postulate three types of risk-taking behavior predispositions, which we called adventurousness, impulsiveness, and rebelliousness. Many of the items we used in constructing indices for these constructs strongly resemble those used in Zuckerman's Experience Seeking, Disinhibition, and Thrill and Adventure-Seeking Subscales (Zuckerman, 1971), and Eysenck's Venturesomeness and Impulsivity Indices (Eysenck, 1958; Eysenck & Eysenck, 1978). Some were borrowed from these scales and others we derived as we developed our understanding of these constructs.

Information Processing and Risk Taking

Sorrentino and Hewitt (1984) tested whether there were differences in the way uncertainty-oriented and certainty-oriented people approach personally relevant information. They found that uncertainty-oriented people chose to undertake ac- tivity that would resolve uncertainty about a new and potentially important ability, whereas certainty-oriented persons actually chose to undertake alternate activity that would tell them nothing new about this ability.

Sorrentino, Bobocel, Gitta, Olson, and Hewitt (1988) explored the interaction between uncertainty orientation, routes to persuasion, and involvement. They found that personal relevance (what some might label involvement) does not increase systematic processing for all persons; uncertainty-oriented persons are more motivated to engage in systematic processing when personal relevance in- creases, whereas certainty-oriented persons become more motivated when personal relevance decreases. This leads us to suspect that those predisposed to be risk takers will be more likely to process information under conditions of personal relevance than will those who are low risk takers.

In a field experiment examining radon reduction behaviors (Ferguson & Valenti, 1988; Valenti & Ferguson, 1988a), we found several interactions for message source and message target with these risk-taking orientations on behaviors to reduce risks associated with radon. We found that individuals high in adventurousness, for example, approach messages about health risks or environmental risks differently than those low in adventurousness. Those high in adventurousness were more like- ly to respond to a message in a government brochure than to the same message in a newspaper. Those high in rebelliousness were more likely than those low in rebelliousness to engage in risk-reducing behavior following a newspaper mes- sage or a message targeting children, both of which clearly specified the action steps.

In the studies reported here we explored two research questions. First, we are interested in how closely our risk-taking behavior factors match the factors Zucker- man (1971), Eysenck (1958), and Eysenck and Eysenck (1978) derived from their research. Second, we are interested in the relationship of risk-taking behaviors to other variables that may be useful to the communicator such as involvement with one's health, health locus of control, health attitude conviction, need for cognition, source confidence, media habits, and demographics. Thus, we have attempted to validate our measures by association with other known indicators of constructs similar to risk taking such as sensation seeking, impulsivity, ven- turesomeness, and uncertainty orientation, and with other behavioral indicators of risk taking such as smoking behaviors and speeding.

METHODOLOGY

Since we began this research program, we have conducted eight separate studies using slightly different versions of the risk-taking questions. Seven studies are reported here. (The eighth, a field experiment designed to replicate Study 6, is

currently underway.) These studies include lab experiments and a survey administered to college students and field experiments administered to general public
populations. We collected data from a total of 1,323 subjects. Although we discuss
each of the studies only briefly, further information on the sampling or selection
strategies and the context of the studies is available in the works cited and from the
authors.

Study 1

This study is part of an experiment conducted with 75 undergraduate and graduate
students in the fall of 1988. We recruited subjects both by offering course credit
and by announcements in classes. Subjects reported for the experiment were told
they would be watching a political debate and they were asked to fill out a pretest
questionnaire prior to watching the debate. The data reported here are from the
pretest. Additional information on this study can be found in Ferguson, Hollander,
and Melwani (1989).

Study 2

This study is also an experiment with college students ($n = 46$) in the fall of 1988,
recruited by offering course credit and by inviting students to watch a presidential
debate. Subjects completed pretest questionnaires prior to participating in the
experiment. The data reported here are from the pretest. Additional details for this
study can be found in Ferguson, Melwani, and Hollander (1989).

Study 3

This study was conducted in the fall of 1988 with 261 members of an introductory
public relations course. Subjects completed a questionnaire that included risk-
taking measures.

Study 4

This experiment was conducted beginning in the fall of 1988. We recruited 283
students from a subject pool of marketing students and from classes in a college of
journalism and communications. Again, subjects completed pretest questionnaires
prior to participating in the experiment. Additional information on this study can
be found in Adler (1989).

Study 5

This experiment was a self-administered survey of 252 members of three specifically targeted groups conducted in the spring of 1988. We administered questionnaires to 79 runners and family members attending a hospital-sponsored health

run. Also, students in a public opinion theory and research methods class taught by the authors administered the same questionnaire to 155 individuals they knew to previously be smokers. Finally, we administered the same questionnaires to 18 members of the state Public Interest Research Group at an environmental seminar (Ferguson & Valenti, 1988).

Study 6

In this experiment, questionnaires were administered to 244 adults at a county fair in the fall of 1988. Interviewers approached visitors to an exhibit at the fair and asked them to complete a questionnaire. The items reported here are from the pretest section of the instrument.

Study 7

In a field experiment begun in the fall of 1987, the authors randomly sampled 837 homeowners in three counties. A telephone interview pretested these homeowners on risk-taking tendencies. Some 706 of these homeowners agreed to participate in a message-testing experiment and were mailed a booklet varying four message factors. Some 317 subjects returned the booklet and about 6 months later were contacted with a follow-up mail questionnaire to measure attitudes and their responses. This data set has 162 subjects. Additional background on this study can be found in Ferguson and Valenti (1988), Valenti and Ferguson (1988a), and Valenti and Ferguson (1988b).

The Merged Data Set

The data from all seven studies were concatenated into one data set for the risk measures and the other variables that occurred across more than one study. The Findings section reports the results of the factor analysis of risk-taking measures as well as the other variables.

FINDINGS

We measured risk taking with 52 different questions derived from Eysenck (1958), Eysenck and Eysenck (1969), Eysenck and Eysenck (1978), Eysenck and Zuckerman (1978), Zuckerman (1971), and Zuckerman (1985). These items were submitted to a principal axis factor analysis. Based on this analysis, we eliminated 10 items that did not load on any of the factors. We concluded from the scree plot of the eigenvalues that a five-factor solution would be a reasonable interpretation of the data. To verify that assumption, we resubmitted the remaining 42 items to a factor analysis forcing a five-factor solution. Table 10.1 presents the factor loadings

TABLE 10.1
Factor Analysis of Risk-Taking Measures

Factor	Factor Loadings						
	1	2	3	4	5	M	SD

Adventurous Risk Taking
(E-Impulsive Risk Taking):

1. I often do things on the spur of the moment.	.73					5.3	1.6
2. I quite enjoy taking risks.	.72					4.8	1.5
3. To broaden my horizons I'm willing to take some risks.	.68					5.2	1.3
4. I'm an adventurous person.	.68					5.3	1.4
5. I welcome new and exciting experiences and sensations, even if they are a little frightening and unconventional.	.62	.31				5.3	1.4
6. I sometimes like doing things that are a bit frightening.	.56			.36		4.6	1.6
7. I avoid taking risks.[a]	.52					4.5	1.6
8. I'd take a job that requires lots of traveling.	.41					4.7	1.9
9. I am a rebellious person.	.37[b]	.34[b]				3.6	1.8

Rebellious Risk Taking
(Z-DIS/Disinhibition):

10. Keeping the drinks full is the key to a good party.		.80				3.0	1.9
11. I like wild, uninhibited parties.		.71				3.7	1.9
12. I enjoy the company of real "partiers."		.70				3.6	1.8
13. I feel better after taking a couple of drinks.		.59				3.6	1.7
14. I think people should have a great deal of sexual experience before they get married.		.48				3.8	1.8
15. I'd like to try a drug that produces hallucinations.		.47			.41	2.2	1.8
16. Something is wrong with people who need liquor to feel good.[a]		.45				3.2	1.8
17. I enjoy watching many of the sexy scenes in the movies.		.43				4.5	1.8
18. I don't like rules.		.40				3.7	1.8
19. I like to date members of the opposite sex who are physically exciting.		.38				5.8	1.3
20. If I were to gamble, I'd make big bets.		.28[b]				2.8	1.7

(Continued)

TABLE 10.1
(*Continued*)

Factor	Factor Loadings					M	SD
	1	2	3	4	5		
Impulsive Risk Taking (E-IMPn/Impulsivity in the Narrow Sense):							
21. I generally do and say things without stopping to think.			.79			3.4	1.8
22. I often get so "carried away" by new and exciting things, that I never think of possible snags.			.73			3.9	1.7
23. I often speak before thinking things out.			.66			3.5	1.7
24. I often get into a jam because I do things without thinking.			.65			3.4	1.7
25. I usually think carefully before doing anything.[a]			.57	.35		3.6	1.3
26. Before making up my mind, I consider all the advantages and disadvantages.[a]			.56	.33		3.2	1.4
27. I'm guided more by my feelings than by facts.			.45			4.3	1.6
28. I'm an impulsive person.	.44		.45			4.2	1.7
29. I never buy anything without thinking about it.			.36			3.6	1.9
Physical Risk Taking (Z-TAS/Thrill and Adventure Seeking):							
30. I would like to go scuba diving.				.78		4.9	2.0
31. I would enjoy water skiing.				.71		5.5	1.8
32. I would like to learn to fly an airplane.				.59		5.1	2.0
33. I would like to try surfing.				.56		4.7	2.1
34. I think I would enjoy the sensation of skiing very fast down a high mountain slope.	.35			.55		4.7	2.2
35. I would like to try parachute jumping.	.37			.55		4.2	2.3
36. I would like to drive or ride on a motorcycle.				.32		4.7	2.1
Unconventional Risk Taking (Z-ES/Experience Seeking):							
37. People should dress according to							

(*Continued*)

TABLE 10.1
(*Continued*)

Factor	Factor Loadings					M	SD
	1	2	3	4	5		
some standards of taste, neatness and style.[a]					.51	3.3	1.7
38. I prefer friends who are reliable and predictable.[a]					.46	2.6	1.5
39. I plan for the future.[a]					.40	2.4	1.4
40. I would like to hitchhike across the country.					.39	2.4	1.9
41. I would never smoke marijuana.[a]		.32			.38	4.3	2.4
42. I'd never give up my job before I was certain I had another one.[a]					.33	3.1	1.8
Principal Axis Factoring, Varimax Rotation							
Percent of variance explained	23.4	8.8	6.5	4.9	4.2		
Eigenvalue	9.8	3.7	2.7	2.1	1.8		
Standardized Alpha	.90	.84	.83	.83	.59		

[a]These items have been reverse coded; high numbers reflect high risk taking.

[b]These items have been excluded from the indices constructed for each factor.

for the five-factor solution with a varimax rotation. The varimax rotation was chosen over the oblique rotation because the loadings were basically the same and the orthogonal solution is more appropriate to our objectives of exploring subcomponents of risk taking.

Risk-Taking Factors

The labels we have given to the factors stem from our interpretations of the factors. Where appropriate, we have included the labels used by Zuckerman (Z) and the Eysencks (E) when it appears that the items are similar enough to represent the same construct. The five factors in our studies appear to replicate three of the four Zuckerman (Eysenck & Zuckerman, 1978; Zuckerman, 1971; Zuckerman, 1985) risk-seeking factors and two of the four Eysenck (Eysenck, 1958; Eysenck & Eysenck, 1969; Eysenck & Eysenck, 1978; Eysenck & Zuckerman, 1978) impulsivity factors. Although we included items that loaded on Zuckerman's (1988) boredom susceptibility (BS) and Eysenck and Eysenck's (1977) nonplanning impulsivity factor, we did not replicate those factors in this data set.

We are not claiming any particular advantage for the labels we use over those chosen by Zuckerman or by Eysenck and Eysenck. We are attempting to describe the behavioral tendency represented by the factor, rather than the drive for the

TABLE 10.2
Intercorrelations of Risk-Taking Measures

	Factor	1	2	3	4	5
1	Adventurous	—				
2	Rebellious	.44^b	—			
		(908)				
3	Impulsive	.23^b	.29^b	—		
		(1155)	(906)			
4	Physical	.57^b	.40^b	.10^a	—	
		(787)	(787)	(785)		
5	Unconventional	.20^b	.32^b	.16^b	.19^b	—
		(1030)	(784)	(1027)	(784)	

Note: The number reported below each correlation coefficient is the number of subjects for whom the measures are available.
$^a p < .01. ^b p < .001.$

behaviors. The adventurous, rebellious, and impulsive factors were labeled in our earlier work and we believe the labels best characterize the phenomena we are trying to describe.

The factor we call adventurous risk taking (called impulsiveness by Eysenck; see Eysenck & Eysenck, 1977) represents self-reports of enjoyment of risk, new and exciting experiences, and spur-of-the-moment decisions. The factor we call rebellious (and which is called disinhibition by Zuckerman; see Zuckerman et al., 1964) represents items such as enjoyment of wild parties, drinking, sex, and drug use. The factor we label impulsive (called impulsivity in the narrow sense by Eysenck; see Eysenck & Eysenck, 1977) represents reports of behaving without thought and being "carried away." The factor we call physical risk taking (labeled thrill and adventure seeking by Zuckerman; see Zuckerman et al., 1964) represents reports of enjoyment of activities such as scuba diving, water and snow skiing, parachuting, and flying an airplane. Our last factor which we labeled unconventional risk taking (called experience seeking by Zuckerman; see Zuckerman et al., 1964), represents reports of preference for nonnormative dress, and unpredictable friends.

To develop the risk indices, we created variables that represent the summed averages of the items representing that factor.[1] Table 10.2 presents the interfactor correlations for the five factors as well as the numbers of subjects for which all data are available. The association between adventurous risk taking and physical risk taking is moderate ($r = .57$) as is that between adventurous risk taking and rebellious risk taking ($r = .44$) and between rebellious risk taking and physical risk taking ($r = .40$). The moderate strength of these correlations led us to conclude that whereas our constructs may share some antecedents, they also are unique.

---

[1]Because not all of the items were included in all studies, some subjects will have scores that are a function of less than all items in the factor.

Risky Behavior

We examined the risk-taking indices as predictors of risky behaviors. One unhealthy behavior is smoking. We asked subjects: "Do you smoke?" If they said "yes," they were asked: "How many cigarettes a day?" If they said "no," they were asked: "Have you ever smoked?"

Table 10.3 presents the mean scores on the risk-taking measures for those who currently smoke, those who have quit smoking, and those who have never smoked. Oneway ANOVAs were conducted to test for differences among these behaviors. Scheffe's post hoc difference of means tests are used to evaluate which groups are significantly different ($p < .01$). Those who have quit smoking score statistically significantly higher on rebelliousness ($M = 3.7$) when compared to those who have never smoked ($M = 3.2$). On the other hand, current smokers score statistically significantly higher on impulsiveness ($M = 3.9$) when compared with those who have never smoked ($M = 3.5$). There are no differences among smokers, quitters, and nonsmokers on the other risk-taking factors.

We also asked respondents how many miles per hour above the legal speed limit they would be willing to drive on an open highway. There is a positive linear relationship between the number of miles per hour over the speed limit respondents were willing to drive and how high they score on all the risk-taking measures, with the exception of unconventionality. A test for linear trends was significant in each case at $p < .01$.

The next stage in this validation process is to explore the relationships between the risk-taking measures and other health constructs.

TABLE 10.3
Risk-Taking Means for Risky Behaviors

Risk Factors	Adventurous	Rebellious	Impulsive	Physical	Unconventional
Smoking					
Current		3.5[ab]	3.9[a]		
Quitters		3.7[a]	3.7[ab]		
Never		3.2[b]	3.5[b]		
Mph Over Limit					
0 mph	4.3[af]	2.5[af]	3.2[af]	3.9[af]	
1–5 mph	4.5[ab]	2.9[a]	3.6[ab]	4.3[ab]	
6–10 mph	4.9[bc]	3.5[bc]	3.7[ab]	4.8[bc]	
11–15 mph	5.2[cd]	3.9[bd]	4.0[b]	5.4[c]	
16–20 mph	5.4[cde]	4.1[cd]	3.7[ab]	5.7[c]	
21+ mph	5.8[de]	4.8[d]	4.3[b]	5.8[c]	

Note: Numbers reported here represent mean score on seven-point scales.

[abcde]Those means that do not share superscripts are significantly different from each other (Scheffe's ad hoc difference of means tests, $p < .01$). [f]Linear trend analysis significant at $p < .01$.

Risk Taking: Cognitive and Affective Involvement

Involvement is a strong indicator of readiness to process information about topics of relevance. In our definition, involvement refers to the extent to which something is personally relevant; it is a motivation to act. Theorists have suggested several dimensions of involvement (Adler, 1989; Chaffee & Roser, 1986; Gibbs & Ferguson, 1988; Grunig, 1976; Grunig & Childers, 1988; Nowak & Salmon, 1987; Roser, 1986; Salmon, 1986). This research uses an index designed to measure affective and cognitive involvement with one's own health. (See Gibbs & Ferguson, 1988, for a discussion of the assumptions leading to the constructed index.) Table 10.4 presents a principal axis factor analysis of the 23 items that yielded six

TABLE 10.4
Factor Analysis of Involvement with Health Items

Factors	1	2	3	4	5	6
Positive Affective Involvement:						
1. I'm happiest when I feel physically fit.	.84					
2. When I am healthy I feel good.	.75					
3. I see a strong connection between myself and my health.	.75					
4. I cope better with my daily activitites when I feel healthy.	.60					
5. When I'm healthy I feel proud of myself.	.56					
6. I am happy when I can stick to a healthy diet.	.53					
7. Being around physically fit people makes me feel good about myself.[a]	.51					
8. I feel elated after strenuous physical activity.	.43					
Nonactive Cognitive Involvement:						
9. I don't have a great deal of knowledge about how to stay healthy.[a]		−.76				
10. I do not know much about health issues compared to most people.[a]		−.74				
11. I have a great deal of knowledge that helps me to stay helathy.		−.71				
Active Cognitive Involvement:						
12. I think about the possibility of developing health problems.			.59			
13. I frequently think about health issues.			.58			
14. I'm more secure when I can find health information easily.			.58			
15. I get angry when I don't have the health information I need.			.56			
16. Health messages inspire me to take care of myself.			.54			

TABLE 10.4
Factor Analysis of Involvement with Health Items

Factors	1	2	3	4	5	6
Negative Affective Involvement:						
17. Being ill depresses me.				−.73		
18. I get frustrated when I get ill.				−.69		
19. I get nervous when I know I'm getting sick.			.31	−.60		
Health Noninvolvement:						
20. I believe that thinking about your health is a waste of time.[a]					.80	
21. Health issues do not concern me.[a]					.52	
Health and Weight:						
22. I never think about my weight.[a]						.72
23. Diets frustrate me.						.50
Principal Axis Factoring, Oblique Rotation						
Percent of variance explained	27.1	10.0	8.5	6.7	5.2	5.0
Eigenvalue	6.5	2.4	2.1	1.6	1.3	1.2
Standardized alpha	.84	.81	.76	.73	.67	.51

[a]These items have been reverse coded; high numbers reflect high involvement.

factors; two are labeled positive and negative affective involvement with one's health, two are labeled active and nonactive cognitive involvement, one is labeled simply noninvolvement, and one is labeled weight involvement.

The items representing these factors are summed and averaged into an index. Table 10.5 presents the significant correlations between the risk-taking measures and types of health involvement. Positive feelings or emotions about one's health are associated with high scores on adventurous risk taking (r [$n = 500$] = .19, $p <$ .001) and physical risk taking (r [$n = 500$] = .20, $p < $ .001), and with low scores on unconventional risk taking (r [$n = 500$] = −.17, $p < $ .001). High scores on impulsive risk taking are associated with having negative feelings about one's health (r [$n = 498$] = .15, $p < $ .001). They are also associated with low scores on active cognitive involvement (r [$n = 260$] = −.20, $p < $ .001). High scores on health noninvolvement are likely to be associated with low scores on impulsive risk taking (r [$n = 260$] = −.17, $p < $ .01) and on unconventional risk taking (r [$n = 260$] = −.26, $p < $ .001).

Health Locus of Control

Since Rotter (1966) developed the locus of control (LOC) construct, a great deal of research has provided evidence for how this situational orientation affects both

TABLE 10.5
Correlation of Risk Taking with Health Involvement

Health Involvement Factors:	Risk Taking Factors				
	Adventurous	Rebellious	Impulsive	Physical	Unconventional
Nonactive Cognitive (n = 261)					
Active Cognitive (n = 260)			$-.20^b$		
Health Noninvolvement (n = 260)			$-.17^a$	$.15^a$	$-.26^b$
Negative Affect (n = 498)			$.15^b$		
Positive Affect (n = 500)	$.19^b$			$.20^b$	$-.17^b$
Weight (n = 256)					

Note: For the sake of parsimony only correlations that are significant at $p < .01$ are presented in the table.
[a] $p < .01$. [b] $p < .001$.

judgment and behavior. Based on social learning theory, Rotter proposed that those high in an internal orientation, or locus of control, viewed events or conse-quences as coming from their own actions, whereas those with an external orienta-tion regard events as determined by outside forces such as chance, fate, or powerful others.

Fiske and Taylor (1984) reported that health LOC is a better predictor of chronic illness-related behavior than it is of preventative behaviors. Research find-ings indicate that those high in internal LOC are more likely to seek information and make better use of it than are externals (Phares, Ritchie, & Davies, 1968) and they are more likely to take action to cope with their problems (Sullivan & Rear-don, 1986).

The ten items measuring health LOC are from the Health Locus of Control Index (Wallston, Wallston, Kaplan, & Maides, 1976). High values on this index represent internal LOC. Some of the items include the following: (a) If I take care of myself, I can avoid illness; (b) People who never get sick are just plain lucky; and (c) Good health is largely a matter of good fortune. Table 10.6 presents all of the items in this index.

The three health LOC indices were correlated with the risk-taking indices. Adventurous risk taking is positively correlated with Type I internal health LOC (r [n = 250] = .18, $p < .01$). The higher the adventurousness score, the more likely subjects are to say they are responsible for their own health or illness. Impulsive risk taking, however, is negatively correlated with Type II internal health LOC (r [n = 247] = $-.15$, $p < .01$). In other words, those high in impulsiveness perceive their own health as out of their control.

TABLE 10.6
Factor Analysis of Health Locus of Control Measures

Factor	1	2	3
Type I:			
1. Whenever I get sick, it's because of something I have done or not done.	.65		
2. When I feel ill, I know it is because I have not been getting the proper exercise or eating right.	.64	.30	
3. I am directly responsible for my health.	.62		
4. If I take care of myself, I can avoid illness.	.60		
5. People's ill health results from their own carelessness.	.57		
Type II:			
6. I can only do what my doctor tells me to do.[a]		.74	
7. No matter what I do, if I'm going to get sick I will get sick.[a]		.57	
Type III:			
8. Good Health is largely a matter of good fortune.[a]		.40	.63
9. People who never get sick are just plain lucky.[a]		.30	.62
10. Most people do not realize the extent to which their illnesses are controlled by accidental happenings.[a]			.41
Principal Axis Factoring, Varimax Rotation			
Percent of variance explained	26.3	21.9	11.2
Eigenvalue	2.6	2.2	1.1
Standardized alpha	.74	.67	.62

Note: Only factor loadings greater than .30 are reported.

[a]These items are reverse coded, thus a high score on any question here reflects a high internal locus of control and a low score reflects a high external locus of control.

Conviction

Abelson (1986, 1988) proposed a model of conviction that may prove to be very useful to help us understand the conditions under which attitudes will change. Conviction refers to the degree to which an attitude or belief is clung to, possessed, or valued. This is very similar to the notion of attitude importance (Krosnick, 1986, 1988), which was labeled centrality and defined as the extent of the links

TABLE 10.7
Factor Analysis of Conviction About
Health

Loadings from Unrotated Factor Matrix	
1. I am extremely concerned about health issues.	.84
2. I've often told others in my family about my views on health.	.79
3. I think about my health often.	.79
4. I've often expressed my ideas about health to my friends.	.77
5. I hold my views on health strongly.	.75
6. My health beliefs are important to me.	.71
7. I've held my views about health a long time, compared to most people.	.68
8. I would be willing to spend a day a month working for a group that shares my beliefs about health.	.63
9. I can't imagine ever changing my mind about my health habits.	.45
Principal Axis Factoring	
Percent of variance explained	56.2
Eigenvalue	5.1
Standardized alpha	.90

between the self and the attitude object. The nine items we use in this study are from Abelson's (1988) validation.

Factor analysis of the nine health conviction items suggested a one-factor solution. Table 10.7 presents the items and the loadings from the unrotated factor matrix. These items were summed and averaged into a Conviction Index. The risk-taking measures were then correlated with the Conviction Index. We find positive correlations between conviction and adventurous risk taking (r [$n = 493$] = .13, $p < .01$), and physical risk taking (r [$n = 493$] = .13, $p < .01$).

Need for Cognition

Need for cognition (NFC) is a concept believed to measure differences in tendencies to engage in and enjoy thinking (Cacioppo & Petty, 1984; Cacioppo, Petty, & Morris, 1983; Petty & Cacioppo, 1986a, 1986b). NFC reflects an individual difference in the likelihood of effortful information processing. NFC was measured with 15 items from the Cacioppo and Petty scale (1984). The items were submitted to a principal axis factor analysis. The scree plot suggested a one-factor solution. The items and factor loadings are reported in Table 10.8. Adventurousness is positively correlated with NFC (r [$n = 372$] = .25, $p < .001$). Impulsiveness, however, is negatively correlated with NFC (r [$n = 371$] = $-.30$, $p < .001$).

TABLE 10.8
Factor Analysis of Need for
Cognition Measures

Loadings from Unrotated Factor Matrix

1. I would rather do something that requires little thought than something
   that is sure to challenge my thinking
   abilities.* .70
2. I try to anticipate and avoid situations
   where there is a likely chance that I
   will have to think in depth about
   something.* .68
3. I think only as hard as I have to.* .68
4. I like to have the responsibility of
   handling a situation that requires a lot
   of thinking. .66
5. Thinking is not my idea of fun.* .64
6. I really enjoy a task that involves
   coming up with new solutions to
   problems. .58
7. Learning new ways to think does not
   excite me very much.* .54
8. I find satisfaction in deliberating hard
   and for long hours. .53
9. I prefer complex to simple problems. .53
10. The idea of relying on thought to make
    my way to the top appeals to me. .52
11. The notion of thinking abstractly is
    appealing to me. .49
12. I like tasks that require little thought
    once I have learned them.* .47
13. It is enough for me that something gets
    the job done; I don't care how or
    why it works.* .46
14. I prefer my life to be filled with puzzles
    that I must solve. .44
15. I prefer to think about small daily pro-
    jects rather than long term projects.* .35

Principal Axis Factoring

Percent of variance explained	34.5
Eigenvalue	5.2
Standardized alpha	.86

Note: Only factor loadings greater than .30 are
reported.
    *These items have been reverse coded; high numbers
represent high need for cognition.

Media and Health Information

To measure media exposure subjects were asked, "In an average week, how many days would you say you watch television/read a newspaper/read a magazine/listen to the radio?" To measure how much subjects rely on these media they were asked, "How would you feel if you were not able to watch your favorite program/read your favorite newspaper/magazine/listen to your favorite radio station?" Finally, to measure use of each of these media for information about health hazards, subjects were asked how likely they would be to watch television/read news-papers/magazines/listen to the radio to learn about health issues. These media use and exposure measures were then correlated with the risk-taking measures. Table 10.9 presents these correlations.

Television exposure is negatively correlated with adventurousness (r [$n = 624$]

TABLE 10.9
Correlation of Risk Taking with Media Use

Media Use Items:	Risk-Taking Factors				
	Adventurous	Rebellious	Impulsive	Physical	Unconventional
Exposure					
Television	−.10[a]			−.12[a]	
	(624)			(503)	
Newspapers					
Magazines					
Radio	.12[a]	.17[b]		.20[b]	
	(500)	(500)		(500)	
Use for Health Info					
Television		−.22[b]			−.13[b]
		(502)			(748)
Newspapers		−.17[b]			−.16[b]
		(499)			(498)
Magazines		−.11[a]			
		(485)			
Radio		−.16[b]			
		(492)			
Reliance					
Television					
Newspapers					
Magazines					
Radio		.17[b]		.14[a]	
		(494)		(494)	

Note: For the sake of parsimony only correlations that are significant at $p < .01$ are presented in the table.

[a]$p < .01$. [b]$p < .001$.

= $-.10, p < .01$), and physical risk taking (r [n = 503] = $-.12, p < .01$). Radio exposure, on the other hand, is positively correlated with adventurousness (r [n = 500] = .12, $p < .01$), physical risk taking (r [n = 500] = .20, $p < .001$) and rebellious risk taking (r [n = 500] = .17, $p < .001$). Use of newspapers, television, radio, and magazines for health information was negatively correlated with rebellious risk taking (r [n = 499] = $-.17, p < .001$), (r [n = 502] = $-.22, p < .001$), (r [n = 492] = $-.16, p < .001$), (r [n = 485] = $-.11, p < .01$), respectively. Also, use of newspapers and television for health information is negatively correlated with unconventional risk taking (r [n = 498] = $-.16, p < .001$), (r [n = 748] = $-.13, p < .001$), respectively. Finally rebellious risk taking and physical risk taking are positively correlated with reliance on radio (r [n = 494] = .17, $p < .001$), (r [n = 494] = .14, $p < .01$), respectively.

Source Confidence

Subjects rated some 10 possible sources of information about environmental and/or health hazards on the confidence or trust they had in the source. The 10 sources were:

1. Environmental Protection Agency (EPA).
2. Newspaper articles.
3. State government agencies.
4. Your doctor.
5. University scientists.
6. The American Cancer Society.
7. Television programs.
8. Government scientists.
9. The American Medical Association (AMA).
10. The Surgeon General.

The scores on the source confidence measures were correlated with the risk-taking indices; see Table 10.10. We found relationships between our risk-taking measures and confidence in "your doctor," government scientists, the Surgeon General, the American Medical Association, the Environmental Protection Agency, and the American Cancer Society. The higher the adventurousness scores, the higher the confidence in "your doctor" (r [n = 727] = .11, $p < .01$) and the EPA (r [n = 725] = .10, $p < .01$). Physical risk taking is positively correlated with confidence in the EPA (r [n = 494] = .17, $p < .001$), the American Cancer Society (r [n = 496] = .11, $p < .01$), the AMA (r [n = 496] = .11, $p < .01$), the Surgeon General (r [n = 496] = .13, $p < .01$), and government scientists (r [n =

TABLE 10.10
Correlation of Risk Taking with Confidence in Sources

	Risk-Taking Factors				
Sources	Adventurous	Rebellious	Impulsive	Physical	Unconventional
EPA	.10[a]			.17[b]	
	(725)			(494)	
Newspaper articles					
State government agencies					
Your doctor	.11[a]				
	(727)				
University scientists					
American Cancer Society				.11[a]	
				(496)	
Television programs					
Government scientists				.11[a]	
				(496)	
AMA				.11[a]	
				(496)	
Surgeon General				.13[a]	−.12[a]
				(496)	(495)

Note: For the sake of parsimony only correlations that are significant at $p < .01$ are presented in the table.

[a]$p < .01$. [b]$p < .001$.

496] $= .11$, $p < .01$). Unconventional risk taking is negatively associated with confidence in the Surgeon General (r [$n = 495$] $= -.12$, $p < .01$).

Demographics

Several demographic variables are measured in these seven studies: age, education, income, marital status, religious preference, church attendance, and gender. Oneway ANOVAs were conducted to test for differences among these groups. Scheffe's post hoc difference of means tests are used to evaluate the significance of the differences ($p < .01$).

Risk taking of all types, with the exception of impulsive risk taking, is a linear function of age (Table 10.11). Younger people tend to have more predispositions toward risk taking than do older people. For education, those with less than a 4-year college degree (and not currently in school) score significantly higher on impulsiveness compared to those who have a 4-year degree or more. Income is also associated with risk taking. Those who report incomes of less than $20,000 or greater than $30,000 score higher on rebelliousness than do those with incomes in the $20,000–29,999 range or above $40,000. Those who report incomes of less than $20,000 score highest on the impulsive, physical risk, and unconventional

TABLE 10.11
Risk Taking and Demographic Measures

Risk Variables	Adventurous	Rebellious	Impulsive	Physical	Unconventional
Age					
18–21 years	4.9[abe]	3.7[ae]	3.9[c]	5.0[ae]	3.6[f]
22–29 years	5.0[a]	3.7[ae]	3.8[bc]	5.0[a]	2.9[a]
30–39 years	4.6[bc]	3.1[b]	3.6[ab]	4.3[b]	3.2[a]
40–59 years	4.4[c]	2.6[b]	3.5[a]	4.0[b]	2.9[a]
60+ years	3.9[c]	2.1[b]	3.2[a]	3.6[b]	2.6[a]
Education[f]					
Some College			3.9[e]		
4-year degree			3.5[a]		
Grad school			3.2[a]		
Income					
Below $20,000		3.3[b]	3.8[be]	4.9[a]	3.6[bf]
$20M–$29M		2.7[a]	3.4[a]	3.9[b]	2.7[a]
$30M–$39M		3.0[b]	3.4[ab]	4.3[ab]	3.1[ab]
$40,000+		2.8[a]	3.3[ab]	4.6[ab]	2.7[a]
Marital Status					
Married	4.4[a]	2.6[u]	3.4[b]	4.1[b]	
Single	5.0	3.8	3.8[a]	5.0[a]	
Other	4.7[a]	2.9[a]	3.5[ab]	4.6[ab]	
Religion					
Protestant		3.1[a]			2.8[a]
Catholic		3.8[bcd]			3.2[ab]
Jewish		4.1[c]			3.2[ab]
Other		3.0[a]			3.0[ab]
None		3.8[abcd]			3.5[b]
Church Attendance					
Regularly	4.5[ae]	2.4[e]		4.2[be]	2.7[ae]
Frequently	5.0[ab]	3.2[a]		4.8[ab]	2.8[a]
Occasionally	5.0[b]	3.6[ab]		5.0[a]	3.0[a]
Never	4.9[b]	3.9[b]		4.9[a]	3.5
Gender					
Males	5.0	4.0	3.6	5.1	3.1
Females	4.8	3.3	3.9	4.6	2.8

Note: Numbers reported represent mean scores on seven-point scales.

[abcd]Those means that do not share superscripts are significantly different from each other. (Scheffe's post hoc difference of means tests, $p < .01$). [e]Linear trend analysis significant at $p < .01$. [f]For education, only data from noncollege students were used.

risk-taking measures. Marital status is also associated with risk-taking tendencies. Generally, single people demonstrate greater tendencies for risk taking.

Religious preference is related to rebelliousness and unconventional risk taking. Those who are Catholics, Jewish, or nonreligious score higher on rebelliousness (M = 3.8, 4.1, and 3.8, respectively) when compared to Protestants (M = 3.1) or others (M = 3.0). Those who report no religious preference score highest in unconventional risk taking (M = 3.5), whereas Protestants score lowest on this measure (M = 2.8). In addition, people who regularly attend church score lower in adventurousness (M = 4.5) than those who occasionally or never attend church (M = 5.0, and 4.9, respectively). Those who regularly attend church score the lowest on rebelliousness (M = 2.4) when compared to the others (M = 3.2, 3.6, and 3.9 for those who attend frequently, occasionally, and never, respectively). Those who never attend church score the highest on unconventional risk (M = 3.5) in comparison with the other groups (M = 2.7, 2.8, and 3.0 for those who attend regularly, frequently, and occasionally, respectively).

Males score higher on all of the risk-taking indices with the exception of impulsiveness, where women score higher.

SUMMARY AND DISCUSSION

We believe we have demonstrated the validity of our constructs through their relationships with both risky behaviors and with cognition and affect. In addition, although we think these data represent an unusually diverse population and the findings are generalizable, we remind the reader that the data presented here are correlational and we are not suggesting they support casual links. Two field experiments currently underway will test for these relationships.

Profiles of Risk Taking

In this section we paint a broad picture of what we think the adventurous, rebellious, impulsive, physical, and unconventional risk taker may be like. Again, we must caution the reader, however, to understand that we have not created typologies of individuals, but rather have measured constructs that are associated with the other variables.

Adventurous Risk Taking. Those who are young, single, male, or who never or only occasionally attend church score high in adventurous risk taking. High adventurousness is associated with driving fast. This risk-taking predisposition correlates positively with good attitudes about health, a feeling of control over one's health, and strong health values. These risk takers like to think. Exposure to television is low, whereas exposure to radio is high, and source confidence is highest for a personal physician or the EPA. We see this risk taker as one who probably is uncertainty oriented and who has been rewarded for exploratory behavior.

Impulsive Risk Taking.   Those who are young, single, female, or smokers score high on impulsiveness. Speeders are impulsive. Those predisposed to impulsive risk taking score low on cognitive involvement with health, have negative feelings about health, do not feel in control of their health, and have little concern about their health. Impulsiveness is associated with a dislike of thinking. This risk taker, we believe, is quite unlike the adventurous risk taker. We suspect that this risk taker is engaging in risky behavior more for the sensations derived from it than from having learned to expect rewards from the results of the behavior. Actually taking the risk becomes the end here.

Rebellious Risk Taking.   Again, those who are young, single, or male score high on rebelliousness. Speeders are also rebellious. Smokers and those who kicked the habit score high on rebelliousness. Those who are Catholic or Jewish or attend church or synagogue only occasionally are high on rebelliousness. This predisposition is associated with high radio use and high reliance on radio, but a low reliance on all media for health information. In our view, this type of risk taker is reacting to others rather than to potential rewards from risk taking. Being known as a "risk taker" probably is one of the rewards associated with this behavior.

Physical Risk Taking.   The young, single, or male tend to exhibit high physical risk-taking tendencies. Physical risk taking is associated with high or low incomes, but not mid-range income. Those who only occasionally or never attend church score high in physical risk taking. Speeders are physical risk takers. Good feelings about health, strong commitment to one's own health beliefs, and concern about health are associated with physical risk taking. A predisposition to physical risk taking is associated with low levels of television exposure, but high exposure and reliance on radio. Confidence is high when the source of information is the EPA, American Cancer Society, the AMA, the Surgeon General, or government scientists. We think this risk taker is quite like the impulsive risk taker in that it is the risky behavior itself and the sensation associated with it that are sought.

Unconventional Risk Taking.   Finally, the young, the single, or males are high in unconventional risk taking. This predisposition is associated with never going to church, being a Protestant, or being nonreligious. Those who do not care about their health, or do not have strong feelings about their health and do not have confidence in the Surgeon General score high on unconventional risk taking. A predisposition for unconventional risk taking is related to little use of newspapers or television for health information. Again, we expect that unconventional risk takers are motivated by the attention they receive from others for taking risks rather than sensations associated with the risk.

Theory of Information Processing and Risk Taking

These findings and our earlier research lead us to conclude that these risk-taking behaviors may have different antecedents. Also, we expect different relationships between these constructs and other variables important to information processing.

We agree with Zuckerman et al. (1966) that risk takers may exhibit a higher need for arousal than non-risk-takers. Thus, messages should be arousing in order to gain their attention. If one thinks of the high risk taker as a young, single person who, as our data suggest, has a relatively high reliance on radio, a successful way of getting this risk taker's attention may be through novel radio public service announcements presenting a message or in the form of a popular song.

Actual processing beyond mere attention will vary with the type of risk taking and will depend on other structural aspects of the message such as target, source credibility, and message content.

Adventurous and physical risk taking are associated with concern for the effects of health risks on the self. We expect that these risk takers will be interested in health information and centrally process that information (Petty & Cacioppo, 1986b). Because these are thoughtful risk takers, we expect them to respond favorably to expert sources and to messages that target the self.

Impulsive risk takers are much more difficult to reach. They do not like to think and we expect that they may process information heuristically (Chaiken, 1987). Instead of a novel frame for the message, these messages may have to be embedded in other arousing stimuli. For example, embedding a "quit smoking" message in a soap opera may be one way of reaching the impulsive risk taker. Because these risk takers do not particularly perceive themselves as in control of their own health, the message may be more successful if the risk target is a significant other. Perhaps the motive to quit smoking would be stronger for these risk takers if they saw potential harm to their children.

The rebellious risk takers may also respond better to a message targeting a significant other. They are not going to respond to experts solving their problems. This risk taker might respond positively to a do-it-yourself kit presented as protecting the significant other rather than the self. These risk takers do not want to be told what to do; they want to be in charge.

Of all the risk-taking predispositions, getting the attention of and persuading the unconventional risk taker will be one of the most challenging goals a public relations person will undertake. These risk takers generally do not use media, they do not have religious affiliations, they do not care about their health, and they do not have confidence in a source as widely respected as the Surgeon General. These risk takers seem to value unconventionality. The source of a message to the unconventional risk taker will have to be as unconventional as they are. For a message to succeed, the risk will have to be seen as a threat to their individuality. Grace Jones might be a celebrity who typifies the unconventional risk taker. A "safe sex" message from Grace Jones that suggests that one's unconventional lifestyle might be threatened, and hence one's own self-identity at risk, if behaviors are not changed, may have some chance of reaching the unconventional risk taker.

Our intention is to extend this research with these risk-taking constructs by examining the effects of variation in the messages for the six experiments outlined in the Methodology section of this chapter. As discussed previously, we expect the message target and the message source to interact with the risk-taking predisposition. Future research will explore the developing theory presented earlier with the goal of aiding public relations professionals who are attempting to reduce risky behaviors.

ACKNOWLEDGMENTS

Although the research described in this article has been funded wholly or in part by the U.S. Environmental Protection Agency under assistance agreement No. (CR 815376-01-0) to Drs. Ferguson and Valenti, it has not been subjected to the Agency's peer and administrative review and therefore may not necessarily reflect the views of the Agency and no official endorsement should be inferred.

The authors thank Peter Sandman, Rutgers University, and Michael Singletary, University of Tennessee, for comments on earlier versions of this chapter.

REFERENCES

Abelson, R. P. (1986). Beliefs are like possessions. *Journal for the Theory of Social Behaviour, 16*, 223–250.

Abelson, R. P. (1988). Conviction. *American Psychologist, 43*, 267–275.

Adler, A. E. (1989). *Personal relevance and cognitive and affective involvement: Processing a message about AIDS*. Unpublished master's thesis, University of Florida, Gainesville.

Ball, I. L., Farnill, D., & Wangeman, J. F. (1984). Sex and age differences in sensation seeking: Some national comparisons. *British Journal of Psychology, 75*, 257–265.

Birenbaum, M. (1986). On the construct validity of the sensation seeking scale in a non-English-speaking culture. *Personality and Individual Differences, 7*, 431–434.

Brown, L. T., Ruder, V. G., Ruder, J. H., & Young, S. D. (1974). Stimulation seeking and the Change Seeker Index. *Journal of Consulting and Clinical Psychology, 42*, 311.

Cacioppo, J. T., & Petty, R. E. (1984). The need for cognition: Relationship to attitudinal processes. In R. McGlynn, J. Maddux, C. Stotlenberg, & J. Harvey (Eds.), *Social perception in clinical and counselling psychology* (pp. 113–139). Lubbock: Texas Tech University Press.

Cacioppo, J. T., Petty, R. E., & Morris, K. (1983). Effects of need for cognition on message evaluation, recall, and persuasion. *Journal of Personality and Social Psychology, 45*, 805–818.

Chaffee, S. H., & Roser, C. (1986). Involvement and the consistency of knowledge, attitudes and behaviors. *Communication Research, 13*, 373–399.

Chaiken, S. (1987). The heuristic model of persuasion. In M. P. Zanna, J. M. Olson, & C. P. Herman (Eds.), *Social influence: The Ontario symposium* (Vol. 5, pp. 3–39). Hillsdale, NJ: Lawrence Erlbaum Associates.

Corulla, W. J. (1988). A further psychometric investigation of the Sensation Seeking Scale Form-V and its relationship to the EPQ-R and the 1.7 Impulsiveness Questionnaire. *Personality and Individual Differences, 9*, 277–287.

Eysenck, H. J. (1958). A short questionnaire for the measurement of two dimensions of personality. *Journal of Applied Psychology, 42*, 14–17.

Eysenck, H. J., & Eysenck, S. B. G. (1969). *Personality structure and measurement.* San Diego: Knapp.

Eysenck, S. B. G., & Eysenck, H. J. (1977). The place of impulsiveness in a dimensional system of personality description. *British Journal of Social and Clinical Psychology, 16*, 57–68.

Eysenck, S. B. G., & Eysenck, H. J. (1978). Impulsiveness and venturesomeness: Their position in a dimensional system of personality description. *Psychological Reports, 43*, 1247–1255.

Eysenck, S. B. G., & Eysenck, H. J. (1980). Impulsiveness and venturesomeness in children. *Personality and Individual Differences, 1*, 73–78.

Eysenck, S. B. G., Pearson, P. R., Easting, G., & Allsopp, J. F. (1985). Age norms for impulsiveness, venturesomeness and empathy in adults. *Personality Individual Differences, 6*, 613–619.

Eysenck, S. B. G., & Zuckerman, M. (1978). The relationship between sensation seeking and Eysenck's dimensions of personality. *British Journal of Psychology, 69*, 483–487.

Ferguson, M. A., Hollander, B., & Melwani, G. (1989, May). *The dampening effect of post-debate commentary: The Bentsen/Quayle debate.* Paper presented at the meeting of the Political Communication Division, International Communication Association, San Francisco.

Ferguson, M. A., Melwani, G., & Hollander, B. (1989). *Motivated media use and predebate analyses: Dampening effects on judgements of presidential candidate.* Unpublished manuscript, University of Florida, Gainesville.

Ferguson, M. A., & Valenti, J. M. (1988, July). *Risk-taking tendencies and radon messages: A field experiment testing an information processing model for risk communication.* Paper presented at the meeting of the Mass Communication and Society Division, Association for Education in Journalism and Mass Communication, Portland, OR.

Fiske, S. T., & Taylor, S. E. (1984). *Social cognition.* Reading, MA: Addison-Wesley.

Fulker, D. W., Eysenck, S. B. G., & Zuckerman, M. (1980). The genetics of sensation seeking. *Journal of Personality Research, 14*, 261–281.

Gibbs, J., & Ferguson, M. A. (1988, May). *Grunig's decision-situation theory: A replication of research.* Paper presented at the meeting of the International Communication Association, New Orleans.

Grunig, J. E. (1976). Communication behaviors occurring in decision and nondecision situations. *Journalism Quarterly, 53*, 252–263.

Grunig, J. E., & Childers, L. (1988). *Reconstruction of a situational theory of communication: Internal and external concepts as identifiers of publics for AIDS.* Paper presented at the meeting of the Association for Education in Journalism and Mass Communication, Portland, OR.

Krosnick, J. A. (1986). *Policy voting in American presidential elections: An application of psychological theory to American politics.* Unpublished doctoral dissertation, University of Michigan.

Krosnick, J. A. (1988). Attitude importance and attitude change. *Journal of Experimental Social Psychology, 24,* 240–255.

Litle, P., & Zuckerman, M. (1986). Sensation seeking and music preferences. *Personality and Individual Differences, 4,* 575–578.

Looft, W. R., & Baranowski, M. D. (1971). An analysis of five measures of sensation seeking and preferences for complexity. *Journal of General Psychology, 85,* 307–313.

Neary, R. S., & Zuckerman, M. (1976). Sensation seeking, trait and state anxiety, and the electrodermal orienting reflex. *Psychophysiology, 13,* 205–211.

Nowak, G. J., & Salmon, C. T. (1987, August). *Measuring involvement with social issues.* Paper presented at the meeting of the Association for Education in Journalism and Mass Communication, San Antonio.

Petty, R. E., & Cacioppo, J. T. (1986a). *Communication and persuasion: Central and peripheral routes to attitude change.* New York: Springer-Verlag.

Petty, R. E., & Cacioppo, J. T. (1986b). The Elaboration Likelihood Model of persuasion. In L. Berkowitz (Ed.), *Advances in experimental social psychology* (Vol. 19, pp. 123–205). New York: Academic.

Phares, E. J., Ritchie, D. E., & Davies, W. L. (1968). Internal external control and reaction to threat. *Journal of Personality and Social Psychology, 10,* 402–405.

Roser, C. (1986). Cognition and affect in persuasion: An empirical analysis of involvement. Doctoral dissertation, Stanford University, Palo Alto.

Rotter, J. B. (1966). Generalized expectancies for internal versus external control of reinforcement *Psychology Monographs, 80,* 1–28.

Rowland, G. L., & Franken, R. E. (1986). The four dimensions of sensation seeking: A confirmatory factor analysis. *Personality and Individual Differences, 7,* 237–240.

Salmon, C. T. (1986). Perspective on involvement in consumer and communication research. In B. Dervin & M. J. Voigt (Eds.), *Progress in communication sciences, VII* (pp. 243–268). Norwood, NJ: Ablex.

Slovic, P. (April, 1987). Perception of risk. *Science, 236,* 280–285.

Sorrentino, R. M., Bobocel, D. R., Gitta, M. Z., Olson, J. M., & Hewitt, E. C. (1988). Uncertainty orientation and persuasion: Individual differences in the effects of personal relevance on social judgments. *Journal of Personality and Social Psychology, 55,* 357–371.

Sorrentino, R. M., & Hewitt, E. C. (1984). The uncertainty-reducing properties of achievement tasks revisited. *Journal of Personality and Social Psychology, 47,* 884–899.

Sorrentino, R. M., & Short, J. C. (1986). Uncertainty orientation, motivation, and cognition. In R. M. Sorrentino & E. T. Higgins (Eds.), *The handbook of motivation and cognition: Foundations of social behavior* (pp. 379–403). New York: Guilford.

Sullivan, C. F., & Reardon, K. K. (1986). Social support satisfaction and health locus of control: Discriminators of breast cancer patients' styles of coping. In M. L. McLaughlin (Ed.), *Communication yearbook* (Vol. 9, pp. 707–722). Beverly Hills, CA: Sage.

Valenti, J. M., & Ferguson, M. A. (1988a, October). *Risk-taking tendencies and radon messages: A field experiment.* Paper presented at the Symposium on Radon and Radon Reduction Technology, EPA, Denver.

Valenti, J. M., & Ferguson, M. A. (1988b, December). *Health and environmental risk-taking attitudes: Two studies on the effects of adventurousness, impulsiveness and rebelliousness.* Paper presented at the Symposium on Science Communication, Los Angeles.

Wallston, B. S., Wallston, K. A., Kaplan, G., & Maides, S. A. (1976). Development and validation of the Health Locus of Control (HLC) scale. *Journal of Consulting and Clinical Psychology, 44,* 580–585.

Watson, C. G., Anderson, R., & Schulte, D. (1977). Responses of high-and-low emotional deficit patients to exciting, grating, and neutral stimuli. *Journal of Clinical Psychology, 33,* 552–554.

Zuckerman, M. (1971). Dimensions of sensation seeking. *Journal of Consulting and Clinical Psychology, 36,* 45–52.

Zuckerman, M. (1979). *Sensation seeking: Beyond the optimal level of arousal.* Hillsdale, NJ: Lawrence Erlbaum Associates.

Zuckerman, M. (Ed.). (1985). *Biological bases of sensation seeking, impulsivity, and anxiety.* Hillsdale, NJ: Lawrence Erlbaum Associates.

Zuckerman, M. (1988). Behavior and biology: Research on sensation seeking and reactions to the media. In L. Donohew, H. E. Sypher, & E. T. Higgins (Eds.), *Communication, social cognition, and affect* (pp. 173–194). Hillsdale, NJ: Lawrence Erlbaum Associates.

Zuckerman, M., Bone, R. N., Neary, R., Mangelsdorff, D., & Brustman, B. (1972). What is the sensation seeker? Personality trait and experience correlates of the Sensation Seeking Scales. *Journal of Consulting and Clinical Psychology, 39,* 308–321.

Zuckerman, M., Eysenck, S. B. G., & Eysenck, H. J. (1978). Sensation seeking in England and America: Cross-cultural, age, and sex comparisons. *Journal of Consulting and Clinical Psychology, 46,* 139–149.

Zuckerman, M., Kolin, E. A., Price, L., & Zoob, I. (1964). Development of a sensation-seeking scale. *Journal of Consulting Psychology, 28,* 477–482.

Zuckerman, M., & Neeb, M. (1980). Demographic influences in sensation seeking and expressions of sensation seeking in religion, smoking, and driving habits. *Personality and Individual Differences, 1,* 197–206.

Zuckerman, M., Persky, H., Hopkins, T. R., Murtaugh, T., Basu, G. K., & Schilling, M. (1966). Comparison of stress effects of perceptual and social isolation. *Archives of General Psychiatry, 14,* 356–365.

Zuckerman, M., & Ulrich, R. (1983). Sensation seeking and preferences among 19th century nature paintings. Paper presented at the Conference on Psychology and the Arts, Cardiff, Wales.

Author Index

Subject Index